Seekir.   ...

Seeking the Church

An Introduction to Ecclesiology

Stephen Pickard

scm press

© Stephen Pickard 2012

Published in 2012 by SCM Press
Editorial office
3rd Floor, Invicta House
108–114 Golden Lane,
London EC1Y 0TG

SCM Press is an imprint of Hymns Ancient & Modern Ltd
(a registered charity)
13A Hellesdon Park Road
Norwich NR6 5DR, UK

www.scmpress.co.uk

British Library Cataloguing in Publication data

A catalogue record for this book is available
from the British Library

978-0-334-04410-9
Kindle 978-0-334-04481-9

Typeset by
Manila Typesetting Company
Printed in Great Britain by
CPI Group (UK) Ltd, Croydon

Contents

Acknowledgements

This book is the fruit of an extended stay at Ripon College Cuddesdon in Oxford from August 2010 to December 2011. During that period, I had the privilege of teaching a semester course on Ecclesiology. This gave me the chance to reconsider the subject having taught ecclesiology for many years. I am grateful to the students of that course for their engagement and good humour in the early stages of the formulation of what eventually became the present book.

The book would never have been written were it not for the generous offer of a Visiting Professorial Fellowship from the Principal of Ripon Theological College, Canon Professor Martyn Percy. I am deeply grateful to Martyn, colleague and friend, for his support and care at a critical period in my own vocation in the Church. The faculty, students and staff of the College welcomed my wife and me, and during our stay we found great blessing and refreshment and in the process made lasting friendships. It was a privilege to have been part of such an exciting, wise and hospitable community dedicated to the nurture of the ministry of the Church.

I am grateful to all those friends and colleagues who have generously commented on various chapters of the book. In particular I want to thank Phillip Tolliday for his customary sharp and insightful comments on the manuscript. Thanks are also due to Matthew Anstey, Bruce Kaye, Michael Lakey and Duncan Reid. It will be clear to readers of this book the debt I owe to the late Daniel Hardy, one time supervisor, theological mentor and wise guide. I am grateful for generous research grants to assist me in the writing of this project from the Australian Research Theological Foundation and the Public and Contextual Theology Strategic Research Centre (PACT) of Charles Sturt University, NSW, of which I am a member. I remain of course responsible for any errors and shortcomings of the present work.

Thanks are also due to Dr Natalie Watson, Senior Commissioning Editor for SCM Press, for making the publication of this book possible.

My wife, Jennifer, as ever, has been a source of great encouragement and joy to me during the writing of this book.

This book is dedicated to the students and faculty of Ripon College Cuddesdon in Oxford. May they continue to be a blessing for the Church and Christ Jesus.

Seeking the Church
Sources and Tasks

Seeking God, seeking one another

Human yearning, divine restlessness

We humans seem to spend much of our lives seeking the company of others. Indeed, we appear to be hard-wired to invest considerable time and energy searching for sustaining relationships in society. The desire for human company goes hand in hand with the very normal human need for solitude. This is no surprise, for life together has many dimensions. I want to suggest at the outset of a book on the Church that our desire for human companionship somehow involves seeking God, and our search for God similarly involves an attraction to others. I say 'somehow', because the way God belongs to our seeking and finding the company of others is complex and rich and belongs to the deepest wonders of being a creature of God.

The simple yet profound insight into the interconnectedness between the move towards God and to one another comes from the fourth-century monastic Dorotheos of Gaza who described the pathway to God and others in the following way:

Suppose we were to take a compass and insert the point and draw the outline of a circle. The centre point is the same distance from any point on the circumference. . . . Let us suppose that this circle is the world and that God is the centre; the straight lines drawn from the circumference to the centre are the lives of [human beings] . . . To move toward God we move from the circumference along the various radii of the circle to the centre. But at the same time, the closer they are to God, the closer they become to one another; and the closer they are to one another, the closer they become to God. (Paraphrase in Bondi 1991, pp. 14f.)

For Dorotheos, seeking the company of God and others went hand in hand. Here is a simple clue to what being the Church is all about. It involves a desire for God and a corresponding desire for one another.

While the two movements, towards one another and to God, cannot ultimately be separated, they can be differentiated in order to grasp more clearly the significance and dynamics involved. With respect to the move towards God, Augustine's prayer in the opening sentences of his *Confessions* comes immediately to mind: 'Lord you have made us for yourself and our hearts are restless until they find their rest in You.' This divine attraction to God is captured in the Anglican Collect for Pentecost 18 based on Augustine's words:

Almighty God,
you have made us for yourself,
and our hearts are restless till they find their rest in you:
pour your love into our hearts and draw us to yourself,
and so bring us at last to your heavenly city
where we shall see you face to face;
through Jesus Christ your Son our Lord,
who is alive and reigns with you,
in the unity of the Holy Spirit,
one God, now and forever. Amen

The basis of this prayer is the fundamental human condition of being created in God's image. Thus, Augustine begins his *Confessions* by recalling his life as a creature bearing God's image. The concept is rich and inviting. However, Augustine's prayer suggests that our being created in God's image is not simply a finished matter. Evidently, the image of God is something which we have to grow into. This future orientation is implicit in the unfulfilled desire and restlessness of the human heart, which continues to seek after God, and the Sabbath rest, which comes as a gift. For a variety of reasons, some of which remain elusive and difficult to understand, the image of God we bear is incomplete or marred and requires repair, healing and fulfilment. Growing into the image of God clearly involves a journey of multiple dimensions. Certainly countless people through the ages have found Augustine's prayer resonates with their deepest desire for God.

One contemporary theologian of the Church speaks about this journey towards God in terms of attraction.

> Creatures are created to move towards God. When creatures somehow lose that towardness – becoming obsessive at some point, separating from the whole of things and serving only themselves – then the creation loses its order. To lack attraction to others and to God is to suffer the inertia of self-attraction: in Luther's terms, to be 'twisted into self'. (Hardy 2010, p. 47)

On this account, seeking God involves being untwisted through attraction to God. This process involves human seeking and divine attraction; the movement comes from both God and the human person. This suggests that the human cry for God has its deepest origin in the life of the Triune God. The human heart's restlessness for God is matched by God's restless desire for human beings to find their joy and *shalom* in God. In this process, we are drawn into the fullness of relation with God. There is thus a corresponding restlessness in God active through the Spirit of Love drawing all things toward Christ (John 12.32).

What about the corresponding move toward one another? I want to suggest that this too is part of the divine working. The movement towards each other and the way in which the Triune God is involved is identified in the following prayer.[1]

---

1 Composed by Sathianathan Clarke at the Sri Lankan March 2012 meeting of the Archbishop of Canterbury's Working Group on Theological Education in the Anglican Communion.

Almighty God,
You have made us for each other
And your heart is restless till we find our joyous rest in each
other around you:
Gift to us, O Triune God, the love that binds and energizes
you,
so that we might be blessedly drawn toward each other while
being drawn closer to you.
And bring us to that renewed Kingdom
where your earth will be filled with the Glory of God
and where we can face each other without fear or shame.
because your own face has been fully unveiled;
Through Jesus Christ and in the power of the Holy Spirit
One God now and forever. Amen.

This prayer echoes and reorientates Augustine's prayer yet retains the selfsame divine restlessness. The above two prayers suggest that being drawn into the purposes of God is a complex process which consists (a) in the attraction between God and human beings and (b) a movement in which people are drawn together. These complementary movements are a gift of God through Christ in the Spirit. The result is an overflow of joy and peace between people and empowerment of human life. The Spirit of God, who empowers human beings and God to come into closer relation, is the same Spirit at work between human beings drawing them closer to each other. The Spirit works in both directions simultaneously. This means that the experience of human empowerment through deeper shared life is never just a human achievement but also a work of the Spirit, who is between all things drawing all things into the holiness of God. As human beings find their life together in God, they share a foretaste of the coming kingdom. It is earthed in the here and now. It is a foretaste and provisional, but none the less genuine. It gives concrete reality to the prayer, 'Your kingdom come, your will be done on earth as it is in heaven.'

I have suggested that our movement toward God is correlated to our movement toward one another. These two moves are simultaneous and generative of community with God and each other. One way to formulate this divine–human attraction as it relates to the Church is as follows: 'All God's creatures are moved by God to their fulfilment in him; the Church is doubly so moved, as one among God's creatures and as a creature that embodies that movement for others' (Jensen 1999, p. 172). This statement captures the divine initiative underlying the movement toward God and each other, and it also brings into focus the sense that the Church embodies this movement in its own life.

Seeking God, seeking one another, embodying this search through the life of the Church; these things are mutually involving, and part of the purpose of this book is to show why and how this is the case.[2] One consequence of this approach to the Church is that the doctrine of the Church is not a second-order matter for theology but belongs in the middle of things. Our understanding of God and of what it means to be a creature in God's world living in the company of others are all richly intertwined. This means that the doctrines of God, creation, anthropology and ecclesiology are mutually involving doctrines, but more of that as the book unfolds.

Ecclesia: roots and wisdom

Our seeking of God is a shared activity, which involves companionship with others. It is for this reason that the Roman Catholic theologian Karl Rahner stated: 'a Christian has to be an ecclesial Christian' (Rahner 1997, p. 345). The word *ecclesia* (from the

---

2 I do not think that Edward Schillebeeckx gets to the nub of the issue in his apologia for the connection between God and the Church. He wrestles with the relationship between people's search for God and the Church (1990, pp. 59f.). He notes that '[b]elief in God has a basic tendency to form communities', though he recognizes that, for many, the institutional Church and its faith 'is no longer endorsed by and from human experience'. There is nonetheless a continuing search for a 'religious more' or 'religious surplus' that remains 'vague and unsatisfied'. He proposes that 'this "more" takes specific historical form in various religious or "church societies"', and as such institutionalization of the quest for the 'religious more' 'remains essential for belief in God'. Yet, this approach leaves the intrinsic relation between God and Church obscure.

Greek *ek*–out and *kaleo*–call) literally means 'called out' (Gooder
2010, p.10). The word has a political function in the classical
Greek institution of democracy as the assembly of the citizens.
With this in mind, Elizabeth Schüssler Fiorenza states that 'democratic equality, citizenship, and decision making power are constitutive for the notion of *ekklesia*' (2007, p. 71). Fiorenza observes
that the Greek ideal of full citizenship operated within a 'kyriar-
chal notion of equality', which severely restricted the vision of a
radical democratic ideal, which included women as equal participants in the life of the Greek *polis*.

In the context of Israel, *ecclesia* (a translation of the Hebrew
qahal) is a reality emerging in response to the call and summons
of Yahweh (Coenen 1975). This dynamic quality of assembly,
especially for worship, is carried over into the self-understanding
of the post-Easter communities born of the gospel and called out
by God. The English rendering of *ecclesia* in the New Testament
as *Church* loses something of the dynamic quality of *ecclesia*. The
move from *ecclesia* to *Church* obscures the dynamic relational
element (being called-out together) and suggests the Church has
a more solid, steady-state character than it actually has. This
unfortunate shift in emphasis can give the impression that the
study of the Church (ecclesiology) is bent toward the shoring up
of the ecclesiastical status quo. This only serves to confirm for
many that the restrictive democratic ideal of *ecclesia* in the Greek
polis – an ordered political and social patriarchy – is transferred
into the life of the Church.

The above brief discussion of *ecclesia* clarifies what a concern
for the doctrine of the Church involves. Given the theological and
political roots of *ecclesia* and the deployment of this word in the
New Testament it is possible to identify at least three dimensions
to the study of ecclesiology (literally 'words/reasoning concerning
the called-out ones of God'): *foundations, dynamics and purpose*.
Concern for *foundations* is usual in the doctrine of the Church.
However, attending to *dynamics* draws attention to the emergence
and endurance of the Church and associated themes of movement
and energy. While foundations and dynamics are important, they
need to be allied to purpose.

Ecclesiology therefore is an inquiry which also attends to the *purpose* of the Church. How might we depict this purpose? No doubt there are a variety of possible approaches. As I read the New Testament, I am brought up sharp by the statement in the Letter to the Ephesians that it is 'through the Church' (*dia tou ecclesia*) that the 'rich variety' of the wisdom of God is known in the cosmos (Eph. 3.10). I treat this matter at some length in Chapter 6, though for the moment I simply flag this reference as a powerful and instructive way to understand the purpose of the Church. It certainly raises the stakes about being the Church and how the Church lives and acts in the world. The Ephesians text suggests that the purpose of the Church has to do with displaying, embodying, and so manifesting divine wisdom.

This holy vocation of the Church is empowered, as suggested above, through attraction to God and in company with others. Accordingly, seeking after God is fundamentally a pilgrimage in the company of others. The accent is on movement, energy and dynamics. To develop a doctrine of the Church from this perspective – which is at the heart of this book – implies a critique of those ways of being the Church more in tune with 'steady-state' and change-resistant approaches to Church and institutional life.

Seeking the Church: historical and theological markers

The remainder of this chapter offers a brief consideration of some key issues in ecclesiology concerning origins, emergence and development of the Church as witnessed to in Scripture. In Scripture, we are offered insight into human yearning for God, the way the divine attraction works, and some of the tensions that run through this story. The tensions are varied and inter-related, for example, between dynamic and permanent features of being the Church, between the now and the not yet of the Church, between the Church and the kingdom of God, between Jesus and the kingdom of God. Yet, throughout the scriptural narrative the basic orientation is towards movement, energy and dynamics as people are attracted to God and each other.

It is not possible in the space of this chapter to provide a comprehensive account of the origin and development of the Church in the Bible. In any case, that is not to my concern. In what follows, I briefly trace the emergence of the Church in Israel and the history of Jesus. This inquiry raises important issues for ecclesiology regarding the foundation of the Church and the relationship between the Church and the kingdom. This leads to a final reflection on the task of ecclesiology within the economy of theology. In brief: it is a preliminary fix on the question of origins and some of the theological issues that arise for the Church. Chapter 2 will further develop some of these lines of inquiry.

Emerging Church: Israel, Jesus and the kingdom

Holy Scripture bears witness to three phases in the emergence of the Christian Church: (a) the formation of the Jewish nation and evolving messianic consciousness; (b) the coming of Jesus and his proclamation of the kingdom of God; (c) the post-Easter Church of the resurrection.

Israel, the Elect Community

From an historical point of view, the Christian Church traces its roots back to the God of Abraham, Isaac and Jacob, Sarah, Rebecca, Rachel, David and Jonathan, Ruth, and Rahab. Israel as the elect people of God is essential to the story of the Church, which emerges into bright light with the coming of the longed for Messiah. However, the fact that the Canon of Scripture of the Christian Church includes the Hebrew Scriptures indicates, among many other things, that there is a story to be told about how the Church of Jesus Christ springs from deep sources in Israel's history. The Jewish roots of the Church have become a significant feature of modern ecclesiology. As Edward Schillebeeckx succinctly states, 'Jesus himself was a Jew, not only by descent but also in his heart' (1990, p. 148). Furthermore, '[t]he activities and speeches of the apostles, as recorded in the book of Acts, give abundant evidence for the Jewishness of the earliest Church' (Wilson 1989, p. 43 and more generally on the topic, pp. 39–51). The sources of the Church reach back to Genesis, to primal origins, to creation and prehistory, to the covenants of Noah and Abraham and the subsequent emergence of Israel. From this perspective, we are not surprised that the New Testament evidence 'is irrefutable about the beginnings of the Church: in its origin, Christianity was Jewish to the very core. The essentially non-Jewish character of today's Church is a matter of history, not a question of origins' (p. 43).

The formation of a nation given over to the worship of Yahweh the Lord had a long, complex and at times violent history. Tribal groupings were always in tension with the drive for more cohesive and powerful corporate identities (Gottwald 1979). Questions of authority and rule through prophetic and monarchical traditions were similarly fraught with conflict. Religious traditions and the quest for purity of worship within a theocratic society gave a particular and distinctive focus for the emergence of a sense of a people chosen by Yahweh. Conflicts with other nations, exodus traditions, liberation, exile and restoration formed the crucible in which Israel's messianic consciousness was born. And this in two respects: first and primarily, in relation to God's Anointed One to usher in the new age of freedom and prosperity; and second, and as a consequence, that Israel was destined to become a blessing for the nations.

It is not difficult to see how the Christian Church, which grew out of Jewish soil, would exhibit so many of the tensions and challenges of Israel in its own subsequent history. To acknowledge the deep roots of the Church in the Jewish people is to acknowledge (a) how intertwined the Church is with Israel, and (b) that the question of the Church cannot be separated from the question of Israel. After all, the Church shares with Israel a common heritage enshrined in the Hebrew Scriptures reaching back to primal origins in Genesis and the faith of Abraham.

This brief discussion raises a fundamental theological question concerning the relation between the Church and Israel. On this matter, Wolfhart Pannenberg states that 'there is an abiding link between the Church and the Jewish people, a link that Paul then describes in terms of the root of the olive tree that carries the wild branches that contrary to normal rules have been grafted into it (Rom. 11.17–18)' (1998, p. 472). How might we understand this 'abiding link'? There is of course a long and contested history concerning this question. In the twentieth century, Karl Barth set an important marker when he developed an answer on the basis of the doctrine of the divine election of Israel. For Barth, 'the Church is older than its calling and gathering from among Jews and Gentiles which begins with the ascension or the miracle of Pentecost. It is manifested at this point, but it has already lived a hidden life in Israel' (1957, p. 211). This leads Barth to state that the Church 'is the goal and therefore the foundation of the election of the people of Israel' (p. 211). The Church thus exists in the midst of Israel from the beginning, 'since it is from the first the natural root of the existence of Jesus of Nazareth' (p. 212). In this context, Barth can refer to the 'pre-existent life of the Church in Israel, which as such is the prototype, prevision and prophecy of the elect in and from Israel' (p. 213). Barth's Christological doctrine of election leads him to the conclusion that the elect of Israel 'is ultimately reduced to the person of one man, Jesus of Nazareth' (p. 213). The pre-existent Church in Israel finally concentrates itself in a singular person, event and time. One thing is abundantly clear from recent scholarship: the Church is welded to Israel in history and theology notwithstanding all the attendant tensions and difficulties. Precisely how this relationship is understood is the contested issue.

Reflection on the relation between the Church and Israel has continued over the long history of the Church. For the sixteenth-century Anglican ecclesiologist Richard Hooker (1554–1600), the reason was properly theological as well as practical. It was a question of the unity of the visible Church. He considered that this unity had 'continued from the first beginning of the world to the last end. Which company being divided into two moieties, the one before, the other since the coming of Christ' (Hooker 1954, p. 285).

Exactly how far back we might locate the origins of the Church is an interesting if teasing theological question. For example, there is an ongoing discussion in New Testament studies as to whether the author of Ephesians thought of a pre-existent Church in Christ before the foundation of the world (see Best 1998, pp. 334–5).

In the ecumenical environment of the past century, and in particular in the wake of the horrors of the Holocaust, the question of the Jewish people is both urgent and unavoidable. Moreover, false developments in that relationship must be avoided.[3] It is for this reason that over the last decade and a half Christians, Jews, and Muslims have been involved in 'scriptural reasoning' to explore the sacred scriptures of our common traditions.[4] The Church's connectedness to Israel is most clearly seen in the depiction of the Church in the New Testament as 'the people of God', a matter taken up in Chapter 2.

The long history of the formation of the nation of Israel; their developing consciousness as an elect community of Yahweh and the emergence of a messianic hope are predicated on a sense of a people on the move. Critical here is the motif of the 'promised land'. The narrative of movement and travel – through Abraham's journeys, occupation of the land of promise, various sojourns in Egypt, exile, liberation and return – eventually gives way to a more settled and established period with the post exilic reconstruction of Jerusalem and the Temple as the national heart of Israel's religious traditions. Yet this Temple identity contains the seeds of its own evolution and transformation embodied in the messianic hopes of the people. The elect community remains a community *en route* in travel mode. This of course meets with some strong and unsurprising resistance from those authorities charged with the guardianship

---

3 Pannenberg points out that it is critical that 'Christian theology today ought to handle the Church's relation to the concept of the elect people of God with the openness that we find in Paul's statements on the theme' (1998, p. 477). Pannenberg is acutely aware of the dangers of the Church abrogating to itself 'the sense of exclusive election'.

4 For further see the *Journal of Scriptural Reasoning* established 2002.

and advocacy of established institutions for religious and political life. This tension comes to the fore when we consider Jesus, the nascent Church, and the coming kingdom.

Jesus and the kingdom of God

A second phase in the emergence of the Christian Church is relatively short; approximately 33 years, the span of the life of Jesus of Nazareth. Its twin co-ordinates are symbolized by the feasts of Christmas and Easter. As recorded in the Gospels, the life of Jesus is clothed in messianic categories and focused on the coming kingdom of God. With Jesus a new epoch has arrived in the history of Israel. In Mark's Gospel, a clear distinction is drawn between the work of John the Baptist and Jesus. Thus Mark 1.8 – 'I have baptized you with water but he will baptize you in (the) Holy Spirit' – 'suggests that the time of eschatological fulfilment of scripture (cf. vv. 2–3), is divided into periods' (Collins 2007, pp. 154f). While this 'qualitative contrast' is not absolute, nonetheless, the opening chapter of Mark's Gospel 'suggests that John is portrayed as a prototype of Jesus'. Jesus proclaims 'The time is fulfilled and the kingdom of God has drawn near' (1.15), implying 'that the prophecies of scripture and the hopes of the people are in the process of being fulfilled', and this is related to 'the fulfilment of history with the kingship of God'.

The Lutheran theologian Wolfhart Pannenberg appeals to the category of sign in his discussion of the relation of Jesus to the kingdom. 'Executing his earthy mission, he [Jesus] gave signs of the divine rule (Matt. 11.4–5) by his work of healing, by his proclamation of the good news of the saving nearness of God, and by his communion meals as signs of fellowship in God's kingdom' (1998, p. 43f). Accordingly Jesus is the sign by which the Father 'reveals himself and his kingdom' (p. 44). But 'the reality of God's kingdom that has dawned in the message and history of Jesus Christ' (p. 95) is 'a sign of the future of God's lordship . . .' (p. 44). Pannenberg's account of the identity of Jesus with the 'divine dominion, which he announced' in terms of sign, means that the identity 'is also not without distinction' (p. 43). His point is that while Jesus in his words, deeds and history embodies the coming kingdom, it does not exhaust it but points to it, even while it instantiates it in the present. In this way, Jesus embodies the mystery of salvation.

In this second moment of the emergence of the Christian Church, we note a number of things. First, the proclamation of Jesus in word and deed initiated a radical nearness of the kingdom of God. The character of this is well captured in Origen's phrase that Jesus was 'the *autobasileia*, the "kingdom-in-person"' (quoted in Jensen and Wilhite 2010, p. 13). Second, Jesus is the 'kingdom-in-person' in association with the outpouring of the Spirit. Both Jesus and the Spirit are profoundly implicated in this action of God. One important consequence is that the kingdom of God is an eschatological reality, which remains essentially open-ended awaiting further determination and fulfilment.

Third, the advent of the Messiah generated significant controversy and disturbance in Judaism. Whether Jesus was primarily a reformer/renewer of Judaism or represented its radical transformation – a matter for continuing scholarly debate – nonetheless, his appearing regenerated the life of faith and community. Older patterns and understandings were deconstructed and reconstructed in such a way that a new momentum for the future kingdom arose from deep within the Abrahamic tradition of faith. For example, the Temple as the centre of faith and life was radically transformed in terms of his own body (John 2.18–22). This entailed a move beyond the settled and established religious forms and discourse. If Jesus' resurrected body embodied the new temple tradition of Israel, the seed is sown for a seismic shift in the character of the kingdom. Henceforth, it can break free of ethnic, cultural, linguistic, social, political, and geographic boundaries. The reciprocity between steady-state religious forms and faith as a dynamic, moving, energetic activity of a people is recovered. This transformation is encapsulated in the parables of the Gospels. When the kingdom of God comes near in Jesus new possibilities are generated and previously established and fixed measures by which human life is ordered and secured are disturbed. The subsequent history of the Christian Church is a story of how this new reality has been the catalyst for new developments and also suffered domestication through ecclesiastical systems of control.

From kingdom to Church

The third phase in the emergence of the Christian Church is initiated by the resurrection of Jesus. The scriptures speak of this as a work involving both Father and Spirit and, it needs to be stressed, not in any sense an achievement of Jesus (Rom. 1.4; 8.11) (Pannenberg 1998, p. 17). The emergence of the post-Easter Church is marked by the outpouring of the Spirit. In John's Gospel, this overflow of the Spirit is communicated by the risen Christ (20.22–3). In Luke's Gospel, the risen Jesus' promise of the Spirit (24.49) is subsequently fulfilled at Pentecost (Acts 2). The trigger for this fulfilment for Luke is the ascension of Christ. This post-Easter period is the time of the *ecclesia* of God. The Church 'had its origin when the step was taken to proclamation of Jesus' resurrection and exaltation' (p. 28). In this third phase, two key issues for ecclesiology have arisen: (a) Did Jesus found the Church and if so what kind of Church did he envision? (b) How ought we understand the relationship between the Church and the kingdom? These two questions are closely related, as I hope will become clear below.

Founding the Church

Why the question matters

In regard to the founding of the Church by Jesus, it is pertinent to ask: why does that matter?; what does it mean to 'found' the Church?; and by what method might we determine if Jesus did found the Church? The fact that there is a Church, which worships Jesus as Lord and saviour, would appear strange if not absurd, to say the least, if there wasn't some fundamental connection between the Christian Church and the person of Jesus Christ. The alternative is to suppose that the Church is simply the invention of some enthusiastic if misguided individuals who once knew or knew of Jesus. Certainly, the Churches of world Christianity have an interest and deep investment in the lineage they trace back to Jesus. At stake in the question of the founding of the Church is the credibility of its existence and ideals.

What then does it mean to found the Church? In the usual sense of 'found', we might expect to speak about someone initiating the conditions for something. This might, for example, be a charismatic or highly influential person who inspires others to begin a new venture without specifying further details. Some might want to include playing a significant part in the actual groundwork of the enterprise be it an organization or group of some kind. Perhaps this might be taken to include some basic blueprints or outlines of the way the new entity will function and what its purpose is. However, minimal requirements for founding would seem to involve a key role in establishing the initial conditions for whatever was to emerge, and this would probably involve some basic ideas about purpose and intent.

An historical critical approach

How then might we decide if Jesus really did found the Church? In New Testament studies, this matter belongs to an historical critical inquiry. In this respect, there has been and continues to be an unsurprising diversity of opinion. Some, like Georg Strecker – in the early twentieth-century tradition of Albert Schweitzer – are confident that it was not Jesus' intention to establish a Church. The reason for this was that Jesus' message was about repentance and the kingdom of God. Such a message was a direct challenge to any institutional religion let alone the creation of a new organization or body (2000, p. 261).[5] Joachim Jeremias is among those who

---

5 Strecker is equally clear that in, for example, the Matthean community 'the story of Jesus as a whole is foundational for the being and self-understanding of the Church' (2000, p. 389). The odd thing about such a

offer a more qualified approach. He argues that it would be an 'anachronism' to ascribe to Jesus the intention of founding an *ecclesia*, if that implied the kind of organization developed in a later period (Jeremias 1971, pp. 168–70). Jeremias suggests that *ecclesia* is most appropriately translated 'people of God'. With this in view he states that 'the *only* significance of the whole of Jesus' activity is to gather the eschatological people of God' (p. 170). This was a similar position to that of the Anglican New Testament theologian Alan Richardson. He concluded that while 'Jesus intended to found the Church', nonetheless the concept was inadequate to express the full truth that 'Christ is not so much the "Founder" of the Church as he is himself the Church, since the Church is not a company of likeminded people, but the body of those who have been incorporated into the *persona* of Christ, *totus Christus*, the head and the members . . . [which] Church came into being with the pouring out of the Holy Spirit by the risen and ascended Lord' (1958, p. 310).

Contemporary Roman Catholic scholars differ on the matter. Karl Rahner recognizes that historical evidence might not allow us to trace the structures of Catholicism back to Jesus' words and deeds (Avis 1993, p. 129). Nonetheless, he argues for a 'genetic connection' between apostolic developments and the structures of Catholicism. Rahner argues that there is a corporate dimension to the salvation announced by Jesus and concludes that Catholic structure is more than merely subjective reality and 'springs from the very essence of Christianity'. Avis notes that Edward Schillebeeckx, 'abandons even Rahner's subtle and elusive appeal to *ius divinum*', arguing that Jesus did not intend to found a new religious community. Instead, his emphasis was on 'faith in his message that led to communal discipleship'. While Schillebeeckx ends up affirming the Church as a divine foundation by Jesus, he

---

conclusion is that Strecker is apparently able to make a distinction between knowledge of what Jesus intended and knowledge of what the community of Jesus intended. 'He [Jesus] certainly did not create a Church in our sense of the word, embracing both Jews and Gentiles; according to the conviction of many New Testament scholars, he did not even express any desire that a Church should exist' (Käsemann 1969, p. 252).

wants to make it clear that this divine foundation fundamentally concerns humankind rather than institutional structure as such.

Following a survey of the debate, Jensen and Wilhite conclude on a positive note stating that there appears to be reasonable agreement that Jesus did establish a body of followers: he initiated followers into a body by baptism; he gathered followers by a ritual meal; he commissioned his followers to teach about the kingdom and practice its values. The key elements seem to be calling, gathering and commissioning. This leads them to state that while it may fall short of a consensus view there does seem overwhelming support for the conclusion Jesus founded the Church (2010, p. 11). They state '[t]hat the Church's origin is grounded in the life and work of Jesus himself should be recognized as an uncontested starting point for ecclesiology' (p. 12). 'Grounded in' is more nuanced than 'founded by' and most certainly involves 'founded upon' (Avis 1993, p. 129). This is helpful as far as it goes, though it also shows how impoverished the discussion can become without attending to more distinctly theological concerns concerning the founding of the Church.

A theological approach

The historical critical method for inquiry into the founding of the Church can take us only so far, and even then ecclesial interests of scholars are never wholly absent from assessments of the evidence. For example, the question of what kind of Church Jesus may have envisioned is open to a variety of views. Answers to this question can appear circular given the interest particular churches have in finding support for their particular ecclesiological position in the scripture. The spectrum includes the more Catholic institutional hierarchical position, which sees a critical link between Jesus and the first apostles, which gives rise to the Petrine office. It also includes the more fluid Free-Church theories of association, where the essence of the Church is found in Jesus' presence in any gathering of two or three in his name. Such ecclesiological filters have been challenged in modern times by the development of historical critical methodologies.

While a more overt theological inquiry into the question of the Church's founding is no guarantee of impartiality, it does open up a very different approach. A theological response enquires into the founding of the Church in terms of the action of God in Christ through the Spirit. In other words, the ecclesial question is brought into relation to the doctrine of God.

From this perspective, an argument can be mounted that both the Son and the Spirit are mutually involved in 'constituting' the Church. This double agency of Christ and the Spirit belongs to the witness of scripture. On the one hand, Paul can identify Jesus Christ as the foundation of the body of Christ (1 Cor. 3.11). On the other hand, for Luke, 'the Church seems to be founded by the "power" of the Spirit' (Pannenberg 1998, p. 15). Indeed, 'the story of Pentecost in Acts 2.1ff. gives expression to the fact that the Spirit does not simply assure each individual believer alone of fellowship with Jesus Christ, and therefore a share in eternal salvation, but that thereby he [sic] founds at the same time the fellowship of believers. For this story does at all events demonstrate that the Spirit was given to all the disciples in common and that therewith the Church had its beginning' (p. 13). From this perspective, it is an outpouring of the Spirit, which constitutes the post-Easter community of disciples.

Recognition of the Spirit's specific role in constituting the Church is the fruit of Orthodox theology in the twentieth century, which has flowed into ecumenical ecclesiology (Jensen 1999, p. 179). John's Gospel weaves the work of the Spirit and Jesus Christ in such a way that the Spirit leads people into the truth of Jesus and does so by glorifying Jesus rather than bearing witness to himself (16.13–14). For John, 'Jesus, by the Spirit's work, is with his own, being "in" them as they are in him' (14.20) (Pannenberg 1998, p. 18). This Johannine concept of Christ indwelling through the Spirit corresponds to Paul's language of adoption in Christ through the Spirit (Rom. 8.14–16). It leads Pannenberg to state that '[t]he christological constitution and the pneumatological constitution of the Church do not exclude one another but belong together because the Spirit and the Son mutually indwell one another as Trinitarian persons'. Thus he concludes, 'the Church is the creation of both the Spirit and the Son' (quoted on p. 18). Pannenberg is not alone in this matter. The Reformed theologian, Colin Gunton, with reference to the seventeenth-century Puritan Robert Owen, argues for a greater emphasis on the eschatological Spirit *constituting* the Church alongside the Son who *institutes* the Church (Gunton 1989, pp. 62–5, 73). This has the advantage of retaining a stronger link to the pre-Easter accounts of Jesus' community formation. However, both scholars seem concerned to correct an over-emphasis on Christology, when it comes to the question of the founding of the Church.

One effect of the over-emphasis on Christology has been to give undue weight to official Church structure and ministries via excessive claims for historical links to the past. Recovering the importance of the Spirit in ecclesiology also involves reappraisal of the more usual isolation of the Spirit to the region of inner illumination. While it is through the Spirit that faith recognizes Jesus the individualistic focus inevitably omits the constituting work of the Spirit for the *ecclesia*. The Reformation focus on the Church as the creature of the divine Word (*creatura verbi divini*) appears incomplete, if it fails to recognize the Spirit's action in constituting the fellowship of believers as Church (Schwöbel 1989).

Kingdom, Church and eschatology

Church and kingdom

I noted above that the question about the founding of the Church was related to the question about the relationship between the Church and the kingdom. The key issue here is one of eschatology. It is the eschatological Spirit of Christ who founds the Church. The particular character of the mutual relationship between Christ and the Spirit is captured in John Zizioulas' remark: 'the Spirit makes of Christ an eschatological being' (quoted in Pannenberg 1998, p. 17). The orientation is towards the future, to the consummation of the coming kingdom. The character and dynamic of the Spirit and Christ in constituting the

Church means that the community of faith is neither the final nor the finished product. The Church is essentially unfinished and in motion on the way, so to speak. It is an anticipation of a future renewed world and humanity (Eph. 2.15; Rom. 8), in which God will one day be 'all in all' (1 Cor. 15.28). For this reason, Church and kingdom are not identical, but nor are they entirely disconnected realities.

How then might we develop an understanding of the relationship between the Church and the kingdom? The Australian theologian Christiaan Mostert notes that the 'idea that the Church is an eschatological community, closely connected to the kingdom or reign of God, has not been prominent in ecclesiology' (2011, p. 25). He argues 'that the early Christian community understood its own existence in eschatological terms, as the 'vestibule' of God's reign (Bultmann)'. Mostert employs the concept of 'anticipation' to argue that the Church is an anticipatory sign of the kingdom. Getting the relation right is important; the Church being 'a function of the kingdom rather than the kingdom being in some sense a function of the Church' (p. 26).

Mostert develops his argument using two key moves in Rudolf Bultmann's discussion concerning Jesus, kingdom and Church. First, he notes Bultmann's famous phrase, 'the proclaimer became the [one] proclaimed' and enquires into the conditions under which 'the bearer of the message of the reign of God became the *content* of the message' (p. 27, quoting from Bultmann 1965, p. 33). By virtue of the resurrection, Jesus was 'proclaimed as messianic and as the core of God's salvific work in the world' as good news. Mostert gives particular attention to Bultmann's evocative notion that 'the earliest Church regarded itself as the Congregation of the end of days', 'the vestibule . . . of God's Reign that [was] shortly to appear' (p. 31). As vestibule of God's reign the Church understood itself as the *eschatological* congregation.

Critical for Mostert is the idea that the present reality of the Church is 'defined by the future; the end breaks into the present' (p. 32). He argues for a view of time 'in which present and future are not neatly sequential but present together. Yet, the difference between the present and the future cannot be obliterated';

'we have only the first-fruits of our redemption' (quoting from Welch 1958, p. 128). Mostert's argument for the Church as an eschatological community is not a reason for confusing it with the kingdom though 'its relation to the kingdom is as much one of association as of dissociation' (p. 33). He appeals to Hans Küng, who, in an earlier generation, described the Church as 'the eschatological community of salvation':

> The Church is not the earthly form of the kingdom, but neither is it a fill-in, a compromise solution, an ersatz kingdom for the kingdom of God which was awaited in vain. The eschatological community of believers is not in opposition to the reign of God, nor are the two unconnected; the Church is directed towards and belongs to the coming reign of God. (quoting from Küng 1967, pp. 94–5)

The relationship between the Church and kingdom developed above contrasts sharply with that of Alfred Loisy who, in the early twentieth century, famously once said that 'Jesus proclaimed the kingdom of God and along came the Church' (Loisy 1976, p. 166). Loisy, the Catholic modernist critical of an over-institutionalized Church, emphasized a relationship of disassociation between the Church and the kingdom. Mostert, a Reformed theologian writing a century after Loisy and in the light of a Protestantism in decline, argues that the relation between kingdom and Church is as much one of *association* as *disassociation*. The critical element in more recent discussions is eschatology. The recovery of this dimension of early Christianity enables ecclesiology to move beyond a steady-state Church which values established form and precedent over the inner movement, dynamism and orientation to the future consummation of all things in God.

As is well known, the tendency to over-identify the Church with the kingdom has been a perennial problem in Christianity and has led to all kinds of excess, institutional hubris and sectarian behaviour. A humbler and more open ecclesiology emerges when the Church is understood as a sign and anticipation of the coming kingdom. Precisely because the Church is a creature of the divine Word and Spirit, it is a genuine foretaste of the coming kingdom.[6] It is not and cannot be an empty sign but rather an embodied sign. What it points to actually constitutes its present life. However, precisely because it is genuinely born of the eschatological Spirit of Christ the Church is also necessarily provisional and unfinished. The basis for this is the double agency of Christ and the Spirit in the creation of the Church, a matter developed further in Chapter 4. From the point of view of practical ecclesiology, the above discussion means 'that the kingdom of God provides the context for the Church's existence; the context for its specific form of the presence of God's Spirit within it; and the framework of reference for the relation to the political community and its constitutional order and law (Pannenberg 1998, p. 97).

Conclusion: emerging Church in brief

Scripture witnesses to three periods in the emergence of the Church: first, the development of Israel as God's people with a messianic consciousness; second, the coming of Jesus and the irruption of the kingdom of God; and third, the community of Jesus arising from the Easter resurrection and the coming of the Spirit at Pentecost. Through the continuities and discontinuities associated with these three periods critical issues arise concerning the founding of the Church, its relationship to Israel and the kingdom of God. The recovery of the eschatological dimension of early Christianity and the agency of the Spirit in relation to Christ has been a central insight of modern theology. It has had a significant impact on contemporary ecclesiology. Probably the most important development in this has been the move from a steady-state approach to ecclesiology – regardless of the particular ecclesial tradition – to a more dynamic openended ecclesiology appropriate to the character of the founding

---

6 Of course, the manner in which the Church's creaturely existence is formed by, for example, the Divine Spirit, is both rich and complex and often contested (McIntyre 1997 Ch. 8).

of the Church, as observed in scripture. As yet, I haven't said anything about the variety of ecclesiologies that can be discerned in Scripture and how they have filtered into contemporary practices (see Bockmuehl and Thomson 1997). I will try to identify something of this variety in Chapter 2. However, before moving to that discussion, this chapter closes with a reflection on the task of ecclesiology.

The task of ecclesiology

Church as an article of faith

The Nicene Creed of the ancient Church states that '[w]e believe in one holy catholic and apostolic Church'. The earlier Apostles Creed refers to 'the holy catholic Church'. Perhaps the most significant feature of both affirmations is the fact that they are located within the third section of the respective creeds under the article about the Holy Spirit. It is no coincidence nor simply a matter of pragmatics that Jürgen Moltmann wrote a book with the title *The Church in the Power of the Spirit* (1977). It is the Lord and giver of life who is worshipped, who speaks through the prophets, who is the Lord and giver of life to the Church. The fact that affirmation about the Church is located firmly within the ancient statements of fundamental Christian belief makes it abundantly clear that the Church is an article of belief. The Church is not merely *context* for our belief but is involved in that very belief about God the Holy Trinity. In this sense, the Church belongs within the Spirit of the Triune God and cannot be discerned apart from faith in this God. The 'Church is the subject of an article of faith and of the creed, a mystery to be believed and confessed' (Bender 2005, p. 168).

But what kind of article of faith is the Church? Another way to put this is to ask: does one believe *in* or believe 'the Church'? The Church is not the object of faith, we do not believe *in* the Church; at least not in the same way that we believe in God, Christ and the Holy Spirit. It is not *credo in ecclesiam* but *credo ecclesiam*. Barth was clear: '*Credo in Spiritum* sanctum, but not *Credo in ecclesiam.* I believe in the Holy Spirit, but not in the Church. Rather I believe in the Holy Spirit, and therefore also in the existence of the Church, the congregation' (Barth 1966, p. 142). And a little later, '*Credo ecclesiam* means that I believe that here, at this place, in this visible assembly, the work of the Holy Spirit takes place' (p. 143). The Holy Trinity is the great and infinite yet wholly personal reality of God. It is this God to whom the creation owes its life, energy and purpose, and it is in the one Lord and Father of our Lord Jesus Christ in the power of the Spirit that the body of Christ in the world owes its origin. As such, we believe only *in* God, in whose power and presence the Church is born and is sustained.

The above comments echo the earliest Creeds, which 'speak of believing *in* God and in the Holy Spirit but of believing the Church' (O'Grady 1969, p. 281). For the same reason, the oldest Church order in Christianity, the *Traditio Apostolica* of Hippolytus of Rome dating around the year 215, asks very precisely in the third baptismal question: 'Do you believe in the Holy Spirit in the holy Church for the resurrection of the body?'[7]

Believing 'the Church' recognizes that its existence and authority are real and significant within the purposes of God. Certainly, believing 'the' Church avoids the danger of equating belief in the Church with belief in God. Over-identification at this point has been a failing of the Church through the centuries; a matter that will be addressed in Chapter 3 of this book. It may be more accurate to refer to the Church as an article of faith *within* the folds of the *object of faith*, which is the Triune God. The above reflections suggest a close association between God and the Church, though specifying the nature of this relation is both important and somewhat illusive. On the one hand, it is critical not to confuse the two entities and thus fall into idolatry. On the other hand, we ought not separate the two such that the real relation is fractured or denied.

---

7 O'Grady also makes the point that for the same reason 'the great scholastics explained the article *credo . . . unam, sanctam, catholicam et apostolicam Ecclesiam* as identical with the one that precedes it, *credo in Spiritum Sanctum*'.

When Karl Barth considered the matter, he developed an understanding of the relation between Christ and the Church on the basis of the divine and human natures of Christ (see Bender 2005, p. 174). The Church's relation to Christ was analogous to the way in which the humanity of Christ was enfolded within or participated in the divinity – *enhypostasis*. Moreover, the only Church Barth had in mind at this point was the earthly visible Church; the form through which the eternal God chose to be manifest. Barth's Christological approach points to the fact that the mystery of the union between Christ and his body the Church (Eph. 5.32) is of such a kind that the two entities ought not be severed or diminished by any reductionist account of the body of Christ. We may not believe in the Church directly, nonetheless when we believe in the Triune God, we simultaneously bear witness in our believing that we are *of* the *ecclesia* of God, *in* the *ecclesia* of God and *for* the *ecclesia* of God. The Church is no longer at a distance but participates in our believing in God. This indeed is a great mystery, not in the sense of a puzzle but a profound indwelling that resists final determination and analysis (cf. Eph 3. 21).

This approach recalls the beginning of this chapter, where I suggested that seeking God involved seeking the Church; that seeking the one necessarily involved seeking the other. I stated that it was the purpose of this book to show why and how this was the case. The nexus between God the Spirit and the Church is such that it is almost impossible to believe the articles concerning the Spirit without at the same time believing the Church and the articles, which necessarily follow (baptism, forgiveness of sins, the resurrection of the dead, life of the world to come). To put the matter another way, the character of the belief enjoined upon us in regard to the Spirit is, as stated in above, an *ecclesial* matter. Spirit and Church are given in and with each other, mutual indwelling without confusion of identity. It means that there is a genuine sense in which it is entirely accurate to state that 'we believe in one holy catholic and apostolic Church'. It points to the fact that the Church as renewed human community is a creature of the Spirit and the Word. The creedal injunction *credo ecclesiam* presumes the kind of ontology that leads the Apostle Paul to refer to the great mystery of the Church as

Christ's body.[8] The Church, enfolded as it is in the creedal articles concerning the Spirit, is rightly an article of faith though never the direct object of that faith.

The Church in the economy of theology

We have noted the longstanding location of the Church within the economy of salvation as embodied in the ancient creeds. Unfortunately, however, when it comes to critical theological inquiry regarding the faith the Church has often been relegated to the purely practical domain. One result of this has been that the Church has occupied a somewhat marginal place in the treatment of the great doctrines of faith. In the typical modern theological curriculum, the doctrine of the Church has usually been located in field D among the practical concerns of Christianity, such as liturgy, mission and ethics. The divisions are increasingly unsatisfying, but to the extent that they continue, the place of the Church in the economy of theology is both diminished and misunderstood. Of course, the Church is an intensely practical matter – it is after all the ecclesial practices of Christianity that we look to in order to determine how adequately the Church attends to its risen saviour and Lord. And indeed, practical ecclesiology does precisely that. However, when the doctrine of the Church is omitted from reflection on the central or core doctrines of Christian belief, faith remains disconnected from the living of life together. This means that the essential ecclesial nature of faith is diminished and the doctrine of God is robbed of something of its inner dynamism.

This state of affairs has been highlighted by Daniel Hardy: 'It is habitual in most theology, if not to exclude ecclesiology altogether, at least to place it in another category from doctrine as such' (2006, pp. 267f). Hardy has in mind theology in universities

---

8 The image of the Church as the body of Christ is not simply a metaphor, but a proper designation of the nature of Church as Christ's risen ascended and hence transformed crucified body. For further discussion, see Chapter 2.

in Britain and the USA. He identifies a number of reasons for this situation: the relative late emergence of ecclesiology as a loci in theology as a result of an emerging self-consciousness of the broken and separated condition of the Church; preoccupation with defence of the Christian faith in the face of challenges; the development of universities where 'high ground' concerns in defending the faith became institutionalized; emphasis in universities on research with consequent marginalization of practical matters. The negative assessment of ecclesiology is noted by Gerald Mannion and Lewis Mudge who state that for some ecclesiology 'has connotations of institutionalism and prelacy, and perhaps also of precious self-concern' (2008, p. 2).

However, it is possible that we are in a period of ecclesiological thaw. The doctrine of the Church appears to be enjoying a renaissance and has become an increasingly popular topic at both the practical and, to some extent at least, the theoretical level.[9] This ought not be surprising, given the emergence of twentieth-century ecumenism as a consequence of the missionary movement of the nineteenth century. It was the experience of mission beyond the established denominational boundaries of Europe and North America that played a significant role in the rise of ecclesial consciousness among the divided Churches. This, combined with the Churches' response to successive world wars in the twentieth century, placed ecclesiological issues on the agenda. The renewal of Trinitarian theology and the recovery of the communitarian aspect of the doctrine of God also played an important part in the contemporary renewal of ecclesiology. It means ecclesiology can no longer be regarded as a secondary matter. This is echoed in Daniel Migliore's comment that

the Church is not incidental to God's purposes. God enters into covenant with creatures and seeks their partnership. If there is communion in the eternal life of God and God wills us to share in that communion, then questions regarding the nature of the

---

9 See, for example, the publications from the *Ecclesiological Investigations Research Network* – www.ei-research.net. See also the overview in Kärkkäinen 2002.

Church and its mission in the world today, far from being matters of secondary importance to the understanding of the Christian faith, are quite central. (Migliore 2004, p. 248)

The Lutheran theologian Jaroslav Pelikan has brought the matter
into sharp focus: 'the doctrine of the Church became, as it had never
quite been before, the bearer of the whole of the Christian message for the twentieth century, as well as the recapitulation of the
entire doctrinal tradition from preceding centuries' (Pelikan 1989,
p. 282). Was this a sign of the failure of Christianity – a retreat into
its religious 'enclave'[10] – at least in the West? Or was it indicative of
an intuition about community and sociality; something quite central
and creative in the life of faith in the world? Part of the purpose of
this book is to show that it is the latter situation. Pelikan's comment
points to the fact that ecclesiology is not a second order in contrast
to a 'first order' issue; nor is it a 'low ground' compared to 'high
ground' matter in theology. Rather, Pelikan's comment suggests the
possibility of ecclesiology as the principle of coherence for the central themes of Christianity. Minimally, it means that there may be
a way of thinking theologically, which locates ecclesiology firmly
within the economy of theology. What exactly this might encompass
is signalled in the following statement of Mannion and Mudge:

Authentic ecclesiology asks what the coming of Jesus Christ
means as expressed 'in the form of a community' (Bonhoeffer).
Ecclesiology looks at the Churches' forms of governance, liturgical life and corporate witness as primary instruments by which
the gospel is lived and communicated. Ecclesiology becomes the
normative study of communities which make social and symbolic space in the world for the workings of grace. In such a
perspective, ecclesiology becomes far more than an afterthought
at the end of the book. It becomes far more than an institutional
setting for the protection and promulgation of truths reached
in other ways. It becomes fundamental to Christian theological

---

10 Bellah refers to 'lifestyle enclaves' signalling retreat from the public
to the private domains of life (Bellah et al., 1985, pp. 71–5).

reflection as such. Seen as 'fundamental theology', ecclesiology concerns the nature of the social space which makes language about God, and therefore faith itself, possible. (2008, p. 3)

This is a wide-ranging agenda and indicates what a complex and dynamic entity the Church is. Nicholas Healy offers a somewhat complementary and practical orientation when he states:

> Putting it boldly, ecclesiologists have something like a prophetic function in the Church. They reflect theologically and therefore critically upon the Church's concrete identity in order to help it boast in its Lord, and boast only in its Lord. They attempt to assess the Church's witness and pastoral care in the light of Scripture and in relation to a theological analysis of the contemporary ecclesiological context. They propose changes in the Church's concrete identity that will conserve, reform or more radically restructure it, in order to help it embody its witness more truthfully and better demonstrate the superiority of its way of life. Contextual ecclesial praxis inform ecclesiology, and ecclesiology informs contextual ecclesial praxis, in a practical hermeneutical circle. (2000, p. 46)

The task of ecclesiology

The complexity of the above projects means that particular care is required not to lose the distinctly *theological* reference in relation to the Church. This is the reason for pursing the rather simple but important issue, with which I began this chapter and returned to in the discussion above regarding the Church as an article of faith; that is, to seek God involves seeking the Church. In the Christian tradition, the God sought is the Triune God of love. To be a seeker of such a God will necessarily lead into deeper communion with the world of this God and its peoples. From this perspective, ecclesiology concerns a journey into the unmeasurable 'height, length, depth and breadth of the God of love' (Eph. 3.18); a journey undertaken in the company of others. There is of course much more to be said about this movement towards God and the Church, but that is the task of the book.

Put simply, the task of ecclesiology is the study of the Church of the Triune God. As flagged earlier in this chapter such study involves attention to foundations, dynamics and purpose. This can be specified more sharply in terms of the following three-fold focus: (a) the conditions for the Church's emergence; (b) the means by which it is sustained and (c) the purposes of its life in the world. Much hangs on that final phrase 'life in the world'. Ecclesiology is never a hermetically sealed inquiry but necessarily includes multiple engagements informed by God's active wisdom in the world. Indeed, part of the task of ecclesiology is not only to draw upon but point to God's wisdom manifest in the world. And all this is not simply that the Church might become puffed up with its own self-importance but rather contribute to the flourishing of society. On this account, ecclesiology necessarily involves 'assembling all that is needed to promote the fullness of human society' (Hardy 2010, p. 79). The doctrine of the Church ought to have an osmotic and dynamic feel about it always orientated beyond its own life, always reaching deeper into the world of which it is a creature in its own particular way. In this sense, ecclesiology ought to be able to show how and why blurred boundaries between the Church and society are to be expected and embraced.

An ecclesiology for pilgrims: a brief tour

The book is intended as a mini systematic ecclesiology and this is reflected in the way the chapters unfold. In this chapter, I have covered some of the familiar territory and questions, which arise in ecclesiology regarding sources and tasks. In Chapter 2, I consider how contemporary theology, including feminist theology, has inquired into the doctrine of the Church in relation to biblical images, models, paradigms and practices for understanding the nature of the Church. Chapters 1 and 2 provide a preliminary map of the territory of ecclesiology.

Chapter 3 examines some of the recurring false tracks in the doctrine of the Church in terms of 'natural ecclesial heresies'. It examines some basic problems in ecclesiology related to Christology and anthropology and explores the implications of such problems for practical ecclesiology: the divide between the Church and world; ministry and leadership; and mission. Chapters 1 to 3 are a prelude to the more constructive part of the book, which constitutes Chapters 4 to 9.

Chapters 4 and 5 provide the theological groundwork for the ecclesiology developed in the book. Chapter 4 focuses on the theme of sociality, as it relates to creation and redemption; the nature of the bond in Christ and the ways in which this ecclesial bond is mediated in the world. Chapter 5 is a critical engagement with the social doctrine of the Trinity as a basis for a renewed sociality. The sociality relevant to the Christian Church is then examined in Chapter 6 in terms of the traditional marks of the Church as one, holy, catholic and apostolic. These marks are reviewed for their relevance to the Church today through the lens of some key twentieth-century theologians.

Insofar as every ecclesial body has some visible structure and leadership, Chapter 7 explores the nature and purpose of the structuring of ecclesial life – its polity and ministry. The key issue here is the way in which structure embodies and facilitates God's presence and work in the world. Chapter 8 considers how an ecclesial body maintains itself, is enriched and expands. This is developed in terms of energy necessary for the journey of faith and its importance for understanding the nature of the Church. Energy is the interpretive key for worship, word, sacrament, service and witness. The final Chapter 9 develops the notion of 'slow Church' for pilgrims of the coming Church.

The book, as I have indicated, is intended as a brief systematic ecclesiology. As such it has a certain generic quality, which hopefully extends its mobility and usefulness for the student, teacher and theological scholar regardless of ecclesial affiliation. On the other hand, I write as an Anglican theologian. This will become apparent as the book unfolds, as I draw on occasions upon my own tradition to illustrate ideas and commend particular arguments. However, I trust that what I have written will prove of value for people of the Churches and indeed all who seek the God who is in all, through all and above all.

Questions

1 'A Christian has to be an ecclesial Christian'. What reasons could you give for this statement by Karl Rahner?
2 Of what value is the Old Testament for the doctrine of the Church?
3 'And I, when I am lifted up from the earth, will draw all people to myself' (John 12.32). What value might this text have for a theology of the Church?
4 Luther said the Church was a *creatura verbi divini*. What did he mean and how important is the Spirit in the creation of the Church?
5 'Jesus proclaimed the kingdom and along came the Church' (Alfred Loisy). Is this fair?
6 'We believe in the one, holy, catholic and apostolic church'. In what sense do we believe *in* the Church?

Further reading

Gregory Afonsky, 'The Church and the Kingdom of God', in *Christ and the Church: In Orthodox Teaching and Tradition*, New York: St Vladimir's Seminary Press, 2001, pp. 33–40.
Paula Gooder, 'In Search of the Early "Church": The New Testament and the Development of Christian Communities,' in Gerard Mannion and Lewis S. Mudge (eds) *The Routledge Companion to the Christian Church*, New York and London: Routledge, 2012, pp. 9–27.
William Henn, 'Why Do We Need the Church at All?', in *Church: The People of God*, London and New York: Burns & Oates, 2004, pp. 6–21.
John McIntyre, *The Shape of Pneumatology*, Edinburgh: T & T Clark, 1997, chap. 8.
Natalie K. Watson, *Introducing Feminist Ecclesiology*, Cleveland, OH: The Pilgrim Press, 2002, Chs 1 and 2.

2

Ecclesial Portraiture

Scriptural images and ecclesiology

The New Testament offers a remarkable variety of images and metaphors to refer to the Church. Some images are more striking and appear more central than others though all offer insights into different ecclesiological streams that flow through the New Testament (Collins 2003). Avery Dulles discusses how images function in a primal way (1974). Images can tap the wells of human experience and imagination and operate as powerful symbols that can transform life and society. Good quality images – that is, those which resonate with experience of life with God in the world – can endure over time and continually refresh understandings of what it means to be the Church.

A variety of images for the Church

The classic study of the images of the Church by Paul Minear half a century ago identified 96 different images, metaphors and analogies for the Church (1961, pp. 268–9). 'Image', as the word suggests, generates mental pictures of entities. For the most part, images of the Church, such as 'little flock', function as metaphors. That is, they convey an understanding of one thing in terms of another.[1]

---

1 The word 'metaphor' derives from the sixteenth-century Old French *métaphore*, in turn from the Latin *metaphora*, 'carrying over', which is the latinization of the Greek *metaphorá*, 'transfer', from *metaphero*, 'to carry over', 'to transfer', itself a compound of *meta*, 'between' + *pher*, 'to bear', 'to carry'. Metaphors compare things without using 'like' or 'as'. As such,

Minear distinguished between minor and major images. Among the minor images, he included the Church as 'the salt of the earth', 'the boat', 'the ark', 'branches of the Lord', 'God's building', 'the bride of Christ', 'citizens with the saints', 'the poor', 'the exiles'. He grouped the major images into three categories: (a) those related to the Church as 'the people of God'. These images highlighted the connection of the Church to its antecedents in Israel and the coming kingdom of God and included 'Israel of God', 'the holy nation', 'Abraham's sons', 'the little flock', 'the elect of God', 'the holy temple', 'the holy city', 'the remnant'; (b) those images that bore witness to the Church in its cosmic and universal dimension. Included here were the Church as 'new creation', 'the new humanity', 'kingdom of God', 'communion in the Holy Spirit'; (c) images that concern the Church as a fellowship of faith such as 'the saints', 'household of God', 'the faithful', 'disciples', 'servants'.

Minear noted that his categories were provisional and many images served all three. His interest lay in analysis of each image and what this indicated about the character of the early Christian Church. Whether any particular image was intended primarily as figurative or non-figurative, whether it had ontological or purely functional significance or whether all dimensions of the operation of the image were relevant, were matters that it was exceedingly difficult to specify.

Assessing Minear's contribution

A number of things are striking with regard to Minear's seminal work. First, the Pauline notion of the Church as 'the body of Christ' does not appear in the images identified above, because Minear devoted a chapter to this image. It is hard to resist the claim of the 'body of Christ' to be a master image with ontological weight. He noted the phrase 'is not a single expression with

---

a metaphor is a figure of speech that constructs an analogy between two things or ideas. The analogy is conveyed by the use of a metaphorical word or phrase that carries over the meaning from one thing to another.

an unchanging meaning. Paul's thought remains extremely flexible and elastic' (1961, p. 173). The 'body of Christ' language of Paul was multi-layered involving reference to Christ's body, the body of the Christian, incorporation into the risen Christ, participation in the Supper of the crucified Lord, the functioning of the gifts and ministries of the body, specifying the proper relations between Christ as head and the members of his body, and embodying the oneness of the new community transcending separated bodies such as Jews and Gentiles. In this connection, Minear noted that, for the Apostle, death and life were 'primary categories for ecclesiology, and the death and life of Christ were the primary clues to the fundamental choice . . . The Church had its existence at the point where that choice was seen and made' (p. 178).

Minear also noted the way in which the twin images of *body* and *koinonia* explained each other and were mutually involving especially in the sacrament of the Supper. Paul's depiction of the Church as the body of Christ remains central to the Church's self-understanding, and it continues to inform ecclesiological reflection across the churches. It can provide the basis for a radical ecclesiology as a counter to prevailing systems of exploitation and control.[2] However, the image of the body of Christ is also the subject of feminist critique. In this case, in terms of the body image, 'it has to be a *male* body which becomes the place of salvation' (Watson 2002, p. 42). Natalie Watson argues that the metaphor of the Church as the 'body of Christ' suggests that women are required to deny their own bodies and become part of a new, different and male body in order to obtain salvation' (p. 43). The argument gathers force from its link to the variety of ways in which women have and continue to suffer diminishment in the life of the churches. Retrieval of the idea of the Church as the body of Christ will depend on how well the Church 'affirms and celebrates women's bodies as part of this corporate body

---

2 For example, Izuzquiza (2009) develops a radical political and economic ecclesiology in relation to the 'body of Christ' in preference to 'the people of God'.

and which understands the Church as incomplete without them' (p. 44). This is an important issue, especially when set alongside the strong realist position regarding the nature of the body of Christ image proposed by the Lutheran theologian Robert Jensen. Influenced by Orthodox ecclesiology, Jensen argues that 'the Church is personally identical with Christ' yet he recognizes that they can be distinguished from each other (1999, p. 213, and generally pp. 211–16). The identity between the Church as the body of Christ and the risen Christ is both profound and theologically challenging.[3]

A second aspect of Minear's work, which remains underdeveloped, is his discussion of the Church as a *koinonia*. This identifier of the Church has become, in the wake of Vatican II and the ecumenical movement of the second half of the twentieth century, probably the most important way to speak of the Church of Jesus Christ. It is closely related to the 'body of Christ' image and has given rise to communion ecclesiology (see Tillard 2001).

A third area, which has assumed greater ecclesiological significance, has been a recovery of the Church as a pilgrim people of God. This image is 'the 'earliest and most inclusive image . . . [which] marks Christianity's consciousness of being a new Israel' (Hodgson and Williams 1996, p. 225). This was the key image employed at Vatican II.[4] Minear's discussion of this image of the Church linked it to the life of Israel from whence it sprang. He gave less attention to the movement forwards into the future. As

---

3 Compare Jensen with Hodgson and Williams (in Hodgson and King 1996, p. 225): '"Body" is basically an ethical and social metaphor for Paul, not an organic one . . . It is not in the literal sense of being an organic extension of the incarnation, but rather in the sense that the self-giving love of Christ (his "body" given for us) now defines and constitutes its unique communal structure.' This traditional symbolic interpretation is a counter to Jensen's argument for the ontological significance of the body of Christ image.

4 McGrath notes that the Council was 'careful to avoid the direct identification of the "people of God" with "the Roman Catholic Church"' (2007, pp. 407f).

noted by Jeremias earlier, 'people of God' is entailed in the concept of *ecclesia*. *Ecclesia* is 'a new communal reality constituted by the call of God. It is a distinctive form of human life in relationship with God and others' (Migliore 2004, p. 252). But as the people of God the *ecclesia* is on a journey. The image draws attention to the travelling and missionary dimension of the Church. It is not surprising therefore that the *ecclesia* of God is such a significant aspect of the ecclesiology of Luke/Acts. The Emmaus Road story at the end of Luke 24 becomes paradigmatic for the Church's life. It is essentially an image of travel; first to Emmaus, then back to Jerusalem, then finally after Pentecost it continues into the Mediterranean world. The body which breaks bread and hears the Word is a body on the move. The theme is picked up in the Letter to the Hebrews though in this context the people of God are wanderers of the earth orientated to the future world (Heb. 2.5, 8.6, 11.14–16); a 'household' on the move (Heb. 3.6). Strecker captures it well, 'The Christian community, however, is not only portrayed as waiting for the coming reality of salvation but it understands itself as the eschatological community of the end-time that is also wandering through time' (2000, p. 617). The wandering elect are aliens and exiles (1 Peter 1.1, 1.17, 17, 2.11); a *diaspora*, who are persecuted and marginalized in a pagan environment, in which they bear witness to their faith (1 Peter 2.15, 3.1, 3.15).

Reinterpreting the images for a travelling Church

In the contemporary contexts of the Churches of the world, particularly in the West, but certainly not restricted to this, the images of the Church are in flux and being reimagined and reinterpreted. Migliore offers a fourfold schema: people of God images; servant people; body of Christ; community of the Spirit (2004, pp. 252–4). All such classifications have their strengths and weaknesses. In our time, I believe we need to highlight the communitarian, dynamic and outer-directed dimensions of the images of the Church. To that end, I offer three basic categories to reinterpret the images of the Church in scripture: (a) images concerning *connecting and community*; (b) images associated with *movement and energy*; and (c) images concerning the Church's *mission and witness* in the world.

In respect to *connecting* and *community*, the organic and living image of the Church as the 'body of Christ' is fundamental. This same organic networked sense of the Church belongs to the image of the 'vine and branches'. The community dimension of course is present powerfully in the image of the Church as *koinonia*. Other images that feed into this dimension include 'household of God', 'the new creation', 'the vine and branches' and 'little flock'.

In relation to images of *movement and energy*, the obvious ones are 'the people of God', 'the new Israel', 'people of the way', 'strangers and exiles'. They are images that involve journey through space and time. In this context, such images invite reflection on questions about purpose, membership, relationship to other peoples and groups, and orientation towards a destination.

Images concerning the Church's *mission and witness* require more careful thought. For example, the images of the Church in I Peter – 'a chosen race', a 'holy people', a royal priesthood' and 'holy nation', 'God's own people' – can and have functioned in the past in a somewhat enclosed and at times sectarian manner. However, the context of I Peter is missional and challenging – 'that you may proclaim the mighty acts of him who called you out of darkness into his marvellous light'. The image of Christians as 'God's ambassadors' (2 Cor. 5.18–21) belongs to this dimension. This depiction of Christians has often been interpreted in an individualistic sense, but the Apostle Paul understood this in terms of the life of the whole Church. In the future, the ecclesial dimension of this image could be usefully explored.

Space does not permit a fuller discussion of the images of the Church and their significance for ecclesiology (for further discussion see Preston 1997). The images I have briefly noted belong to the witness of scripture. They offer a window into the rich diversity in New Testament ecclesiology and continue to inspire and inform the Church's seeking after God and its discipleship in the world. In the slipstream of scriptural images, the Church will continue to seek for companion images to make sense of its engagement with God and life in the world. For example, movements of new monasticism have recovered an ancient image of the Church as 'sanctuary'. This image refers not simply to an enclosed community but a place for refugees and the forgotten. The image of the Church as a 'pioneer people' picks up a theme from Hebrews concerning Jesus as pioneer (Heb. 12.2), but gives it an intentional ecclesial focus. Seeking companion images is a way of being faithful to the trajectory of the scriptures. It points to the continuing task of interpreting the faith afresh in changing contexts. Scripture images and their companion images remain open-ended and somewhat plastic. They invite new imaginative endeavours and in the process they generate a wealth of new ways of understanding the nature and purpose of the Church. They are also not simply to be identified as 'metaphors', 'similes' or for that matter 'images', but, as Robert Jensen shows, they can also operate as highly rich and interlinked concepts such as 'people of God' and 'body of Christ' (see 1999, pp. 189f). The images of the Church can give rise to different models of being the Church.

From images to models

Five models of the Church: Avery Dulles

Images and models of the Church are related. For example, the Roman Catholic ecclesiologist Avery Dulles notes that '[w]hen an image is employed reflectively and critically to deepen one's theoretical understanding of a reality it becomes what is today called a "model"' (1974, p. 21). Drawing upon the work of Ian Ramsey and others in the sciences, Dulles refers to models in theology as 'analogue models' or 'disclosure models' because of their capacity to explain and explore phenomena (p. 26). However, because the phenomenon of the Church is a mystery hid with Christ in God it is not measurable in the same way as, for example, a chair is. Rather a spiritual discernment is required, and even then we cannot grasp the whole. This means that the models we deploy to inquire into the mystery of the Church and make sense of its complexities will not be identical with the Church but approximate, partial and have a functional purpose. This suggests that deployment of models is a way of responding creatively to the complexity of the Church. In this sense, 'the term "model" refers to a theoretical construct that is employed to deepen our understanding of a complex reality' (Migliore 2004, p. 255).

Dulles' *Models of the Church* has become part of the stock-in-trade of discussions of the Church. He identifies five models: the Church as institution, mystical communion, sacrament, herald and servant. Each model draws upon and develops certain key images and writings from scripture. The 'institutional' model appeals to those scripture texts that point to order, structure, office and apostolic tradition in ministry. Matthew's Gospel has been important in this respect.[5] Thus texts relating to the Petrine office and the image of the Church as 'rock' (Matt. 16.18) as well as the later so called Catholic Epistles have been important for the development of this model. The moderate institutionalism associated with the Church as 'mystical communion' draws upon two Pauline biblical images: (a) the 'body of Christ' – an organic rather than sociological image – vivified by the spiritual life principle of the Holy Spirit; and (b) 'people of God' – with roots in the community of Israel and its deployment in the New Testament to indicate a chosen people gathered for a purpose. Dulles – perhaps with a critique of his own Church in mind – argued that both these images suggested a flat hierarchy, democratic order and a focus on the quality of the relationships in the Church as a whole. This model emphasized the personal dimension of the Church knit together by the Holy Spirit. This personalist

---

5 Strecker notes that Matthew's community is a mixed Church of good and bad in which there are strong ethical demands that relate to the development of the institution of penance (18.15–20); to 'binding and loosing'; baptism is a legal act, a rite of initiation (3.13–17); the Lord's Supper is linked to the power and authority of the Church to forgive sins (26.26–8). Strecker states that 'Matthew's Church is to be understood as an "institution"' (2000, pp. 389–91).

dimension transcends organic and juridical categories.[6] The model of the Church as sacrament to some extent mediates between the institutional and communion models offering a way to understand how the spiritual reality of the Church is manifest through the visible forms and structures. It owes its formulation in the twentieth century to the Roman Catholic theologian Henri de Lubac. It was an important concept at Vatican II. This model can claim less obvious biblical warrant though Dulles (1974, p. 69) suggests it may have resonances with the Pauline concept of marriage as a 'mystery' analogous to Christ and the Church (Eph. 5.32).

The foregoing models are the familiar territory of more Catholic ecclesiologies. The model of the Church as herald of the divine Word is a feature of Protestant ecclesiology. In this model, emphasis is firmly on hearing and responding to the preached Word of God. This kind of model belongs to a 'call' type ecclesiology centred on Jesus Christ, scripture and proclamation. This model is exemplified in the Reformed theologian Karl Barth, and can be traced to the Reformation tradition of Luther and Calvin. Important here is the image of the Church as those summoned by a herald to become a new community of witnesses to the Lordship of Christ in the world. This model is informed by a strong eschatology and for this reason it distinguishes sharply between the Church and the kingdom of God. This also means the Church lives in a precarious situation in relation to its Lord and any attempt to secure its form in fixed visible structures is a sign of what might be termed a 'steady state ecclesiology'. Not surprisingly the model will find the biblical image of the 'little flock' important for the reality of the local gathered congregation (Matt. 18.20).

The servant model of the Church, unlike the previous four models, gives priority to the interface between the Church and the world and in doing so gives greater recognition to the Church

---

6 Dulles (1974, p. 52) draws at this point on the theology of Herbert Mühlen who coins the word 'personalogical' to identify the work of the Spirit of the body.

following in the footsteps of Christ beyond the familiar boundaries of the Church. The servant ecclesiology has strong echoes in Bonhoeffer's idea that '[t]he Church is the Church only when it exists for others' (p. 88). While the servant model might not have any direct biblical foundation, Dulles refers to an 'indirect foundation' in the servant songs of Isaiah (such as Isa. 42.6–7), the servant ministry of Jesus (Luke 4.16–19) and the prophetic intent of the beatitudes of Matthew's Gospel (Matt. 5.1–16) (pp. 93f). Yet, this 'indirect foundation' simply highlights the close connection in this model between Christology and ecclesiology; images for Christ the servant are the ultimate basis for the servant model of the Church.

A Protestant response: Daniel Migliore

Dulles' fivefold model of the Church has exercised considerable influence in the study and teaching of ecclesiology across the Christian Churches. It is interesting to see how the schema is reinterpreted and redeveloped by a Protestant theologian such as Daniel Migliore (2004, pp. 254–62). He shows how the institutional model also operates within Protestantism through its patterns of organization, tests of orthodoxy, and books of order. However, he finds the most compelling critique of this model coming from Latin American liberation theology and the emergence of base communities (p. 256).

When Migliore refers to the mystical communion model as 'an elite community of the Spirit', we are not surprised that his critique is focused on the way the Church, particularly in the West, has uncritically borrowed patterns of spirituality and intimate community from a culture dominated by bureaucratic and depersonalized life. To this extent, the Church becomes a place of escape and the mystical communion becomes a closed therapeutic community. The sacramental model of the Church, as in the former model, has a tendency to 'ecclesiocentrism' preoccupied with the internal life of the Church and its liturgy. The risk is loss of the Church's social witness and service. Liberation theology shows how this model can have a proper outward directed function as the Church embodies in both its liturgy and social engagement God's redemptive work in the world. The Church as herald is critical for the Church's faithfulness to the proclamation of the gospel. However, it can generate a patronizing, self-righteous and uncaring Church that needs to learn how to listen as well as teach.

Migliore gives most attention to Dulles' fifth model of the Church as '*servant* of the servant Lord'. It is a model that has been enriched by liberation theology through 'Christian base community' and 'house Churches' wherein the service includes solidarity with the poor and downtrodden, and struggles for justice against oppressive forces. The danger of course is the 'virtual equation of the Church with an agency for social improvement' (p. 260). Feminist theologians have called attention to the misuse of the servant model as a subtle means to maintain oppression against women by extolling submission and denial of freedom rather than fostering friendship (John 15.15).

Both Dulles and Migliore are at one in their view that no one single image or model of the Church is capable of saying everything that needs to be said or all that needs to be embodied in the visible life of the Church in the world. From this perspective, both are clear that no model ought to dominate and all models are to be constantly referred back to their origin in the risen Christ and the power of the Spirit.

From model to paradigm

However, when one model becomes dominant in the discourse and understanding, it functions more accurately as a paradigm according to Dulles. For example, the Roman Catholic Church of the Counter-Reformation understood itself as the *societas perfecta* based on analogy with the secular state. This dominant model operated *de facto* as a basic ecclesial paradigm. However, in the course of the late nineteenth century and into the mid twentieth century, the official Roman Church appealed to the analogy of 'the mystical body'. This gave way at the Second Vatican Council to the image of the 'people of God', which became so significant that it began to function in a comprehensive explanatory way to understand the nature of the Church; that is, it became a dominant paradigm. However, in the post-conciliar period of the 1970s, the model of the Church as servant emerged as a key model, which began to function as a frame of reference for discourse and practice concerning the Church and to this extent attained a paradigmatic status.

The transition from model to paradigm, in Dulles' view, is a sign of dominance of a particular model of the Church. Three decades on, the matter of dominant models and/or models vying for dominance in the Church is problematic. We are in a period of history when pluralism and diversity abound which means the question of models of the Church will remain a contested and essentially unfinished business. Of course, this may be precisely how it ought to be from a theological point of view. The triune God is a God of abundance and variety and it would be odd and somewhat worrying if the Church restricted itself to a single model to explain and explore the spiritual reality of the Church. Herein lies the great danger of all models. Having emerged to some extent out of the lived experience of people of the Church, models can become rarefied, resistant to reinterpretation, change and even death. The 'model' can become zombie-like (Reader 2008, p. 20).[7] Dulles reminds us of Paul Tillich's statement that 'images are not created or destroyed by deliberate human effort. They are born or they die.' The same is true of their offspring, models and their cousin paradigms.

However, the matter may be both more interesting and complex than suggested by Dulles. The philosopher of science Michael Polanyi refers to frameworks (rather than paradigms) as ways of seeing or being orientated (1958, pp. 103, 106, 165, 212–13,

---

7 John Reader, following the sociologist Ulrich Beck, states: 'Zombie categories are "the living dead", the tried and familiar frameworks of interpretation that have served us well for many years and continue to haunt our thoughts and analyses, even though they are embedded in a world that is passing away before our eyes.' (2008, p. 1).

266–8).[8] It may be more accurate to speak of frameworks in which we dwell – functioning like water in relation to the fish. In this sense, we are often unaware of the fundamental paradigms that shape and orientate our lives in the world. The concept of indwelling is more appropriate. Accordingly, it is not simply that a certain model of the Church commends itself in such a manner that it dominates the discourse and becomes the controlling paradigm. Rather, the paradigm or framework may function as the environment operating at a subliminal level to make any particular model attractive and powerful. The unnoticed character and impact of such frameworks is critical. This also raises the possibility of competing paradigms some operating overtly and others covertly.

An example of the power of a paradigm operating in a covert manner would be the influence of the power and ideology of the Roman Empire as a fundamental shaping force on the early Church (Fiorenza 2007, Ch. 1). Studies of the Gospels, Paul's 'counterimperial gospel', and other literature from the New Testament has served to rehabilitate Christian writings by showing that they 'were critical of Roman imperial power and resisted its structures of domination, because they were written by subordinate and marginalized people' (p. 4). In this case the background imperial paradigm generated an anti-imperial response that can be traced in the New Testament. This means that ecclesial paradigms informed by recurring themes such as the Lordship of Christ and discipleship in terms of service and sacrifice arise out of Christological reflection in the context of and as a counter to prevailing empire ideology concerning Caesar, authority and power. As a result, the emerging ecclesial paradigms offer clues to embedded

---

8 See also references to 'implicit beliefs' and 'indwelling'. The word 'paradigm' comes from Greek (*paradeigma*), meaning to 'pattern, example, sample' from the verb (*paradeiknumi*), to 'exhibit, represent, expose' and that from (*para*), 'beside, by' + (*deiknumi*), 'to show, to point out'. The original Greek term was used in Greek texts such as Plato's *Timaeus* (28A) as the model or the pattern that the Demiurge (god) used to create the cosmos. In our scientific contexts, the word more usually is used to refer to a philosophical or theoretical framework of any kind.

socio/political frameworks of power. This gives a certain force to feminist critique of this anti-imperial approach because 'even such resistance literature will re-inscribe the structures of domination against which it seeks to argue' (p. 4). What is required is a critique of the rhetoric of domination so that contemporary ecclesial forms of violence and exclusion can be exposed. This is not the place to pursue this task. I raise the issue as an interesting and important example of how an underlying paradigm operates on the emergence of dominant images and models of the Church, both past and present.[9]

The image I have of how paradigms work can be likened to the way a sufficiently powerful magnet, when placed underneath a sheet of iron filings, will order the filings into a certain pattern. It is not immediately obvious to the observer that the arrangement of the filings is the result of an underlying force field.

Beyond models: practices and the new ecclesiology

Models and 'blueprint' ecclesiologies

The Roman Catholic theologian Nicholas Healy is critical of the 'models' approach to ecclesiology because of its rhetorical use in what he terms 'blueprint ecclesiology' (2000, pp. 43–6). His concern is not the models themselves but the different and disputed ways in which theologians use the models. For example, it is not the term 'communion', 'but *everything that guides its use*' (p. 45). At this level, what is critical is what the particular theologian imports into the model and the framework in which the model itself operates. It leads Healy to conclude thus:

> Of itself, the model can offer few answers to ecclesiological questions. The model cannot function logically as a normative

---

9 The feminist critique draws attention to the continuing features of empire (submission, violence, exclusion) as it recurs in contemporary contexts, aided and abetted by inscribed patterns of empire in biblical texts that have not been critiqued (de-colonized and detoxified).

principal, but only in a much weaker way, as a concept summarizing the ecclesiological proposals a particular theologian is advancing or analysing . . . This is not to deny a model's heuristic function, but what among its findings is accepted or not is determined by the agenda rather than the model itself. Models may indeed function systematically, but only by gathering together and organizing everything else that is finally more significant than the model itself. (p. 46)

In Healy's view, the search for a 'supermodel is misguided, the method of models itself focuses attention in the wrong place' (p. 46). The right place for ecclesial reflection is at the level of concrete practice, for this domain is always a factor in the construction of every ecclesiology. Healy's critique is timely and to the point. He has not abandoned the appeal to models but identified how they function in ecclesiology.

In association with Healy's approach, I want to suggest that current discussion of models in ecclesiology fails to attend to the dynamics and process by which images and models of the Church die and are reborn in new contexts. Furthermore, the classificatory scheme, in some respects at least, is only a halfway house to understanding the dynamic by which the ecclesia of God emerges and is transformative for the world. This connects with Healy's concern for attention to concrete practices.

As an example of the problem with the 'models' approach to the Church, I want to return to my proposal in Chapter 1, where I suggested a threefold schema for interpreting the familiar images of the Church: (a) images concerning connecting and community; (b) images associated with movement and energy; and (c) images concerning the Church's mission and witness in God's world. I made some preliminary proposals about what images might be relevant to these different dimensions of being the Church. What about the application of this scheme to the models of the Church? From this perspective, the key to a fuller evaluation of the models would be achieved by asking: *how does each model measure up in terms of its capacity for connecting and community, movement and energy, and mission and witness?* This means that the relative strengths and weaknesses of each model would be assessed in terms of quality of community, capacity for generation of energy and movement and degree of outer-directedness in mission and witness. My own view is that, on balance, the models approach is of limited value in identifying and following the dynamics of being the Church. The effort expended to classify different models can end up supporting a steady-state approach to the Church and undermine the capacity of the primal ecclesial images to reinvigorate and redevelop the community, generate energy and focus the mission of the Church. In other words, the strength of the models approach is its weakness. Ecclesial models are not designed to uncover the dynamics, energy, movement and transformation associated with God's work in creation and the Church.

Practices and the new ecclesiology

In an important article, Nicholas Healy discerns a shift in recent decades from preoccupation with models and associated 'highly systematic and ideal ecclesiologies' to concern for the concrete Church, 'its activities and distinctive functions' (2003). This 'turn to the concrete' or 'turn to practices' represents a move from the 'turn to the subject' that has supported 'those liberal and privatistic theologies in which the Christian community has little role to play in the lives of individual Christians' (p. 288). By contrast, the turn to practices implies a turn to the community of faith and those activities by which its identity is formed and endures. As Hardy states, 'the Church is embodied in its practices, and its practices embody a living relationship among its members and the triune persons of God. The measure of the Church lies within this relationship and is embodied within Church practices' (2010, p. 65). Healy welcomes this new ecclesiology typified in theologians like Stanley Hauerwas, Greg Jones and Alasdair MacIntyre. He suggests that this new approach 'retrieves some important aspects of premodern ecclesiology' especially its concern for 'proper performance, traditions and customs' (2003, p. 288).

However, precisely in order to strengthen this new approach Healy raises some critical issues that remain underdeveloped. In the first place, he notes that there is 'no settled definition of what a practice is'. Furthermore, beyond general agreement about the importance of practices for formation of character and ecclesial identity and the recognition that such practices are often unnoticed or overlooked, there is considerable diversity about different kinds of practices (clearly structured though complex, such as sacraments; loosely structured such as 'honouring the body', 'dying well', hospitality). Some are said to be constitutive of the Church (such as sacraments, proclamation), others necessary but not constitutive (such as theological inquiry, confession). Needless to say, there is little consensus on the above classifications.

Healy notes that the focus on practices can serve either (a) a reforming function in ecclesiology using insights from sociology and ethnography or (b) the retrieval of practices to face the challenges of secularism and decline of 'orthodox Christian identity and Church life' (p. 291). The aim in this latter move is to restore the 'Church's centre' which is under threat from 'liberal constructivism' or 'reactionary conservatism'. Retrieval of practices provides 'new disciplines and practices of formation'; it nurtures the sense that the people of the Church are 'resident aliens'. This move is often associated with a counter-cultural identity, in which the Church is called, in the words of John Milbank, to 'exhibit the exemplary form of human community'.

Healy argues that many practices – because they are so loosely structured and capable of manifold forms of expression – are more accurately attempts to obey a precept of the Church. An example would be 'hospitality'. Furthermore, practices are the work of human agents and the intention underlying the practice affects the meaning. The meaning of the practices cannot be neatly determined and made normative without concern for the intention of the active agents. Moreover, an agent's sense of what Christianity is – the theological context for action – affects the intention of an action. For example, my Church background affects what I think I am doing when I participate in the Eucharist. When intention is recognized as informing the meaning of practices, there is obviously wide scope for weak or erroneous intentions, which only serve to *distort* a Christian practice or perform a *different* practice. Healy uses the example of the Roman Catholic practice of dipping one's fingers into holy water and crossing oneself upon entering a church. In short, he argues that 'practices as concretely performed are not patterns of behaviour with sufficiently fixed meanings that they can do the task required by them by this version of the new ecclesiologies' (p. 295). 'Repeated performance of behaviour patterns does not, of itself, issue in the right formation of Church members nor the acquisition of Christian virtues. Character is indeed formed through practices but only as they are performed with appropriate intentions and construals. Without such, practices may foster as much as halt the decline of the centre and the absorption of the Church into the world.' Healy thus concludes that the 'failure of the new ecclesiologies to address the confusions and complexities of practices . . . may be considered an example of the "fallacy of misplaced concreteness"'.

Healy argues that the emphasis on practices is also in danger of ignoring some important theological issues. When, for example, core practices and doctrines are understood pneumatologically as the work of the Holy Spirit – the real subject and constitutive ground of practices – the danger is that the work of the Spirit through alternate, prophetic and critical voices in or beyond the Church is effectively silenced. The price of over-sacralization of practice is ironically the loss of capacity for reform and growth in holiness. The particular way in which practices are settled and undergirded by reference to the Spirit attributes 'too limited an account of human action within the Church', nor can it show how the Spirit 'might work salvifically in our mis-performance of Church practices, or in our performance of non-Christian practices', nor does it help the Church to respond to the prophetic voice of the Spirit of God (p. 299).

Healy's main concern seems to be with evident mis-performance of ecclesial practices. This appears problematic for those ecclesiologies, that invest great store in the Church's integrity and faithful witness being tied to faithful and true practice. Healy has in mind the work of Stanley Hauerwas. Thus, for Healy, in the new ecclesiologies, 'ordinary concrete mis-performance or non-performance and its effect upon character formation and Church witness is left out of the picture' (p. 301). In other words, the intent to commend Christianity as a habitable form of life may remain unconvincing if it all depends on practice given (a) the human predilection for mis-performance and/or (b) correct performance with ambiguous intentions which may be confused, sinful and faithless.

Healy argues for an approach to practices and the turn to the concrete that places much greater weight on theology as a contemplative enterprise that includes an account of the doctrine of the Triune God and the gospel. This means ecclesiology has to be set within a more developed doctrine of the Trinity in such a way that 'the action of the Holy Spirit is accounted for in a way that does not bind it to the Church's practices' (p. 302). Healy finds some creative possibilities in this respect in the theology of Thomas Aquinas whose ecclesiology is framed by 'Christ who is the Head of all humanity, his Body'. On this account the Church is never centre stage but is placed within the larger Body of Christ and the doctrine of God (p. 305). Moreover, the Church is a people *in via* (on the way) participating in the passion of Christ and following the wisdom of the cross. For Aquinas, obedience 'trumps all other virtues, practices, precepts and principles' (p. 306). Healy's intent is to strengthen practices and the direction of the new ecclesiology. To do so, he wants to develop a much more robust understanding of the work of the Word and the Spirit informing and reforming ecclesial practice so that the people of God might be 'transformed into the visible communal embodiment of the gospel'. (p. 302).

Practices, embodiment and feminist ecclesiology

The focus on practices as the groundwork for ecclesiological reflection resonates with feminist critique of traditional ecclesiology and a recovery of women's contribution to being the Church. The Anglican feminist theologian Natalie Watson addresses these issues, when she considers feminist perspectives on ecclesiology (2001). Watson notes that 'most feminist ecclesiology has been generated out of women-church movement'. She joins those who are critical of such ecclesiology 'for failing to engage deeply enough with influential ecclesiological traditions which still shape women's experience within the Church' (p. 60). Watson argues for a 'critical, constructive feminist ecclesiology [that] will enable women to participate in ecclesial self-reflection and the informed critique of patriarchal models'. Underlying this approach is the recognition that sexual difference in ecclesiological construction does make a difference; that the bodies of women 'embody the body of Christ' and that as a result women have their own particular contribution to make to the embodiment of Christ's presence in the world. Critical for Watson is a reclaiming of the traditional sites and modes through which ecclesial reflection has occurred – that is, word, sacrament and care of the other. The patriarchal framework through which these practices of being the Church have traditionally been filtered requires unmasking ('dis-covering') and reinterpreting.

Watson's focus is accordingly on revisioning performance as a means to subvert 'the gendered symbolism that has structured ecclesiological discourse in the past'. Such a focus, for example, leads to a critique of the submissive asexual feminine (as either 'virgin or mother') or the asexual celibate priest. In both cases, representation of Christ falls short of embodiment. Ecclesiology in the concrete is ecclesiology within the framework of sexual difference. This can lead to a reconsideration of 'gendered ecclesiology' and the development of a 'feminist narrative ecclesiology' (p. 63). This narrative includes re-membering and re-telling the stories of 'a complex religious praxis of making space in all aspects of the life of the Church in participation and subversion of parts of ecclesial life, such as female forms of eucharistic piety, as they are expressed by medieval mystics, or forms of the veneration of saints, which are particular women's practices of faith' (p. 65).

Watson attends to the three 'power-centres of patriarchal ecclesiology: word, sacrament and care for the other'. She notes the word of God 'has always been a site of fundamental ambivalence' and a place that women have been excluded from (that is preaching/teaching) and kept 'illiterate' (p. 66). In the area of sacramental celebration, women have been rendered 'incapable of representing Christ physically'. Watson, following the feminist Denise Carmody, identifies this as a 'permanent sin against women', made even more corrosive of being the Church, because the sacramental celebration is 'the embodied interaction between the individual, the divine and the community'; the 'dynamic centre of ecclesial life', where 'women's being Church, essentially manifests itself' (p. 67). The restriction of the sacramental celebration to men (and the denial of this to women) results in a truncated theology of divine embodiment given the failure to recognize how women as well as men contribute to the 'sexual dimension inherent to being human'. This leads Watson to the third domain of care and attention to the other. The issue is sharply stated: 'we cannot restrict ourselves to attributing some aspects of Christlikeness to men and others to women, such as attributing Christlike authority to men and Christ-like submissiveness and humility to women. Being Christ-like to each other means that both men and women represent Christ's presence to each other in each and every respect of the embodied reality of the Church'. Watson articulates a basic project of feminist theology, that is, to make women visible. This requires women to 're-member the Church' and to 'dis-cover their history . . . which is one of both oppression and empowerment' (p. 72).

Watson's proposals belong to Healy's 'turn to the concrete' associated with the new ecclesiology. There is a strong emphasis on community performance of the story of the gospel. Such performance is both a telling and an embodiment. Women are particular actors in the story with their own particular sexual identity that contributes to the whole. Without their contribution the whole is diminished. To tell and embody the story of Christ in its fullness women have to share in the whole story and the practices through which it is performed. Healy's approach would support this, and for this reason his cautionary qualifiers on the turn to the concrete are also relevant to Watson's project.

Conclusion

Ecclesial portraiture is a complex yet important way to understand the nature and purpose of the Church. This chapter has explored the question of portraiture by attention to the images, models, paradigms and practices by which the character and vitality of the Church can be understood. I suggested a more dynamic way of understanding the images of the Church; a way more in keeping with a 'travelling ecclesiology'. To this end, I located the discussion of images in terms of three areas: how communities are formed; where they find their energy and how they embody their life in the world. Images fed into various models of the Church, and in this chapter, I have outlined and critiqued some well-known models (institution, mystery, sacrament, herald, servant). As with images, so with models the basic challenge was to show how they served a more dynamic understanding of the Church and how they interrelated. At particular times and places some images and models gain a significance, which leads them to be associated with basic paradigms for the Church.

However, all three elements in ecclesial portraiture (images, models and paradigms) have increasingly given way to an emphasis upon practices by which the Church is the Church. While this emphasis is not unproblematic, is does draw attention to those particular concrete practices that mark the being of the Church. The focus on practices continues to be an important and valuable element in feminist critique of the doctrine of the Church. I want to return to the issue of portraiture at the end of this book and offer my own proposal. But this necessarily follows a more constructive attempt in ecclesiology (Chapters 4 to 8). As a prelude to this constructive work, the next chapter clears the ground so to speak. In it, I examine some perennial problems for the doctrine of the Church and its impact on matters to do with practical ecclesiology.

Questions

1 How might the biblical images of the Church serve the Church in an age of mission?

2 What contemporary images of the Church might be important for ecclesiology as a complement to biblical images?
3 Which model(s) of the Church connect with your own journey in Christianity?
4 What is the problem with 'blueprint ecclesiologies'?
5 What contribution does feminist theology make to the doctrine of the Church?

Further reading

Raymond F. Collins, *The Many Faces of the Church: A Study in New Testament Ecclesiology*, New York: Crossroad Publishing, 2003.

Everett Ferguson, 'The Body of Christ', in *The Church of Christ: A Biblical Ecclesiology for Today*, Grand Rapids, MI: Eerdmans, 1996, pp. 91–103.

Nicholas Healy, 'Blueprint Ecclesiologies', in *Church, World and the Christian Life: Practical-Prophetic Ecclesiology*, Cambridge: Cambridge University Press, 2000, pp. 25–51.

Matt Jensen and David Wilhite, 'Models', in *The Church: A Guide for the Perplexed*, Edinburgh: T & T Clark, 2010, pp. 16–58.

Natalie K. Watson, 'Reconsidering Ecclesiology: Feminist Perspectives', *Theology and Sexuality* 14 (2001), pp. 59–77.

3

Natural Ecclesial Heresies
Some Implications for Practice

Heresy and the Church

Heresy as systemic default

The word 'heresy' comes from *haeresis*, a Latin transliteration of the Greek word originally meaning *choosing* and/or *choice* or in an extended sense *school of thought*. The word eventually came to denote warring factions and a party spirit by the first century. The word appears in the New Testament and was appropriated by the Church to mean a sect or division that threatened the unity of Christians. Heresy eventually became associated with departure from orthodoxy in Post-Apostolic times. Thus Irenaeus of Lyons (c.120/140–c.200/203) defined heresy as deviation from the standard of sound doctrine. McGrath offers a contemporary definition: 'a heresy is a doctrine that ultimately destroys, destabilizes, or distorts a mystery rather than preserving it' (2009, p. 31).

Are there particular kinds of heresies to which the Church is prone? Put in a slightly different way: Are there perennial issues that trip the Church up, so to speak? The purpose of this chapter is to uncover what I call the natural heresies of the Church, that is, those heresies that are peculiar to the being of the Church. I hope to show in this chapter how such heresies are closely related to those heresies that have traditionally occupied the attention and energy of the Church, such as Docetism, Arianism and Pelagianism.

I make a distinction between the heresies, which emerge from time to time in the Church, that involve conflict and disputation and require resolution by established authorities for faith, and the particular heresies that appertain to the Church as Church. In the former case, the Church is called to decide on matters of faith; in the latter the Church itself is the subject of the heresy.[1] This can make the matter exceedingly complex. My concern is this latter kind of heresy, which involves the very nature of the Church. But there is an important relationship between the heresy which challenges the Church's teachings regarding the faith and those heretical features of the Church as such. My argument in this chapter is that the natural heresies of Christianity have an inescapable ecclesial dimension. My intention is to uncover and track what happens when basic heretical moves in Christian theology are transposed into the realm of ecclesiology. Strictly speaking there are not two different kinds of heresies, that is, doctrinal and ecclesial. Rather, there are two different modes in which the heretical impulse operates, doctrinal and ecclesial. Focusing on heresy in its ecclesial mode relocates it to matters concerning performance (and dispositions) rather than restricting heresy to ideas and cognition.

When the Church is the subject of the inquiry the heretical element or impulse will be often concealed or unnoticed. This recalls the discussion in Chapter 2 with respect to paradigms and frameworks. The 'heretical' will to a large extent be embedded in fundamental frameworks that influence the practices of the Church rather than opinions, views or doctrines that gain currency in the Church. It will come as no surprise to find recurring patterns and echoes of earlier ecclesial distortions and mistakes. However, tracing their form and dynamic in new situations is neither a simple nor an uncontested matter.

Inquiry into natural ecclesial heresies is important, because it may help to unearth some of the reasons why the Church in every age wrestles with similar sets of difficulties. My thesis is that many of the problems to do with the relationship between God, the Church and the world can be traced to theological and ecclesiological misunderstandings and/or mistakes that generate

---

1 The Donatist heresy might spring immediately to mind as a heresy pertaining to the being of the Church. It would be interesting to trace the antecedents of this heresy back to the doctrine of God.

'natural ecclesial heresies'. I call them 'natural', because they function as systemic defaults for the ecclesia, which can be traced back to the doctrine of God. Overcoming such defaults is neither simple nor assured. It is as if the default is hard wired into the being of the Church. On the other hand, the Church has resources it can draw upon to respond faithfully and live beyond the defaults that disrupt and diminish its life. Such matters can sound somewhat ethereal. However, anyone in the least familiar with Church life knows only too well the sense of being overwhelmed by work and stress. Sometimes, this can occur due to poorly formed personal habits, but often such experiences are symptoms of deep rooted and systemic problems in the practices and understanding of the community of faith. These practices often embody beliefs about how the Church and its leaders are effective, achieve success and deliver measurable outcomes. This rationalistic temper in a competitive environment is evidence, I believe, of a form of ecclesial Pelagianism, in which God has been displaced from the centre of life. Here is a toxic heresy at the root of the system. My thesis is that the Church's systemic defaults – such as ecclesial Pelagianism – constitute its particular heretical trajectories. Because they are of a systemic character, they remain hidden and deeply embedded, and for this reason they are all the more dangerous and distortive of the Church's practice of the gospel.

The natural heresies of Christianity

The natural heresies of Christianity were examined by Friedrich Schleiermacher in *The Christian Faith* (1928, p. 97). In a brief but insightful discussion, he identified the four natural heresies of Christianity: Docetic, Ebionitic, Manichean and Pelagian. He recognized his choice of four heresies could appear quite arbitrary. He went on to state that 'these names [Docetism et al.] are here intended only to denote universal forms'. The four categories he had identified covered 'the number of different ways in which the distinctive fundamental type of Christian doctrine can be contradicted while the appearance of Christianity remains'.

What then was the nature of Christianity in relation to which the natural heresies would necessarily arise? From his well-known definition of the essence of Christianity, in which 'all religious emotions are related to the redemption wrought by Jesus of Nazareth' (p. 98), Schleiermacher argued that there were two ways in which heresy might arise. Given the basic definition – for without it the system ceases to be Christian – 'either human nature will be so defined that a redemption in the strict sense cannot be accomplished, or the Redeemer will be defined in such a way that He cannot accomplish redemption' (p. 98).

With regard to the former (human nature), redemption meant that people were both in need of it and capable of receiving it. This could play itself out in two ways. First, if the need of human beings for redemption was posited in such a way that their inability to receive redemption was 'absolute' (that is unlimited), their ability to receive redemption effectively disappeared. This 'annulled' the fundamental formulae – albeit in an indirect manner – that human beings had both a need and capability of receiving redemption. Such a situation arose when the inability of human beings to receive redemption was caused by the 'dominion' over it of an 'original Evil'; 'an Evil-in-itself as being original and opposed to God' (p. 98). This deviation was Manichean.

A second scenario with regard to human nature arose when 'the ability to receive redemption is assumed so absolutely' that 'hindrance to the entry of God-consciousness' is 'infinitesimal'. The result was that the need for redemption was 'reduced to zero, at least in the sense that it is no longer the need of one single Redeemer', because at any particular moment a stronger person can be the vehicle to elicit the God-consciousness. In other words, redemption 'would not need to be the work of one particular Person, but would be a common work of all for all . . .' (p. 99). This aberration was Pelagian.

When attention shifted from the human being to the Redeemer, heresy could arise in relation to the definition of the Redeemer. The fundamental formulae required that for Christ to be the Redeemer and thus 'enjoy an exclusive and peculiar superiority over all others', there had to be an 'essential likeness' between him and human beings. As with the human being so with the Redeemer, there were two basic directions in which problems might arise. First, where the difference between Christ and human beings is made to be 'unlimited', such that there is no 'essential likeness' between the two, Christ's 'participation in human nature vanishes into a mere appearance'. From Schleiermacher's point of view, this meant that human God-consciousness was essentially different from Christ's and so could not be derived from Christ and 'redemption is only an appearance'. This aberration accorded with Docetism, the Christological heresy in which it only seemed (Greek, *dokeo*) that Christ shared in human nature.

Heresy in relation to the Redeemer could also occur when Christ was so like those who had to be redeemed, in an 'unlimited' manner and thus absolutely that 'no room is left for a distinctive superiority as a constituent of his being'. This meant that the Redeemer also was in need of redemption – 'however absolutely small' – and thus the basic relationship between Christ as Redeemer – who has both an exclusive and peculiar superiority over all others – and human beings is effectively annulled. This heresy, in which Jesus was regarded as 'an ordinary man', was the Nazarean or Ebionitic heresy.

Schleiermacher drew attention to the natural connections between the various heretical forms. For example, if it was the case that human beings were 'essentially infected with positively original evil' (Manichean), this meant that the Redeemer could not participate in human nature (Docetism). Alternatively, where the capacity for higher God-consciousness was no different in Christ than all others (Ebionitic), redemption was a human activity and Christ was unable to contribute anything substantial (Pelagian). In terms of his nineteenth-century European context, Schleiermacher considered current manifestations of 'Supernaturalism' as approximating to Docetic/Manichean heresies and 'Rationalism' approximating the Ebionitic and Pelagian heresies.

For a succinct and insightful account of the dynamic of heresy and its fundamental forms, Schleiermacher's analysis stands out although it is marginalized in contemporary discussions of heresy (McGrath 2009, pp. 92–6). What contribution to an understanding of heresy in the Church might be gained, if Schleiermacher's analysis is transposed into ecclesiological categories?

Heresy: ecclesial transpositions

Does a Docetic Christology have an ecclesial counterpart? For example, could Docetism infect the form of the *ecclesia* and how might this be identified and tracked through various practices? It is these kinds of questions that I want to examine in this chapter. My purpose in doing this is twofold. First, to understand the theological roots of a number of significant contemporary aberrations in the practice of being the Church. Second, to gain a clearer sense of the kind of challenges facing the Church in the world and the resources available to meet those challenges.

The four natural heresies identified by Schleiermacher transpose into two fundamental ecclesial heretical forms, namely, *sacred inflation* (the ungrounded Church) and *desacralized ecclesia* (the disappearing Church). Why and how this is the case and what implications this has for the life of the Church, its ministry and mission in the world is the purpose of the remainder of this chapter.

Sacred inflation: the ungrounded Church

The monist drive in theology

In the history of Christianity, probably the most significant default of the Church has been what I would term 'sacred inflation'. This occurs when the Church's action is overly identified with the acts of God. This is not to deny that the Church of Jesus Christ participates in and is a particular, even special recipient of divine blessing. Indeed, as I argue in Chapter 6, the Church embodies in its life and practices a divine wisdom that befits the Lord of the Church. However, the attribution of sacredness, notwithstanding some careful qualifiers, is a dangerous claim for it risks falling into idolatry with respect to institutional structure, authority and actions. This occurs when the Church's claim to be a mediation of the divine presence and wisdom is over-inflated. This can happen in the most benign, unobtrusive and innocuous ways. For example, it occurs when an inversion takes place and the institution becomes the face and voice of the invisible God in such a way that the Church's structures, ministry and practices acquire quasi-sacral status in a self-referencing manner.

This tendency to sacred inflation of the institutional Church extends back into the early stages of the Christian tradition. What are the theological roots of this deviant ecclesiology? The Reformed Church theologian Colin Gunton locates the matter in what he calls the 'drive towards monism', the result of 'the fact that it [the Church] has never seriously and consistently been rooted in a conception of the being of God as triune' (1989, p. 48). Gunton argues that this monistic drive has been one of the principal reasons for the failure to generate a rich theology of community, substituting instead a hierarchically ordered institutional Church. He traces this problem to early developments in both Eastern and Western Christianity. This development in ecclesiology was at variance with reflection on the doctrine of God and the Trinity, which 'generated an ontology that was distinctively different from those prevailing in the ancient world' (p. 50).

Gunton argues that insights from the emerging doctrine of the triune God were not transferred into ecclesiology. Rather, ecclesiology in the East appeared to be influenced by neo-platonic ideas of earthly hierarchies being an image of the heavenly. In the West, 'the Church appears to have derived in large measure by analogy from the conception of an earthly empire' (p. 51). The Church from the time of Constantine became the domain and habitation of the Spirit, 'a substance which becomes the possession of the Church' rather than the eschatological Spirit drawing the Church towards the consummation (p. 57). In this context, the Spirit is easily domesticated and assimilated to the prevailing institutional structure. As a result the freedom and eschatological orientation of the Spirit is forfeited. The Spirit becomes enfolded in the web of institutional arrangements. A dynamic future-orientated

NATURAL ECCLESIAL HERESIES

ontology of the Church is sacrificed for a steady-state theory of the Church.

Sacrificing the Church's humanity

The resultant sacred inflation takes even more powerful hold when we inquire into the Christology associated with this development. Here the basic default involves placing a 'greater emphasis on the divine Christ than on the human Jesus of Nazareth' (p. 60).[2] Such a development is entirely in keeping with the already noted transference into ecclesiology of the monist drive in the doctrine of God. The singularity of God and a Docetic Christology are natural correlates of each other. This in turn can be traced back to a failure to apply to ecclesiology insights from the theology of the communion of the Triune God. Instead, a monist doctrine of God predominates and within this basic schema Christ's unity with the Father is construed in such a manner that there is no place for the humanity of God. The result is a halfway-house Trinitarianism.

Gunton points out that when ecclesiology is ordered according to a 'monophysite or docetically tending Christology', the effects are disastrous. The Church de facto becomes 'a living organ of salvation'.[3] It is associated with what Nicholas Healy has termed 'blueprint ecclesiologies', which privilege particular and often competing ideal 'models of perfection' of the Church, which are essentially disconnected from the concrete reality of the Church (Healy 2000, pp. 36f). Karl Barth, some years earlier, had referred to an 'ecclesiastical Docetism' 'which paradoxically tries to overlook the visibility of the Church, explaining away its earthly and historical form as something indifferent, or angrily negating it, or treating it only as a necessary evil, in order to magnify an invisible fellowship of the Spirit and of spirits. This view is just as impossible as Christological Docetism' (1956, p. 653). This Protestant

---

2 Gunton doesn't explain why this is the case though his discussion is in the context of the doctrine of election by God 'in His Son or Word'.

3 Gunton is quoting from the Second Vatican Council document on the Church.

retreat into invisibility drains the visible fellowship of theological significance and precisely for this reason generates churches that behave in coercive and unaccountable ways. At the level of performance, there is often little to separate the top down controlling behaviour of those in authority in the heavy institutional forms of the more Catholic varieties or Protestant denominationalism.

A number of things flow from an ecclesiology informed by such a Christology. First, when the divine Christ is transposed into the Church, the Church becomes the singular and determinative authoritative voice of the Divine. The logic of this finds its fulfilment in a doctrine of infallibility and certainty mediated through the authoritative magisterium of the Church. This, we should note, takes two forms; one emphasizing the authority of the Church's teaching office as in Roman Catholicism; the other locating the magisterium in scripture evidenced in various Protestant forms.[4] Second, to secure the living reality of the Church's quasi-divine status the Spirit is assimilated into the institution to become the possession of the Church. Again this pneumatological immanence has both heavy institutional forms (the various cognates of Catholicism) and more free floating ecclesiologies which make a claim for a realized eschatology of the Spirit. In both scenarios, what the Church says and does becomes welded to the voice of the Spirit of the Divine Christ. Third, and perhaps most obviously, the humanity of the Church evaporates, at least theoretically. A Church so identified with the divine Christ cannot recognize its own fundamental humanity and associated finitude, lack, unknowing and boundedness, let alone its failures and sinfulness. The denial of its own humanity is encoded into its self-understanding given that its life and being is determined by a Christ whose incarnate humanity is mere appearance and not substantive to his being. A Docetic Christ spawns a Docetic Church coterminous with a wholly immanent Spirit. The price for such an ecclesiology is high; the humanity of the body of Christ.

---

4 In the Protestant form, the magisterium of interpretation operates through a plethora of designated doctrinal elites with implied claims to be definitive arbiters of truth.

Of course, this state of affairs can't be sustained from a practical point of view. The visible Church is clearly a mixed body and its humanity is palpable and undeniable. The way to deal with this fact, within a fundamentally Docetic ecclesiology, is to locate the realm of the action and voice of Christ within a particular domain of the Church. Historically, the clergy became identified with the 'real' Church of the 'holy ones'. 'The Church does not have its being from the congregation of the faithful – because not all of them are faithful! – but from its relation to a hierarchical head' (Healy 2000, p. 52). This separation of clergy from laity has been a feature of the history of the Church. Although its roots can be located in a Docetic Christology transferred into a similar Docetic ecclesiology, the effect is to create a bifurcated ministry – clergy representing the divine Christ, laity representing the human Jesus – which has all the hallmarks of Nestorianism (Pickard 2009, pp. 112–14).

The foregoing discussion raises an interesting question in relation to Schleiermacher's schema of natural heresies. In that discussion, Docetic and Manichean heresies were correlated. Might there not be a faint echo of this latter heresy in the separation of the two orders, clergy and laity? In so far as the laity represent the human face of the Church and accordingly are a mixed group of sinners, their capacity for redemption may rightly be held under suspicion within the logic of this ecclesiology.

Docetic Church and 'Manichean' world

However, the matter has an even harder edge when it comes to the relationship between the Church and the world according to this ecclesiology. When the Church succumbs to a sacred inflation via a Docetic ecclesiology, it is axiomatic that the Church will be sharply distinguished from the world. The relationship is fundamentally disjunctive. This is in direct proportion to the degree of identity between the Church and God. Such a Church–world relation will be asymmetrical; the basic flow of information and energy will be from Church to world with minimal recognition that the world will have anything significant to contribute to the being and action of the Church. The logic of this is sectarianism though this can operate under different guises. For example, it is just as relevant to a large Church structure as well as the more familiar smaller Church, the reason being that the disjunction has to do with an attitude and predisposition towards the 'other'. This predisposition arises from, among other things, a serious theological flaw (in this case Docetic ecclesiology).[5] In fact, the larger the Church body the more likely a sectarian and negative view of the world as 'other' will dominate driven by a totally false assumption that 'might is right'. The disjunction between Church and world is the clue to the presence of an implicit Manichean-ism. This may not be overt but is implicitly present to the extent that the world is other and is unable to contribute, or refused any contribution to the form and life of the Church.

Ministry in such a Church is similarly asymmetrical; the infor-mation and energy will flow in one direction from clergy to laity; collaboration is not strictly speaking possible and if it happens it does so due to aberrant and unintended system behaviour. The more familiar feature of such a Church will be heavy authoritar-ian forms of leadership. Such a Church provides the ideal environ-ment for the incubation of a plethora of human pathologies and illnesses masquerading as the wisdom of the spiritual elite. This ought not be surprising in an ecclesial form that has, as a matter of theological principle, implicitly and indirectly suppressed its own humanity.

The sacred inflation of the Church is the offspring of two natural heresies of Christianity, Docetism with a whiff of Man-icheism. The result is a Church which sacrifices its humanity and generates a strong top down system of authority and min-istry. Moreover, it establishes a sharp dichotomy between the Church and the world that repeats the basic one-way bossing dynamic traced back to an inadequate doctrine of God. Sacred inflation is evidence of an ungrounded Church derived from an ungrounded God.

---

5 Martyn Percy's critique of Radical Orthodoxy as 'profoundly Docetic' arises in part from the strong Church – world separation implied in its ecclesiological programme (2005, p. 84).

De-sacralized *ecclesia*: the disappearing Church

An ecclesiology from below

The desire for a Church that is more grounded and in touch with the peoples of the world has been on the agenda since at least the mid twentieth century. This is not surprising in the wake of the horrific wars and conflicts of the twentieth century and increasing suspicion of institutions – including the churches – regarding questions of authority and matters of moral concern. We are familiar enough with the tradition of liberation theology and its call for the Church to become rooted in the lives of the poor and oppressed. In the Western world, the Church has been in decline and struggled in the environment of late modern culture. One response to this has been to emphasize reconnection and re-engagement of Christianity with society. In this context, the Church has tried to recover its human face. Such a concern can be discerned in the Vatican II statement on the Church *Lumen Gentium* and in ecclesiology more generally in recent decades. The focus has been on flat hierarchies, collaborative practices, openness to the world and an ethics of compassion in a broken world. This represents a renewed focus on the humanity of the Church seeking the wellbeing of society and creation.

These developments in ecclesiology emphasise incarnation and presence and focus on the visible, empirical, historical Church and its practices. This ecclesiology 'from below' can name the failures and shortcomings of the Church in a way that is resisted when the Church is inappropriately sacralized. The Church with a human face is more able to recognize the brokenness of the world because it is a participant in the same reality. The human condition is neither suppressed nor idealized in such a Church. Theologically, such an ecclesiology requires a more robust and realistic theology of human community; a matter addressed in Chapter 4.

In the shadow of the social sciences

An emphasis on the Church as an historical, empirical organization has much to learn from social theory, anthropology and cultural analysis. Sociological inquiry has opened up new insights and brought a note of realism to the life and practices of the body of Christ (see, for example, Ormerod 2008). A pioneering attempt was made in the 1920s by Dietrich Bonhoeffer in his innovative *Sanctorum Communio*, in which he developed a theology of the sociology of the Church (1963). Over the past century, the application of social theory to religion generally and Church life in particular has increased significantly though the matter remains contested and controversial (Ormerod 2008; Percy 2005, pp. 66–73; Izuzquiza 2009, pp. 42–62). One issue is the extent that the discipline of sociology – itself by no means unified and stable – adds value to an understanding of the reality of the Church. Furthermore its application to the discipline of ecclesiology has remained oddly underdeveloped (Preston 1999, p. 60), and in the view of some, ecclesiology could benefit considerably from deeper engagement (Mudge 2001; cf. Healy 2000, pp. 164–8). Nicholas Healy seems on the mark:

> In contrast to the agnostic, thin-theoretical approach, a theological form of social analysis describes and assesses the Church's concrete identity in light of Scripture, the tradition of its interpretation, and the ecclesiological context, with a view to practical reforms. It will make use of non-theological analyses and construals of the ecclesiological context as it does so, but will subject these to the same criteria. Thus, for example, it cannot assume that congregations should work for the flourishing of the social environment within which they are situated, for the inquiry may conclude that they should challenge or even reject their social environment through counter-practices. The Church's survival in the midst of change is not the point of the inquiry; the point is to discern the movement of the Spirit in our midst so as to improve our witness and discipleship. (2000, p. 166)

Healy advocates a theological form of social analysis in dialogue with other non-theological disciplines, in which he includes not only sociology but history and ethnography or cultural analysis. Neil Ormerod recognizes the contested and conflictual nature of the social sciences and the difficulty theologians have had in 'bringing the social sciences into the heart of ecclesiology'. Ormerod, summarizing the work of Joseph Komonchak, reminds us that ecclesiology (a) is concerned with the concrete history of the Church – not simply what is said about the Church, (b) must engage with the social sciences given that every ecclesiology has an implicit social theory and further 'that the social sciences themselves have an implicitly theological dimension' (2008, p. 651) and (c) is to be placed within the larger field of a theology of history – 'The history of the Church is a moment in the larger history of humanity and so ecclesiology finds its natural home in a larger theology of history' (p. 650).

The above developments in the doctrine of the Church have for the most part been welcomed both from a practical and theoretical point of view. Indeed, it is hard to find fault with an approach to the Church that takes seriously the concrete historical reality of the Church, which exists before the overlay of the idealizations of 'blueprint' ecclesiologies identified by Healy. Moreover, the possibility of engaging with other non-theological disciplines to assist in the explanation of the practices of the Church, and the nature of the interaction between Church and environment ought, in principle at least, to be of great benefit to the Church and hopefully wider society. I say this notwithstanding the lack of agreement in the social sciences regarding appropriate methodologies and applications. The interface is a potentially creative one.

The difference between this second approach to the Church compared to the former Docetic ecclesiology was enunciated by Cardinal Kasper in debate with the then Cardinal Ratzinger: 'One side [Ratzinger] proceeds by Plato's method; its starting point is the primacy of the ideal that is a universal concept. The other side [Kasper] follows Aristotle's approach and sees the universal as existing as concrete reality' (quoted in Ormerod 2008, p. 639). In Ormerod's terms, it is a divide in ecclesiology between 'those who study ecclesiology as an idealist Platonic form in some noetic heaven, and those who study it more as a realist Aristotelian form, grounded in empirical data of historical ecclesial communities' (p. 639). The former regard the latter as being in danger of a sociological reduction of the Church. It is treated like any other human institution. It is this suspicion that I want to explore briefly in terms of the disappearance of the Church. What is the basis for this criticism? Is it justified and, to the extent that it might be, how might it constitute a natural ecclesial heresy?

The disappearing Church?

At this point, I want to introduce Karl Barth's approach to ecclesiology. Barth is anything but a neutral observer. Healy identifies Barth's doctrine of the Church as belonging to an idealized 'blueprint' ecclesiology (2000, pp. 29f). Ormerod considers Barth 'the clearest exponent' of 'methodological purism' or 'exclusion of mediation'; meaning that theology basically has no need of any other disciplines in so far as they are not able to contribute to the distinctly theological understanding of Christianity, in this case, the reality of the Church (2008, p. 639). Yet Barth, as ever, is able to shine a light into the ecclesial cracks and uncover some important issues that can easily remain hidden in an ecclesiology from below.

In Barth's discussion of the marks of the Church, he recognizes that from the point of view of the concrete, historical empirical Church it is patently obvious that the Church is not *unam ecclesiam*. How then, in the face of diversity and division can we speak of the unity of the Church? It is at this point that Barth refers to two tempting heresies that have to be avoided. The Docetic heresy attempts to secure the *unam ecclesiam* 'by escape up or on from the visibility of the divided Church to the unity of the invisible Church' (Barth 1956, p. 677).[6] 'To "flee into invisibility" from the problems of the visible Church is to abandon God's chosen means of redemption' (Bender 2005, p. 183).

However, the opposite temptation is 'not an escape into invisibility but an attempt to establish the unity of the Church only

---

6 Note Barth's use of the word 'monadic' in this section. It is not identical with 'monist' but it has helpful resonances.

in the realm of history, to try to realize the one Church "externally *in abstacto*"' (Barth 1956, p. 678). This corresponds to the Ebionite heresy. That is, in the same way that Jesus Christ was considered to be a human being – an exemplary one at that – nonetheless merely human awaiting the blessing of the Spirit; so too the Church considered as a merely historical entity, perhaps called upon to be an exemplary one at that, nonetheless remains no more than this. In this way, the Church becomes an embodiment of an Ebionitic Christology.[7]

For Barth, it is not a matter of denying the historical empirical reality of the Church. Barth's dialectical ecclesiology maintains the twin realities of the Church: the vertical (the invisible divine action of the Spirit) and the horizontal (visible historical form) can neither be separated nor confused. This means that the historical reality of the Church participates in the spiritual reality of its Lord. To consider the Church of God apart from these fundamental interlocking dimensions is to consider the Church in *abstraction* apart from faith (Bender 2005, pp. 168–70; cf. Barth 1956, p. 655). Thus, while the Church 'does not exist and must not be sought abstractly in the invisible, [it] also does not exist and must not be sought abstractly in the visible' (Barth 1956, p. 654). His point is that while the Church certainly must and does exist in concrete historical forms, nonetheless its 'character, the truth of its existence in time and space, is not a matter of a general but a very special visibility'. This particular or 'special visibility' does not negate its reality as a sinful marred, broken and fragile historical society and organization belonging to fallen humanity. Furthermore, the 'particular visibility' of the Church is precisely the form through which the 'spiritual reality', the 'inner mystery of the Church's spiritual character' is manifested.

Barth's criticism is directed at the 'two dimensional view' of the Church, that is, the Church as purely invisible or as 'generally

---

7 This heresy had strong roots in Jewish culture and religion. It eventually spawned a variety of Adoptionist Christologies in which the transcendent Spirit constituted Jesus as a new being ontologically different from what preceded it.

visible', 'a historical phenomenon like any other'. Barth argues that the character of the Church is three-dimensional involving a 'special visibility' or 'spiritual reality' that requires discernment of its reality according to faith (pp. 656–8). This is the reason for his rejection of doctrines of the Church that bracket out or discount the *theological* reality of the historical community of faith. To do this directly or indirectly represents an abstraction. This occurs when the Church is considered from an 'external' view. This is happening in familiar everyday human activity whether in the political world or by the 'pure historicist, psychologist and sociologist' (p. 655). The ever-present threat of such a judgement is the 'sword which always and everywhere hangs over the *ecclesia visibilis*' (p. 657). This temptation comes to the Church 'from without, from its own humanity' not 'from within' wherein the Holy Spirit awakens the Church to its third dimension, of its invisible reality. Thus, for Barth, 'just as considering Jesus only from the perspective of historical criticism produces an abstraction of his true character, so also the Church is dealt with as an abstraction if conceived apart from the call of God through the Spirit of Christ which bestows its true existence' (Bender 2005, p. 173).

Barth's dialectical ecclesiology may not have escaped Healy's tag of 'blueprint ecclesiology'. However, his approach highlights the nexus between an historicist approach to the Church and an Ebionitic ecclesiology. Moreover, in Barth's Christological ecclesiology, he is well placed to expose the influence on ecclesiology of an incipient Ebionite Christology. The irony of such a theological matrix is that the end result is a church that constantly teeters on the verge of disappearance. The logic of a Church that is both regarded and indeed behaves like any other historical phenomenon is the eventual disappearance of the identity of the reality of the *ecclesia*. A visible concrete form remains, however, it may be theologically vacuous.

A feature of such an ecclesiology is the utter transcendence of the Spirit. The Church is a human work but it is no longer clear how the Spirit is present and or active. An Ebionitic ecclesiology funded from a similar Christology is correlated to a radically transcendent pneumatology. It ends up as a form of ecclesial deism. The result is that the Church is left to its own devices to figure out how to act and order its life. Not surprisingly, the practices of such a church culture are deeply Pelagian and widespread in the contemporary churches of the West.

Church, world and Pelagianism

There are a number of things that flow from the above ecclesial reduction. First, I note the particular way in which the church and the world are related. In an Ebionitic ecclesiology, Church and world implode. Effectively, the reality of the Church disappears in this assimilation of the Church to the world. The Church, when treated as an historical concrete entity without reference to its spiritual ground, effectively forfeits its identity as the ecclesia of *God*. Church and world coalesce and the price is the bond between the Church and God.

The Pelagian stream is a natural fit with the Ebionite ecclesiology, which is constantly morphing into the world. The work and being of the Church is achieved apart from and/or without reference to divine transcendence. The Church remains locked into the phenomena of its life with a consequent loss of inner spiritual capacity.

The heretical impulse: implications for ecclesial praxis

In this closing section of the chapter, I want to tease out some of the implications of the two different kinds of heretical impulses embodied in the above systemic ecclesial defaults.

Church and world

I have already noted and briefly discussed the nature of the relation between the Church and the world according to the natural ecclesial heresies identified. Thus where the Church is the subject of a 'sacred inflation', the relationship between Church and world is disjunctive; the Church is set over against the world, which exists as an alien 'other'. In this relationship, the Church is credited with divine attributes and becomes the habitation of the Spirit. A Docetic Christology and an immanent pneumatology provide the environment for a controlled ecclesial world administered by spiritual elites. Needless to say this is the breeding ground for a range of leadership pathologies. This kind of ecclesiology finds embodiment in a remarkable variety of Church types and is certainly not restricted to any particular one. Ecclesiologies of the 'sacred inflation' type exist on a spectrum, and this will be reflected in the nature of their engagements with society from relative openness to withdrawn and closed. But the fundamental relation is disjunctive. It fosters a sectarian spirit, though this is often masked in larger ecclesial bodies. Moreover, the disjunction between Church and world can go unrecognized. For example, a Church may be entirely oblivious of the extent to which it mirrors in its own life, values, mission and worship the cultural forms and values of the social and cultural environment. An espoused ecclesiology of separation masks a pervasive assimilation that is so seamless that it remains unnoticed.[8] In this way, the world is the alien other over against the Church, and at the same time its values receive religious legitimation. I think particularly of the influence of entertainment culture on Christian worship.

As noted above, such ecclesiologies are most naturally aligned with either soft or hard forms of Manicheanism. The degree and intensity will vary with different Church bodies and depend on a range of factors – theological outlook, sense of place in the society, view of the world etc. Such ecclesiologies are notoriously unable to recognize their own humanity and brokenness. It remains fundamentally alien to the Church's existence and to this extent a troubling puzzle. Harder forms of this state of affairs are manifest in negative judgements concerning the world beyond the Church, which is identified as a region devoid of grace and apparently impervious to redemption.

---

8 For a helpful distinction between espoused and operant theology, see Cameron et al. 2010, pp. 53–6.

Where the Church is regarded simply as any other historical phenomenon (and thereby succumbs to de-sacralized reduction), the Church/world distinction tends to implode. In this case, as I noted above, the Church is assimilated to the world and more often becomes a mirror image of the world and the prevailing cultural values depending on the particular context. This arises because the Church is treated and behaves like any other historical empirical entity. In this case, both ecclesiology and Christology are correlated according to an underlying Ebionite pattern.

What of the Spirit? When the systemic ecclesial default is Ebionitic, the Spirit is dislocated and distanced from the life of the Church. This involves a form of radical transcendence of the Spirit typical of an ecclesial deism. An Ebionitic Christology and a pneumatology of transcendence provide the conditions for Church and world to coalesce. This is easily masked to the extent that the Spirit is reconceived as the common life of the people of the Church. However, the price of this is forfeiture of the capacity for critique of the status quo and loss of a transcendent referent. One practical consequence of this development is anxiety about loss of identity and purpose. In this context, it is no surprise to find a Pelagian spirit alive and active. This in fact is the natural correlate to an Ebionitic ecclesiology.

Institution and individual

Edward Farley noted some decades ago that the overwhelming issue facing the Church of the West was no longer a dominant institutionalism but rampant individualism. 'Individualism is the characteristic perversion of the *ecclesia* not institutionalism' (1975, p. 238). A chief characteristic of this phenomenon was the loss of face-to-face relationships. There is of course a natural and perennial tension between institutional life and the autonomy of individuals of the Church. This is not new and has an important and at times controversial history not only in the Church. The familiar Protestant emphasis on private judgement is one response to a perception of heavy handed institutional control. However, Farley is pointing to something far more serious when he refers to the fragmenting impact of social and cultural individualism which has so infected the life of the *ecclesia* of God.

But does this well attested phenomenon of the Church constitute a systemic default that springs from a natural ecclesial heresy? I believe it does from a number of different but related perspectives. First, within the framework of a long attested and heavily embedded institutional Docetism – with associated practices of top-down control – the phenomenon of pervasive individualism is a natural reaction. The Church lurches from one extreme to another. Second, where the Church loses its transcendent reference and behaves as if it were like any other historical community, the assimilation to the surrounding culture will, unsurprisingly manifest itself in a radical individualism. The natural ecclesial heresies discussed above both resolve into highly fragmented religious societies that mirror the host cultures.

Leadership, anxiety and Pelagian culture

Anxiety has become a fundamental characteristic of contemporary Western society (see Cowdell 2008). The churches have not been immune from this; indeed it infects all facets of ecclesial life. The kinds of systemic defaults I have been outlining in this chapter provide the natural environment for an anxious Church. It would seem that the second of the two basic ecclesial heresies would be most conducive to toxic forms of anxiety. A Church suffering the loss of its own inner transcendence is for the most part a Church left to its own devices, notwithstanding protestations to the contrary. Such a Church naturally defaults into behaviour and practices which are best identified as Pelagian in spirit and temper. This is expressed in discourses and practices that are focused on strategic planning, heavy emphasis on rationalizing resources, obsession with efficient, cost effective processes, tight control via micro-management technique, and the achievement of measurable and successful outcomes. This Pelagian ethos is embedded in management and therapeutic models of ministry and leadership. In such an ecclesial system, the constant experience is dissipation of energy, loss of coherence and fleeting 'success'. Ministry appears more democratic and the discourse may be collaborative, but it often masks a new form of control via bottom up management (see Pickard 2009, pp. 174–9).

When the Church is more indebted to a Docetic ethos, institutional anxiety concerning the state of the Church manifests itself as powerful top down, non-collaborative, tightly controlled ministry and leadership. The discourse can easily fool people into believing that the work being undertaken is all God's work to save a fallen and dark world (the Manichean view of the world is the natural counterpart to institutional Docetism). However, the sacralization of leadership within this schema is not the whole story. While attributing all to God, this kind of leadership is beset with unacknowledged anxieties more in tune with a Pelagian temper. An emphasis upon divine sovereignty and power bolsters competitive work practices that trade on mistrust and lead to subtle and not so subtle forms of authoritarianism. (In the process, people are worn down, fall by the wayside or react and exit in search of a place where the healing balm of the Spirit can do its work.) While reference to the Spirit may receive strong statement the actual practices of leadership betray the anxieties of a Church adrift and struggling to remain faithful. A top-down sacralized leadership operates as a Trojan horse for a Pelagianism that soaks the ecclesial world. At this point, we see most clearly the power of the Pelagian heretical impulse, which transcends the boundaries of the typology adopted in the above discussion. It arises because the sacralizing agenda of leadership within the Docetic Church in fact can't be sustained by human will and collapses. This is evidenced in practices that indicate that reform of the Church – its structures and ministry – is a very human work on behalf of but not in participation with the divine. Yet, it is the Spirit that brings reform and renewal. The Lutheran theologian Robert Jensen states that '[i]f there is to be Churchly reform, the Spirit must do it; it must be done by the triune person who frees the Church to be the own [sic] body of Christ . . . Churchly reform is the risen Christ's self discipline in the Spirit' (1999, p. 213).

Missional distortions

When the Church manifests a sacred inflation with sharp boundaries between Church and world and clergy and laity, mission
is primarily by *attraction*. The litmus test for this is the way in
which the energy of the Church is geared to gathering people into
the sacred fellowship. When, on the other hand, the Church is
regarded and/or behaves like any other kind of organization mission can either evaporate or morph into various kinds of welfare.

Conclusion: beyond ecclesial heresy

This chapter has offered a very preliminary and broad-brush
analysis and theological diagnosis of some of the ills of the
Church that require repair and healing. It has done this by
applying to the Church the natural heresies of Christianity, as
articulated by Friedrich Schleiermacher in the early nineteenth
century. The natural heresies of Christianity have an ecclesial
form and embodiment, which I have tried to identify. In doing
this, I hope I have been able, to some extent, to show how many
of the presenting ills of the body of Christ can be traced to familiar heretical impulses that will inevitably re-emerge in Christianity in any age. This ought not be surprising as it belongs to the
search for the truth of our life with God in the world in every
age. This ecclesial project is the scene of energetic and controversial encounters with others and the Divine – just as it should
be. This is what happens when humans seek the God who is the
transcendent ground of human society and creation and therefore of the Church.

I have also tried to uncover some of the ways in which the
systemic defaults of the Church – the encoded heretical impulses
of the ecclesial system – can be observed indirectly through practical ecclesiology. In this respect, I focused on Church practices,
attitudes towards the world, forms of ministry and leadership,
tensions between the institution and the individual, and ways in
which the Church attempts to manage its inner anxieties and engage
in mission. The point of this exercise was to identify the ways in

which heretical impulses, when transposed into the domain of the Church, eventually manifest in practices to do with spiritual life, ministry and mission. By this stage, however, the heretical impulses have travelled a long way from 'home', but importantly they have not suffered any dissipation of energy. Their effects remain as virulent as ever, but they usually remain unrecognized. For this reason, heretical ecclesial practices are much harder to identify and eradicate.

Much more could be developed in these latter areas and many of the subjects briefly touched on at the end of this chapter have been the subject of significant commentary and analysis in sociological study of Churches and practical ecclesiology. This chapter has offered a theological diagnostic to complement approaches from sociology and organizational psychology. Doctrine, ecclesial practice and spiritual life are finely interwoven, but often we fail to grasp the nature and significance of the weave. To this extent, we lack the capacity and understanding to identify ways to repair and assist the healing of the Church. The embodiment of heretical impulses in ecclesial forms ensures that genuine repair, reform and renewal are constantly thwarted. The result is that, notwithstanding multiple changes and modifications of Church life, the end result is a repetitive steady-state ecclesiology.

In the chapters which follow (4 to 9), I want to consider what a dynamic ecclesiology for the pilgrim people of God might look like. The intent of the present chapter has been to alert the pilgrim to some of the dangers en route so to speak. Such warnings ought not deter the Church from its calling. However, they add a note of realism about the pitfalls and potential ravines that have to be negotiated on the journey. With this in mind the next chapter begins to lay a foundation for the construction of an ecclesiology for pilgrims. This requires a fundamental reorientation of the Church from a steady-state to a dynamic ecclesiology seeking the coming kingdom of God. In this context, to seek the Church is to seek a renewed sociality energized and structured after God's own life. This is the subject of the chapter which follows.

Questions

1 The chapter argues that there are heresies that the Church has to make judgements about, and there are heresies that are systemic to the being of the Church. Why are these latter kind of heresies so difficult to identify and respond to?
2 Make a mind map or matrix of Schleiermacher's fourfold scheme of heresies. Consider how the different heresies relate and how they are applied to the Church.
3 What kind of Church leadership is typically associated with a Docetic ecclesiology?
4 The *de-sacralized* Church emphasises an ecclesiology from below. What are the strengths and weaknesses of this approach?
5 What are the basic ways in which the church and world relate in the natural ecclesial heresies identified in this chapter?
6 If the Church so easily succumbs to the kinds of heretical developments identified in this chapter, what response(s) are possible in order to reform and repair the Church?

Further Reading

Scott Cowdell, 'Organised Religion', in *God's Next Big Thing: Discovering the Future Church*, Mulgrave, Victoria: John Garrett Publishing, 2004, pp. 191–225.

Colin Gunton, 'The Church on Earth: The Roots of Community', in Colin Gunton and Daniel Hardy (eds), *On Being the Church: Essays on the Christian Community*, Edinburgh: T & T Clark, 1989, pp. 48–80.

Alistair McGrath, *Heresy: A History of Defending the Truth*, London: SPCK, 2009, esp. Ch. 8, 'Cultural and Intellectual Motivations for Heresy'.

4

A Renewed Sociality

Connectivity and society

Searching for human society

Among the many puzzles and challenges of contemporary life, one of the more significant and illusive concerns the question of human society. It is not simply a question about whether human society is possible in a deeply fragmented and violent world, though that matter haunts us. Nor is it simply a concern about what kind of society is optimal and makes for human well-being (though, of course, the search for exactly such a society remains a hope and desire for many, particularly those of the world for whom daily life is a grind and without hope). Such concerns belong to the human project across cultures, races and languages. The search for viable, sustaining human society, which enhances quality of life belongs to the purpose of the Church. However, this is often lost sight of. For the sake of the world and the good news of God, this purpose needs to be recovered. How the Church might participate in the renewal of the social ordering of things ought to be at the heart of ecclesiology.

Yet, there is a deeper and quite critical matter, which is often missed or skated over. It can be put in the form of two related questions. What holds human society together? What are the conditions required for human society? A doctrine of the Church ought to be able to offer some clues and directions regarding these two questions and other related fundamental questions about human society: questions about the possibility of human society; the optimal kind of society; questions about human flourishing and questions about how society might be repaired and improved. These are some of the questions that underlie so much of contemporary political, cultural and religious life, and clearly they have multiple dimensions: economic, legal, social, interpersonal, communicative. These matters throw a shadow over all theological reflection on the nature of the Church.

Justifying true society

The gremlin in the system is that we no longer seem to have any confidence about what might justify true human society. This is a question about the foundations of human society. Moreover, we are unsure how to develop an understanding of the conditions necessary to justify true society. Nor, it seems, are we clear, from a religious point of view, how human society might be related to God. These are some of the questions that ecclesiologists need to attend to in the service of a renewed sociality.

In the modern Western world, the question about what justifies a true society is answered principally by reference to a utilitarian philosophy based on a pragmatic assessment of what works best to maximize economic well-being of individuals. This seems to have achieved a god-like status in the minds and hearts of people. This approach underpins a competitive market economy which functions according to Darwinian notions of natural selection where the most powerful and intelligent survive. Welfare and governments often attempt to keep the system in check to some extent. But in other ways they simply collude with the dominant market forces. Within such a framework, society receives its own justification based on the usefulness of its constituent parts (including people) for the maximizing of efficient production and exchange of goods. The end result is that human society and its flourishing is interpreted in terms of economic value. While a doctrine of the Church ought in principle at least to espouse a very different ethos and set of values, too often and perhaps unsurprisingly the Western Church has been deeply infected with economic utilitarianism, as witnessed in its preoccupation with competition, property and wealth, and system management. A theological response to this will have to include a critique of a self-absorbed individualism and offer a richer communitarian focus for society. This is why recent emphasis on the social doctrine of the Trinity, Trinitarian relations and communion ecclesiology have been so eagerly absorbed into mainstream theological discourse on the Church. It appears to offer a counter to the Church acting in a complicit manner with prevailing market values that are essentially non-communal, consumerist and individualist (see Cowdell 2008, pp. 22–41). However, as we will see in this and the following chapter, such responses can be controversial and have not yet borne the fruit they promise.

Beyond utilitarianism

In the last quarter of a century, we have become more aware than ever that a utilitarian approach to social cohesion does not and cannot do justice to the nature of the social bond. Environmental concerns, and recognition that our lives are inextricably woven into the fabric of the planet and indeed the cosmos, have reminded us that we are deeply connected with each other on the earth. This is a condition of our being, prior to any consideration of usefulness or serving the interests of society, its organizations and institutions. Indeed, few things can be more fundamental to our life than our interconnectedness with others and the world. From this point of view, it is no accident that the language of *koinonia* or communion has become almost stock in trade in reflection on the Church. One recent Anglican theology report stated the matter in the following terms:

> The terms 'koinonia' and 'communion' can become so much a part of the discourse of a fractured and divided Church that they lose their force and significance. Koinonia has to do with a fundamental connectivity between God, the world, and all living things, including of course human life. The African word 'ubuntu' captures something of this primary oneness. In the Genesis story human beings are called 'earthlings' or 'groundlings'

(Genesis 2). This underscores the fact that we are 'of the earth' and are intrinsically related to other living things, the whole created environment and God. Such koinonia is encoded into the very being of creation. The story of redemption is a story of Christ rejoining people, races and the rest of creation. This is the good news which overcomes sin and broken bonds. There is no other community on the earth with a mandate to bear witness to the remarkable miracle of our oneness in the triune God. What is even more remarkable is that God invites the body of Christ to become the new experiment in the communion of the Holy Spirit. (IATDC 2008, p. 57)

The context for this comment was reflection on the way bishops served the communion of the Church. Importantly, the report noted that 'koinonia or oneness is given by God in creation and renewed in Christ and the Spirit'. The implications of this for the doctrine of the Church are examined in more detail below, where I draw a distinction between the *basis* for *koinonia* and its *fulfilment* in Christ. At this point, my concern is to draw attention to the importance of connectivity as the key to the nature of the social bond. I want to argue in what follows that such connectivity has ontological weight; that it involves a dynamic that can be traced in the first place to creation, before it becomes the subject of redemption. Furthermore, and not surprisingly, such connectivity finds its headwaters in the doctrine of God and its estuary in the doctrine of the Church. This comprehensive view is encoded in the above statement that 'koinonia or oneness is given by God in creation and renewed in Christ and the Spirit'. This suggests that theologically the proper and only adequate basis for society has to be unfolded in relation to a doctrine of God. It also means that ecclesiology is – among many things of a more practical kind – a theoretical inquiry into the conditions by which human society is grounded and flourishes with God in the world.

Finally, this also points to the fact that ecclesiology is always more than simply a study of Church, as if it were able to be hermetically sealed off from society. Rather, ecclesiology is a discipline that ought to be undertaken in conversation with a range of other disciplines that have direct and indirect bearing on the dynamic and purposes of human society. In other words, to seek a doctrine of the Church is to inquire how human society arises, endures and fulfils its inner purposes.[1] That is why it was stated in Chapter 1 that ecclesiology involves 'assembling all that is needed to promote the fullness of human society' (Hardy 2010, p. 79). While such a conclusion may appear obvious, it is often obscured or ignored because the doctrine of the Church is treated apart from its placement within society. This can be observed when studies of the Bible and theology are subsequently *applied* to the Church and its purpose in the world. Implicit in this manoeuvre is a disconnection between theology, Church and world. There is a failure to recognize that Christianity is necessarily ecclesial in form and that it is possible, indeed necessary to be an ecclesial being without being churchy!

The ecclesial nature of Christianity

Church as social form of Christianity

The foregoing remarks on the significance of connectivity for understanding the basis for human society have already flagged some critical issues for the nature of the Church. The remainder of this chapter will develop an understanding of the Church as renewed sociality.

I argued in Chapter 1 that ecclesiology was not a second-order matter in theology but rather belonged in the mix with primary theological concerns. Indeed, the doctrine of the Church functions as a, if not the fundamental filter for the doctrinal tradition of Christianity. This is more than ecclesiology operating as one perspective

---

1 For too long, the doctrine of the Church has remained disconnected from other disciplines related to human society and this has diminished ecclesiology and tended to lock the discipline in a web of reflections upon scripture and theology with little appreciation of the value or need for interdisciplinary work.

on the Christian tradition – though it can and does perform such a task. Rather, the Church is nothing less than the social form of Christianity. This claim deserves teasing out a little particularly against the background of the excessively individualistic and privatized notions of Christianity – what Edward Farley has described as the contemporary 'peril' of *ecclesia* (1975, p. 182).

Referring to the Church as the social form of Christianity is premised on a relation of co-inherence between Church and Christianity. In the twentieth century, Dietrich Bonhoeffer (1906–45) developed a view of the Church as 'Christ existing as community' (1963, p. 160). Here, the social form of Christianity was not a secondary matter but was derived from the sociality of God:

> Communion with God exists only through Christ, but Christ is present only in His Church, hence there is communion with God only in the Church. This fact destroys every individualistic conception of the Church. (p. 116)

This statement resonates with another of Bonhoeffer's:

> Social community is in essence given with community with God. The latter is not what leads to the former. Communion with God is not without social community, nor is social community without community with God. (Quoted in Hardy 1989, p. 38 from Feil 1985, p. 8)

Daniel Hardy comments on this statement:

> Bonhoeffer derives sociality directly from relationship to God; human sociality arises in (is given with) relationship with God – as a necessary part of it, not as a *post facto* addition to it. Therefore human sociality is inseparable from community with God; human and human–divine community are mutually necessary. (p. 38)

Human sociality being given in and with relationship to God is the key here. It is not an 'add-on' generically derived from being with

God nor is it disconnected from relationship to God.[2] Rather, there exists a fundamental theological link between human sociality and the Triune God. The rich simplicity of this relation was depicted in Chapter 1 in Dorotheos of Gaza's image of people journeying at different points on the periphery of a circle towards God at the centre of the circle: the closer one moved towards God the closer one moved towards each other. This conception is the basis for the claim that seeking God is intertwined with seeking the Church. What it also means is that Christianity is inescapably an ecclesial reality.[3] On this basis, ecclesiology is, as I suggested above, an inquiry into the conditions for human sociality, the dynamics by which this occurs and endures, and the purposes entailed in such a form of life.

Church: created sociality

Foundations for ecclesial life

If it is the case that human sociality is given in and with relationship with God, how does this actually come about? If Daniel

---

2 For example, Church and Christianity might be construed as *disjunctive* realities operating in parallel and essentially unintegrated. This kind of relationship has been a feature of the Christian religion from the Enlightenment. An alternative to this is a *generic* relationship in which Church is derived from a more general conception of Christianity. This is a basic cause and effect quasi-mechanistic type of relation. It can assume more institutionalized forms at the more Catholic end of the spectrum whereby the Church is 'an extension of the incarnation' to carry on the work of Christ. At the more Protestant end is a 'call type' ecclesiology whereby the Church comes into existence as people respond to the call of Christ.

3 Of course, the circle analogy, like all analogies, is useful as far as it goes. I recognize that the analogy also means that persons begin, at the periphery of the circle as individuals and to that extent the analogy undermines the essential relational quality of human beings with God. My concern, however, is with the dynamics of movement which reveal increasing levels of ecclesiality as the fundamental form of relation to God.

Hardy is right, this question cannot be answered *in the first place* by reference to a doctrine of redemption whereby God calls people into a new community called Church. Rather, the question about the *basis* for human sociality is to be located first in relation to creation. This was identified above in the statement that 'koinonia or oneness is given by God in creation and renewed in Christ and the Spirit'. In other words, might we be able to speak of created sociality before we speak of redeemed sociality (Hardy 1989, pp. 21–47)? Is it possible that the basis for a true society is to be located in an originative creative work of God? If so, does this mean that sociality is a constituent of createdness *per se*? It is not clear how such a conception is present in a great deal of current discourse on the Church notwithstanding the renewed emphasis on the doctrine of the Trinity in relation to ecclesiology.

If the concept of created or general sociality can be sustained it would have far reaching consequences. Such a starting point would signal a departure from the more traditional theological approach that locates the *basis* for human community in redemption. Where this latter axiom obtains the immediate effect, is to privilege the Church as the locus of God's activity. One consequence is that it raises serious questions about the status of the rest of the created order, particularly human society. Is this all merely preparatory to the creation of real community? Can human life outside of the Church participate in God's good, true and beautiful ways with the world? For too much of Christianity, the answer has been more often an emphatic *No*. A dualism has operated and the Church has operated like a sect – albeit at times quite puffed up – either separated from the world or assimilating the world to itself. Such a scenario was identified in Chapter 3 as belonging to one of the natural heresies of the Church.

The focus on redemption or perhaps more accurately the omission of creation in the discussion of the Church is almost endemic in ecclesiology. For example, Bonhoeffer's admirable search for a solution to the problem of the basis for true sociality, as helpful as it is, still remains captive to the redemptive motif. While God and society are deeply connected for Bonhoeffer his rationale for this omits reference to creation; focuses on redemption, and privileges the Church as God's sphere of action. How does he do this? The mutual necessity of social community and community with God is simply stated in a definitional manner though it is apparent that it arises from God's 'specific work' in Christ and the cross. Social community is 'the response to the gift of God, fulfilled in his achievement in Christ' (Hardy 1989, pp. 39f). When Bonhoeffer states that 'Christ is present only in His Church, hence there is communion with God only in the Church', the supposition is that the Church is the 'place where this response is made', albeit for the sake of society as a whole (p. 40).

Hardy's point is that this approach effectively sidelines a '"general sociality" or created sociality present in the human condition; there can be no such thing as the social transcendental present in human society as an element of nature, because its place is always taken by the specific gift of God in Christ' (p. 40). He argues that the 'social transcendental', which is the basis for all society and informs its functioning ought not be located in 'God's specific act of redemption in Christ' but be 'traced to the Logos of God operative in creation' (p. 42).

Where sociality belongs to those 'necessary notes of being' (pp. 24f; unity, truth, goodness, beauty), the deep relationality we observe in creation – in the animal kingdom, human society and in the symbiotic life of the natural environment – is no accident or purely evolutionary surprise. Rather it is a form of life inherent in the very nature of creation; its materiality, life forms and of course human beings. Hardy refers at this point to a 'divine ordering' in creation 'that ultimately implants in the human condition the "being with" which is natural to it' (p. 42). Sociality belongs, on this account, to creation and is to be attributed to God's work of creation. Indeed an important trajectory in theological discussion of the concept of the *imago Dei* in Genesis 1 emphasizes the relational understanding of the human person as image bearer of the Divine (see, for example, Grenz 1994, pp. 170–2). This ought not be surprising given the character of the Triune God, whom Christians worship and follow. Indeed, created sociality is exactly what we ought to expect from a Trinitarian account of creation and human life. Such an approach invests the whole world with new possibilities for community, and we ought not be surprised that human society, beyond the boundaries of the ecclesiastical world, abounds with instances of the operation of such a created sociality.

Church: redeemed sociality

Redemption as fulfilment of created sociality

The *basis* for the social transcendental is to be differentiated from its *fulfilment* associated with God's redemptive work. The distinction between *basis* and *fulfilment* is important and easily misconstrued. The truth of God present in creation is the originative work of God. The true form of the social dynamic of being with God is thus not in the *first instance* to be attributed to the 'apostolicity of the Church' but to the *logos* of God in creation (Hardy 1989, p. 42).

However, we are well aware that natural community is not necessarily ideal in its operation or purpose. Genuine created sociality, in so far as it is attracted to and responds to the call of God, will necessarily be in constant stages of reform and transformation. A true society is also a potential to be achieved as human community is assimilated to the holiness of God; a movement concentrated in the offering of worship (see Hardy 2001, Ch. 1). There is a necessary redemptive moment in social life so that created sociality becomes an emergent redemptive sociality. This leads us naturally to inquire into the dynamics by which a faithful sociality emerges and is sustained in a world where broken communities, violence and dysfunction subvert the deeper intentions and purposes of the divine creativity of the God and Father of Jesus Christ. In this context, the Christian community has a story to tell and a form of life to practice, which can bear witness to and be an instantiation of the holiness of the Triune God. This calling of the *ecclesia* is not a judgement of the Church upon the failure of the world but more a response to the abundant graciousness of God who bestows a rich sociality upon the world.

Hardy's fundamental theological insight into the basis for human society is critical, if we are to recognize and appreciate the work of God in creation sustaining and enhancing life and society in ongoing and ever expanding ways. What it means is that the sociality associated with redemption *is not over against but emergent from within* what is given in creation as such. In this case, redemption is not something fundamentally alien but is properly a reconstitution of all that is already present in creation. This can be identified as a 'raising' of the social transcendent to its 'true form' through a dynamic process 'due to the presence of divine sociality and hence the Trinitarian presence of God' (Hardy 1989, p. 42). *An important conclusion of this is that a doctrine of the Church as renewed sociality can be developed in such a way that does not diminish the world.* This, of course, raises quite sharply questions about the purpose and place of the Church in the world. At the same time, it also presumes that the Church has much to learn about the ways of God in the world.

The bond in Christ that forms a truly redeemed community has, accordingly, a double reference to both creation and redemption. The *logos* at work in the world – 'all things came into being through him, and without him not one thing came into being' (John 1.3) – is the *logos* enfleshed, indwelling, reconciling and renewing all things. The sociality of God has an ongoing history. The truth of the work of God in Christ in creation continues in a concentrated form in the incarnation and passion of Christ. In this particular work of God, a redeemed sociality is formed out of created sociality; one new humanity beyond all fractures and hostilities (Eph. 2.15). This work of the divine Trinity requires further examination below.

Church: displaying the bond in Christ

I have been trying to develop an understanding of the Church in terms of connectivity and sociality relevant for a doctrine of the Church that includes both creation and redemption. Fundamental to the argument is the integrative way in which human society is founded by God in creation and renewed and/or reconstituted through redemption. This means that the Church has twin coordinates: creation and redemption. Furthermore only both together enable an adequate theology of the Church.[4] Accordingly, if the Church is a creature of the Word and Spirit – as I suggested in Chapter 1 – it is so because its form and dynamic is original to creation as such.

In the light of the foregoing, *the Church in time and space is that form of sociality that makes explicit what is already present by virtue of God's work in the world.* As such, the Church is an instance and manifestation of a reconstituted sociality due to the presence and work of Christ and the Spirit. The supposition here is that the Triune God is the primary unifier and creator of true sociality. For this reason the writer of the letter to the Ephesians says of the Church, that it is Christ's body, 'the fullness [Greek: *pleroma*] of him who fills all in all' (Eph. 1.23). True sociality comes from the plenitude of the being of God manifest in creation and redemption. Yet, the gift-like character of God's rich bestowal of human community operates through a creative dynamic that is constantly reconstituting and thus raising what is – in this case human sociality – to fullness of life. The emergence of the Church as a specific creation of God is not something that occurs from outside the system[5] but *from within what it already is.* The *ecclesia* of God is always an emergent, creative and new form of sociality orientated towards the holiness of God and thus essentially imperfect and unfinished.

As I have indicated, such an approach provides for a far more integrated and dynamic account of the life of the Church in the world. The twin dangers of dualism and assimilation – natural ecclesial heresies identified in Chapter 3 – can be more

---

4 The redemptive coordinate includes the ongoing and eschatological orientation of the Church.

5 In this sense, we need to eschew any form of 'vitalism' with respect to the way the grace of God actually operates and in this sense reject any notion of grace that requires an insertion from outside the system rather than an eruption from within.

easily identified and avoided. More positively, the Church is freed to be a more generous, open and engaged participant *with the world* as it follows the work and ways of God in creation.[6]

The ecclesial bond in Christ

Identifying the ecclesial bond

Our reflections so far point to the importance of what I would call the 'one-in-Christ bond' or the 'ecclesial bond in Christ'. The manifold ways in which human beings are held together (their 'connectivity' and 'created sociality') and are drawn deeper into God's life (the reconstitutive or raising work of God in Christ and the world) is encompassed in the concept of the 'one-in-Christ bond'. It is another way of speaking about the Church as renewed sociality. Of course, inquiry into the nature of this ecclesial bond in Christ is difficult to pursue for Church life is rich and diverse, and the Church is a complex social reality that resists simple assessments or explication.

How then might the ecclesial bond be depicted? At a general level this bond may be identified as a *one-in-Christ* bond ('you are all one in Christ Jesus', Gal. 3.28; cf. Col. 3.11; John 17.11 22; Eph. 2.14). Yet, as we have already observed the bond in Christ is complex and capable of remarkable expansion (Eph. 1.22). I have suggested that at a primary level (ontological) the one-in-Christ bond is constituted by the sociality of God who is the primary unifier. However, the implication of my argument so far is that the twin co-ordinates of God's sociality, that is, creation and redemption together constitute the one-in-Christ bond. Indeed, it is this rich and dynamic bond in Christ 'through which being

---

6 I discovered an interesting and encouraging example of this kind of approach in the Newcastle Diocese of the Church of England programme 'Local, Sustaining, Christian Presence: a generous, engaged and open approach to mission', 2011.

displays itself' (Hardy 1989, p. 25).[7] The doctrine of the Church takes its cue, so to speak, from one of the fundamental features of the cosmos, that is, a sociality derived from God. The one-in-Christ bond manifests this constitutive feature of reality.

While an appeal to the ecclesial bond in Christ might provide a foundation for reconceiving the doctrine of the Church, it still remains unclear what exactly might be included in the sociality of being with God. Or to put it another way, what might be involved in the complex and rich bond in Christ? Or alternatively, how might the one-in-Christ bond be mediated in the world? The importance of such questions ought not be overlooked. For example, the Christian mystical tradition would provide very different responses to the question of mediation of the bond in Christ compared to other forms of Christianity. Mysticism would usually emphasize a radical soul-realism where mediation is direct between the person and the divine. Participation in the social reality of *ecclesia* is relocated interiorly or at least emanates from a prior interior relation to God. Indeed, any kind of ecclesiology that gives priority to interiority and/or the invisible Church will take minimal account of the various ways through which the one-in-Christ bond is actually mediated in the world.

The problem of the interpersonal

More generally, there is a real danger, particularly in our Western context, that the mediation of the ecclesial bond will be reduced to *interpersonal* relations. This is my fundamental concern with Colin Gunton's critique of Hardy's appeal to sociality (Gunton 1992, pp. 219–23). Gunton's restriction of

---

7 Hardy is discussing transcendentals, those '"necessary notes of being", such as unity, truth, goodness, beauty . . . The forms through which being displays itself, through which being is determinate; they constitute an answer to the search for the fundamental features of the cosmos'. His argument, which I have been drawing upon in this chapter, is that 'sociality' is properly identified as one such transcendental.

the domain of the social to the personal and/or interpersonal effectively severs the social (and all that it includes at the personal level) from createdness *per se*.[8] The problem is that the concept of 'persons-in-relation' appears to be interpreted exclusively in relation *to other persons*. Hardy's category of sociality is far wider and richer, while always retaining the personal dimension. Accordingly, it is persons-in-relation not simply *to other persons* but *to creation and all that this involves*. It is for this reason that sociality belongs to the region of transcendentals, operating as it does at fundamental levels of being in the world.

When the sociality of being in Christ is reduced to interpersonal regions, the result is that significant areas of life are marginalized or ignored as irrelevant to being the people of God. For example, such a restriction cannot give an adequate account of the nexus between Yahweh, people and land in the history of Israel. The link between earth, God and humankind is encoded into the creation narratives of Genesis.[9] It is impossible to understand the emergence of the character of the people of Israel as a community without reference to a complex and multi-layered concept of sociality. The problem with the concept of relationality is that it remains unspecified and too general and does not justify the particularities of human life.

Often this retreat to the personal is in response to a sense of alienation and frustration, that much of the normal course of life no longer seems able to offer media through which God's holy and joyful presence can be manifest. From this point of view the dominance of the interpersonal signals a retreat from the world and all those ways in which the sociality of human beings actually operates and expands. Restriction of

---

8 This may arise at least in part from Gunton's Reformed focus on the Church as redemptive community of persons in relation; and his consequent omission of creation from ecclesial reflection.

9 Thus *adam* (Adam) and *adama* (earth) share a common etymological root 'reddish colour', 'reddish earth'. The wordplay is familiar, hence Adam is 'earthling' or 'groundling'. See Genesis 2.7 and 3.19. For further detail, see Wallace 1992.

the social to the region of the interpersonal feeds a view of the Church as little more than a club or a self-interested and disconnected group of people of marginal significance for society, its concerns and needs. The language of community often masks this basic default (see Chapter 9 for further critique of 'community').

So, what might be the primary ways through which people are one-in-Christ? It is tempting to list scripture, sacraments, worship, ministry and acts of compassion as the essentials of being the Church. It is indeed true that such things are constitutive for being the Church, and they are deeply involved in the forming and transforming of the life of the Church. However, even these elements and activities belong within a wider and prior range of media through which the social transcendental is mediated. If we ignore this prior dimension and thereby fail to relate the 'Church type' forms and activities to their deeper roots, we simply continue to promote false distinctions between Church and world.

Mediating the bond in Christ

Hardy has identified at least five intermediate categories through which the social transcendental is displayed in the world: *place* (or territoriality); *polity* (social organization; including institutions, laws, customs, political leadership); *economics* (mediums of exchange, production and distribution); *interpersonal relationships* (natural and 'spiritual' or friendship); *communication* (language, symbol and culture) (Hardy 1989, pp. 44–7). These categories are by no means exhaustive. The interesting thing about these categories is that they belong to the ordinary materiality of the world including, for example, being bodily, living and dying in a place with others, mediums of exchange. Such media constitute the way we live and relate in the world and as such they represent fundamental features of what sociality consists of. Human beings are bonded to each other and the world through such media. They are the determinate forms through which created sociality is manifest and develops. Theologically we might say that these are the forms through which God's Christ-like work and presence is manifest. The bond in Christ is rooted in these general forms but of course not always apparent and often distorted.

Dimensions of the ecclesial bond in Christ

However, what about the *ecclesial* bond in Christ arising from redemption as such? How is that bond related to the various ways in which and through which human sociality operates as above? This is properly a question about the specificity of the Church in relation to the wider sociality of the world. One way to state the relation is to understand the ecclesial bond *as a way of being connected within the above intermediate social categories*. The latter – place, polity, economics, interpersonal relationships, communication – constitute the fundamental forms and filters through which the ecclesial bond in Christ is displayed and operates. The particularity of the ecclesial bond in Christ is that it manifests what being one-in-Christ entails within the basic forms of created human sociality. *Accordingly, the Church is that form of life that makes explicit what is true about the world created and loved by God.* The presupposition here is that God's work in the life, death and resurrection of Jesus Christ through the eternal Spirit effected a reconstitution of the basic forms of social life. It is this reconstitution that 'forms from created sociality a truly redeemed sociality' (p. 49).

Where then do those various forms and activities associated with being Church fit in this matrix of sociality? For example, scripture – its interpretation and proclamation – belongs within communications. Sacraments might be recognized as instances of a particular form of just distribution of the resource of God. Acts of compassion, friendship and justice might be linked through sacrament to economics. In like manner, ecclesial structure and ministry are determinate forms of polity. Place and associated concepts of territoriality have a long and vital significance for the people of God stretching back into Israel and into modern understandings of worship and pilgrimage. The region of the interpersonal is obviously a fundamental category for the spiritual bonds of friendship and servant ministry. The links between the social categories (place, polity etc) through which the bond in Christ is filtered, and the familiar forms of being the Church (worship, sacraments, preaching, care and witness) are complex and rich. Even this brief discussion suggests that the doctrine of the Church is much broader, intricate and dynamic than is usually assumed in ecclesiology.

The above discussion of the nature of the ecclesial bond highlights the complexity of the Church as a renewed sociality. It is clearly not simply to be equated with a settled community of faith, self-sufficient and disconnected from the world. Rather, Church as renewed sociality involves a complex web of relations covering basic categories of place, interpersonal, economics, polity and communications. *The Church is that body of Christ, which displays through its life and action what the renewal of place, economics, politics, communication and interpersonal life might actually look like.* In this sense, the Church is not set over against the created order, but from within this order it is that body, which is called to make explicit, fulfil and hence display the wisdom of God's own sociality manifest in creation. In this activity and calling, the Church is following the way of Jesus Christ, for he was 'one in whom wisdom reconstituted such dimensions of materiality' – 'bodiliness and life, community, exchange, social organization, interpersonal relationships and communication' (Hardy 1996, p. 251). The Church is called to follow Jesus in the Spirit, as he changes such dimensions of materiality *'from within what they are'*.

Being a part of the slipstream of this dynamic of Christ in the Spirit occurs as 'God's own people' 'proclaim the mighty acts of him who called you out of darkness into his marvellous light' (1 Pet. 2.9). God's acts are manifold and they involve power and light. Such acts are precisely those activities through which people and places are reconstituted and attracted towards God.

This is rightly understood as a movement into light. It is not a movement that leads the people of God out of the world but deeper into the way by which God's light is enabled to shine more brightly through all those features that make up created sociality.

The foregoing considerations have traded on some as yet unexamined issues concerning the doctrine of the Trinity and its relevance to an understanding of the Church as renewed sociality. This matter is the subject of the next chapter.

Questions

1 There are at least two questions that a doctrine of the church ought to engage with:
(a) What holds human society together?
(b) What are the conditions required for human society?
How would you begin to answer these two questions? How would the Scripture reference to Christ breaking down the divide between people and making one new humanity (Eph. 2.14) assist your answers? What other texts/narratives from the Scriptures would you want to explore?

2 Dietrich Bonhoeffer referred to the Church as 'Christ existing as community'. What does this say about the relationship between Christ and the Church? What about the role of the Spirit?

3 'The social doctrine of the Trinity and an emphasis on the church as communion offers a way by which the Church can behave in a prophetic manner in a society driven by market values which are non-communal, consumerist and individualist.' What do you think?

4 'The church is that body of Christ that displays through its life and action what the renewal of place, economics, politics, communication and interpersonal life might actually look like.' Why do you think it is so important that the bond in Christ includes such a variety of elements? How might this relate to the mission of the church?

Further reading

Chris C. Green, ' "The Body of Christ, the Spirit of Communion":
Re-Visioning Pentecostal Ecclesiology in Conversation with
Robert Jenson', *Journal of Pentecostal Theology* 20 (2011),
pp. 15–26.

Robin Greenwood, 'Church: Communal Practice of Good News',
in *Parish Priests: For the Sake of the Kingdom*, London: SPCK,
2009, pp. 52–89.

Brad Harper and Paul Louis Metzger, 'The Church as a Triune
Community', in Brad Harper and Paul Louis Metzger (eds),
*Exploring Ecclesiology: An Evangelical and Ecumenical Intro-
duction*, Grand Rapids, MI: Brazos Press, 2009, pp. 19–38.

Veli-Matti Kärkkäien, Miroslav Volf, 'Participatory Ecclesiology',
in *An Introduction to Ecclesiology: Ecumenical, Historical and
Global Perspectives*, Downers Grove, IL: InterVarsity Press,
2002, pp. 134–41.

5

The Church beyond the Social Doctrine of the Trinity

Renewal in Trinitarian theology

It is clearly incumbent upon an ecclesiology focused on a renewed sociality to give some account of the Trinitarian sources for such an understanding of the Church. This is necessarily the case in so far as ecclesiology is not a stand-alone theme in Christianity, but is rather interwoven with other dimensions of the faith and in particular the doctrine of God. While such interconnections have not been ignored so far, it has yet to become a matter of explicit argument. To talk about a created and redeemed sociality and to refer this to the work of God in creation through the *logos* and subsequent salvific work of God in Christ the Redeemer requires further teasing out to show how the concept of sociality deployed in Chapter 4 might be rooted in the Triune God.

In one sense, we are on familiar ground here, perhaps far more so than in the previous discussion of sociality. I refer to the extensive rethinking of the doctrine of the Trinity and its link to human society which has occurred in the last half century. The volume has grown particularly over the last quarter of a century with the result that theologians such as Gunton, Johnston (2002), LaCugna (1991), Moltmann (1997), Volf (1998) and Zizioulas (1985) are common names in the theological 'household' when it comes to relating the doctrine of the Triune God to human society and the Church. In many respects, this is a positive development. It points to the fact that there is a perceived need for a theologically robust justification for the social nature of Christianity and an implied need for a critique of structure and process that is inimical to true community. The doctrine of the Triune God has a natural reciprocity with issues concerning personhood and human community. Furthermore, an emphasis upon the relational God whose inner Trinitarian life is one of *perichoretic* movement in mutual respect and acknowledgement of the 'other' makes for rich offerings for re-conceiving the doctrine of the Church. When God is understood as a differentiated plurality operating in harmonious mutual relation there is significant scope, it appears, for the Church to be patterned after such a God.

Explication of this ecclesiological patterning derived from the Triune God is a feature of contemporary ecclesiology and leads to the important concept of the Church as a *communion*. However, at this stage I simply want to recognize how important and practical the renewal in Trinitarian theology has been for ecclesiology and for appreciating human society and its needs. Such an emphasis challenges individualistic and atomistic thinking associated with fragmenting cultures of the West. We might not unjustly conclude that the theological instincts of Christian theology are basically right. There is a fundamental relation between the creator and the creation, and this is illuminated through inquiry into the doctrine of the Triune God. It has led to an extended discussion on the social Trinity and its implications for the doctrine of the Church.

Problems in the social doctrine of the Trinity

Projection

Yet, how helpful for ecclesiology is the contemporary emphasis upon social Trinitarianism? To further this matter, I will first note some criticisms of the social doctrine of the Trinity and then make some proposals concerning sociality for a Trinitarian ecclesiology.

There are a number of difficulties of a methodological and substantive kind in the application of the social doctrine of the Trinity to human society and the Church. The first difficulty concerns the problem of idealization and projection. In this respect, I note that it is not uncommon these days to claim a reasonably unproblematic link between the Triune God and the quest for community and renewal of the Church. Jürgen Moltmann offers a good example when he states:

> Father, Son and Spirit . . . do not exist with each other, but rather empty themselves on to each other and live in each other by virtue of love . . . When the Church is such 'an icon of the Trinity', she can become a life-principle of human society: a society without privileges – a society without poverty and need – a society of free and equal persons. Then the Trinity will become our 'social programme', the program of social personalism, or of personal Socialism. We would overcome the possessive individualism of the West as well as the depersonalising collectivism of the East. We would be able to integrate a human 'culture of sharing' symbiotically into the perichoretic texture of nature and to live and become blessed together with the fellowship of the entire creation in the fellowship of the Triune God. (Moltmann 1993, pp. 110–11, quoted in Chapman 2001, p. 245)

This rather lengthy quotation is a good example of a general approach to the Trinity and society by theologians such as Moltmann and Leonardo Boff. Moltmann's statement has a programmatic ring about it. It is also indicative of a method which appears to move somewhat seamlessly from exposition of Trinitarian categories of community, personhood, sociality and relationality to visions of an ideal social, political and ecclesial order. Who knows of such communities on earth?

Colin Gunton follows a similar trajectory to Moltmann. Gunton's conception of God as a relational and communal being flows into his ecclesiology: 'The Church is therefore called to be a being of persons-in-relation which receives its character as communion by virtue of its relation to God, and so is enabled to reflect something of that being in the world' (1993, p. 12). In his Bampton Lectures, Gunton refers to relationality as a universal transcendental rooted in the doctrine of the Trinity and basic to being human. As such, human sociality constituted by the relations to the Triune God is the way to avoid either the ideology of the one (individual) or the many (collective) (1992, p. 223).

There is no doubting the finely tuned theological instincts of Moltmann, Gunton and others concerning the need to recover a sound foundation for human community, as we have already noted in Bonhoeffer. However, in the crisis of a fragmented and dysfunctional society there is a natural temptation to develop blueprint Trinitarian 'models' of society and then project them onto human society as a cure for the ills of contemporary society (see Healy 2000, pp. 34f). Such a projection can be observed in the way in which *divine perichoresis* has been deployed as an ideal for a harmonious and peaceful society characterized by mutual respect and loving self-sacrifice (Kilby 2000). This kind of move ought to be resisted (a) because that is not how good Trinitarian theology actually works and (b) because such a method falsifies how God is actually involved in the dynamic of human society. What usually emerges, is an idealized vision of human society generated from an abstracted theory of Divine operations.[1] This methodological procedure is associated with two further related problems.

Dealing with conflict and tension

Trinitarian projection fails to give an adequate account of conflict or 'creative tension' as a feature of human community (Chapman 2001, pp. 239–54). Indeed, Mark Chapman suggests that rather than 'harmony and balance and mutual reciprocity' being the way in which human beings most perfectly express themselves it may

---

1 The problem of projection is of course not restricted to social Trinitarianism but has been a feature of what David Nicholls has termed 'monolithism' (to be differentiated from monotheism) and refers to a monolithic, undifferentiated monarchic deity. Nicholls makes the point that not all monotheists are monolithites and that care is necessary when assessing the relationship which obtains between divine and political images or concepts (see Nicholls 1989, pp. 234–40, present quote p. 237).

be that 'tension, conflict and debate' may 'prove to be at the heart of human society' (p. 248). If this is the case, Chapman asks, what place is there for conflict in human attempts to model the Trinity? He wonders whether the harmonious understanding of God associated with social Trinitarianism 'perhaps expresses a longing for concord and a conflict-free zone' which is 'divorced from the creative and constructive conflict that can plausibly be shown to be the foundation for democratic human societies' (p. 249). This leads Chapman to examine how a social understanding of the Trinity might incorporate a place for conflict in God. In this respect, he examines the way in which the love of God is reconciled with 'the moral demand for justice'. His point is that a 'harmonious God is of little assistance' in the oppression of exploitation; that God the Trinity is involved 'with the struggles at the heart of human life' and solutions 'to the problem of the Trinity only begins to emerge in the art of living' (p. 254). Chapman is among those critics who challenge the tendency of advocates of social Trinitarianism to propose an idealized doctrine of God in order to support a pre-determined ideology for a reformed social world. Moltmann is not entirely free from this, though Leonardo Boff may be more open to criticism on this account (pp. 243–5; cf. Boff 1988). But this can easily lead to the theological legitimation of a particular social ordering developed independently from theology.

Escape from tritheism?

The twin problems of projection and conflict are associated with a third difficulty, that is the charge of tritheism. This of course is neither new nor surprising and is associated with any account of the doctrine of the Trinity that begins with 'threefoldness' of the divine being and employs the language of personhood (Coakley 2002, p. 116). Advocates of a 'social' (or 'plurality') doctrine of the Trinity over against a 'Latin' (or 'Unity') model are committed to the application of the language of 'person' and/or 'individual' to the Trinity. Sarah Coakley argues that there is an unresolved tension present. On the one hand, analytical philosophers of religion, who are advocates of social Trinitarianism, emphasize the 'three' persons of the Trinity and in so doing appear to trade on quite modern notions of person and individual – associated with self-consciousness and/or centres of consciousness – and import these meanings back into Patristic texts. Yet, on the other hand, systematic theologians, in an attempt to rehabilitate Trinitarian theology by critiquing modern notions of the individual 'construe "person" *as* "relations" (whatever this means exactly)'.[2] Coakley's concern is to investigate the subtlety of fourth-century Trinitarianism in Gregory of Nyssa (c.330–c.395) in relation to contemporary depictions of the Trinity. She argues that 'social' Trinitarianism can take a variety of forms and further that the notion of 'person' can likewise be used in a variety of ways. The danger, of course, lurks in an incipient tritheism aided and abetted by modern notions of 'person' or avoided at the cost of incoherence in proposals regarding 'persons' as relations. Coakley questions whether in fact Gregory of Nyssa supports the position common to modern advocates of social Trinitarianism, that 'one *starts* with the three – whose individual identities are at least initially clearly and distinctively bounded – and that the task thereafter is to account for the unifying *community* which they share' (p. 117).

Clearly, the social doctrine of the Trinity remains contested and is not a 'cure all' for those theologians desiring to recover sociality as fundamental for divine and human reality. The application of a social doctrine of the Trinity to ecclesiology may inadvertently smuggle in more difficulties than perceived advantages. It prompts a question: Can the sociality relevant to creation and redemption reach back into the being of God? This question remains on the agenda for proponents of the 'social' Trinity precisely because their advocacy of a 'yes' to the question raises considerable diffi-

---

2 Coakley shows how the tension between analytical philosophers of religion and systematic theologians is 'in some form replicated in the feminist camp: while Daly [Mary] assumes a threefold 'individualism' in the doctrine (and rejects it), Johnson [Elizabeth] prefers to construe 'persons' in terms of 'relationships' (2002, pp. 110f).

culties that undermine a rich and grounded ecclesiology. A critical engagement with social Trinitarianism signals that further theological work is required.

Nonetheless, I do not believe that it is too much to claim that there is a consensus among theologians of the Trinity that the category of the social is encoded into the theological DNA of the Christian tradition *in its many forms*. The issue is how to give an adequate account of divine sociality – which does not lead into tritheism nor collapse the Trinitarian distinctions – which resonates with an account of the Church as renewed sociality. Both plurality and unity in the divine being belongs to the story of God in the Judaeo/Christian tradition.[3]

Underlying difficulties in social Trinitarianism

I would note the following three features that appear to underlie social doctrines of the Trinity. First, and somewhat unexpectedly, the doctrine operates in a 'top-down' fashion rather than a 'bottom-up' one. The problem of projection and blueprint models of divine sociality, and the failure of such approaches to incorporate or adequately attend to fundamental features of human life such as conflict and tension are symptomatic of rather artificial and speculative attempts to apply supposed knowledge of the inner Trinitarian life of God to the formation and repair of human society. This has all the hallmarks of a top-down approach involving intuitive grasp of the dynamic and nature of divine life. However, such efforts may owe far more to human idealizations of harmonious societies projected onto the divine than we care to admit. However, methodologically the argument is top-down.

Second, and somewhat illuminating for our present concern for ecclesiology, the social doctrine of the Trinity has, as far as I can observe, remained restricted to the sphere of the Church as community of the redeemed. The application of the perichoretic

---

3 Whether of course this is an epistemological and contingent plurality or a matter of ontology as such remains contested.

divine life involving mutuality and respect is proposed in the first instance as a basis for ecclesiology. However, the usual result is a truncated ecclesiology. I mean an ecclesiology which is overly preoccupied with its internal life and insufficiently attentive to the Church's engagement in the world. Theoretically, this problem is related to the earlier noted restriction of the category of 'sociality' to the *interpersonal* neglecting other domains – place, polity, economics and communication. Moreover, the domain of the interpersonal is primarily focused on redemption. This breeds an ecclesial piety disconnected from the wider society and its concerns. Accordingly the concept of *perichoresis* is assimilated into an ecclesiology hermetically sealed from the world. If the perichoretic life of the divine Trinity does overflow to creation as such, this is secondary and consequential. It remains unclear in contemporary theology how the social doctrine of the Trinity has spawned a rich general sociality appropriate to creation. Instead, the social doctrine of the Trinity has remained locked in the orbit of redemptive life. In this way, social Trinitarianism can become party – albeit unintentionally – to the long-standing omission of creation from ecclesiological reflection while at the same time supporting the basic ecclesiological default to redemption. This, I believe, is a clue to some of the deeper problems in the nature of sociality operating in contemporary social doctrines of the Trinity.

Third, the above criticism and dangers associated with the social doctrine of the Trinity suggest that, despite our best intentions, it operates within a static as opposed to a dynamic ontology of being. That this might be the case can be observed in the deployment of the language of 'individual', 'person' and even 'persons-in-relation'. The clue here concerns the way in which concepts such as 'social Trinity', *perichoresis* and relationality are construed to operate. My hunch is that we have not as yet developed a sufficiently dynamic understanding of such concepts in relation to God's sociality. The meaning attributed to the language of 'persons as/in relation', person, individual, 'centres of consciousness'; and the application of notions of mutuality, respect, mutual submission, self-effacement and harmony easily succumb to human idealizations which evidence minimal capacity for transformative and expansive life, let alone respond to the darkness and conflict of the world and human society. Moreover, the language of relation, when applied to the doctrine of the Church, appears to operate in an essentially self-enclosed manner. The quality of overflow associated with perichoretic life similarly appears checked and restricted. It lacks both depth and reach. We might well agree with Moltmann that the divine Trinity is our 'social program'. However, when the doctrine of the Church is shaped by redemptive motifs to the exclusion of creation and is focused on the interpersonal and inattentive to other dimensions of life, the result will be a restricted and/or truncated ecclesiology. This is a sign of a basically static ontology that does not embrace the dynamic ways in which God's transformative work occurs throughout creation. This is ironic given the current emphasis on movement and *perichoresis*, change and restructuring. The frameworks or underlying beliefs restrict and reshape what social Trinitarianism is and can achieve. The 'social' doctrine(s) of the Trinity do not deliver what they promise and are essentially too restrictive and static. As such they cannot provide an adequate basis for a dynamic ecclesial sociality. From a practical point of view the Church can appear sealed and unresponsive to wider society. What is required is a Church that functions (theologically) in an osmotic manner with a semi permeable membrane.

Divine sociality: a preliminary reflection

God: *infinite in all directions*

The foregoing conclusion raises an important question: How might we depict divine sociality and how might this be relevant for the form of the Church? It seems to me that the long Judaeo/Christian tradition of theological reflection on the character and ways of God offers insight into the way in which divine sociality might be understood. In particular, the Church's story of the ways of God in creation, redemption and fulfilment bears witness to a divine being of both infinitely expansive perfection and concentrated holiness.[4] We are in the region of abundance, richness and overflow without measure; beyond human knowing and grasp (for example, Eph. 3.18–20). This finds echoes in the Christian tradition. I think, for example, of the sixteenth-century Anglican theologian, Richard Hooker, who referred to God's being as richness;[5] to Anselm's depiction of the divine as 'that than which nothing greater can be conceived'. More recently Jean-Luc Marion has developed notions of 'excess' and 'saturated phenomena' and Daniel Hardy refers to 'the infinite identity of Jesus Christ' and God's 'magnificent complexity'.[6] We are at the borderlands of deepest mystery, and we do well to recall Austin Farrer's wisdom that 'God is on the verge of conceiving and at the heart of knowing'.[7]

The depiction of God as a being of concentrated holiness and expanding perfection suggests two co-related movements. The first movement concerns the unimaginable expanding vastness of the God of creation. Yet, this dynamic relevant to God's cosmic reach is simultaneously displayed through concentrated holy presence at the micro and personal levels of life. The power and love that marks the dynamism of God in the vast unfolding of time and space is precisely the same dynamism by which the ever-increasing nearness of the personal holy God is perfected

---

4 For a recent erudite discussion of the problem of the being of God, see Pattison 2010. Pattison wants to retrieve the language of being for God but in a more dynamic and open-ended form notwithstanding difficulties regarding the language of being when attributed to God. He refers to God as 'potential being'.

5 For Hooker, God's action in the world was 'the exercise of his most glorious and most abundant virtue. Which abundance doth show itself in variety, and for that cause this variety is often times in Scripture exprest by the name of riches' (Hooker 1954, Book 1, Ch. 1, para. 4).

6 See Marion 1991, p. 23. For reference to 'the infinite identity of Jesus Christ' see Hardy 2004. p. 2; for Hardy on the divine 'magnificent complexity' see Hardy 1996a.

7 I have searched in vain to retrieve this statement by Austin Farrer, which is etched in my memory.

at the micro level.[8] This points to a being whose transcendence and immanence are co-related and mutually enriching.[9] The deep mystery of the nature and dynamic of the divine being is emergent from within the very fibres of the universe in its particularity and immensity.

Testing against scripture

But does such a depiction of God resonate with sacred scripture? The prologue to John's Gospel offers insight at this point. The *logos*, through which everything came into being, who is none other than the *logos* of God and Lord of all things, is the same *logos*, who becomes flesh as human being (John 1.1–14). This interwoven transcendence and immanence involves an unimaginable concentration of truth and grace (John 1.14, *pleros*; full). The theme is repeated in slightly different ways in the

---

8 The nearness of God is a fundamental insight of medieval theology typified in Aquinas: '*Deus est in omnibus rebus, et intime* [God is in all things, and intimately]'. See *Summa Theologica*, Part 1, Question 8, first article.

9 For an insightful discussion of transcendence and immanence developed in terms of 'contrastive and non-contrastive divine transcendence', where the latter includes 'involvement in the world', see Tanner 1988, pp. 36–56. With respect to a non-contrastive account of divine transcendence, Tanner states: 'Only that sort of transcendence prevents God's transcendence and creative agency from becoming competitive. If Christians presume that God is somehow beyond this world and is therefore not to be identified with it in part or as a whole, the theologian in the interest of Christian coherence adds that this non-identity must not amount to a simple contrast. This insistence upon a non-contrastive characterization of God's transcendence forces, in turn, Christian talk of God's creative agency to be worked out in a genuinely radical way: God must be directly productive of everything that is in every aspect of its existence. Anything short of that supposes, I have argued, a diminished divine transcendence. Apparent problems of incompatibility are resolved in this manner – not at the cost of either claim but in taking both to their genuine extremes' (p. 47). Tanner's approach points in the same direction as the argument I am advancing, that is, a radical divine transcendence necessitates a similarly radical divine immanence; they are co-related and co-inhere.

letter to the Colossians. Here Christ is both 'the image [*ikon*] of the invisible God' (Col. 1.15) and the One in whom 'the plenitude [*pleroma*] of God was pleased to dwell' (Col. 1.19). This self-same dynamic of divine life flows through scripture. The letter to the Hebrews refers to the Son, 'through whom he also created the worlds' [the created worlds] . . . 'the exact imprint [impress] of God's very being [*hypostasis*], and he sustains all things by his powerful word' (Heb. 1.3). Important for these present reflections is the fact that in the high Christology of Hebrews we also find the rich humanity of God in Christ, who is our 'brother' (Her. 2.11), who 'shared the same things' and 'became like his brothers and sisters in every respect', that is, flesh and blood unto death (Heb. 2.14, 17). In the context of the epistle, this radical identification of God in Christ with humankind is the basis for the efficacy of the ascended Christ's heavenly intercession.

My purpose in referring to the above scripture texts is to high-light the remarkable way in which the reach of God is infinite in all directions; from the expanding universe to the concentration of divinity in the complex region of the personal down to the micro levels of created life. All things in heaven and earth, at whatever level of life, inanimate/animate, micro/cosmic, personal and con-scious are related, *in some way*, to the living God incarnate in Christ and alive in the Spirit. It leads to the concept of 'the infinite identity of the Lord',[10] an identity realized through the working of the eschatological Spirit.

The sociality appropriate to such a God is of a kind that can never be fully mapped, grasped or conceived. Minimally, it will be a sociality that is capable of laser-like concentra-tion and expansive perfection. It will be a sociality, which continually gathers, reconnects and assimilates all things into conformity with the holiness of God in heaven and on earth. This infinite extension and concentration of divine perfection

---

10 Daniel Hardy refers to the Anglican Church: 'Rooted in the infinite identity of the Lord, it has a "relative identity", but it is always also implicated in the world, implicated in every aspect of life in the world' (1996a, p. 2).

has both creative and redemptive social forms. For example, the redemptive sociality of God comes to explicit concentrated form in Christ's reconciling work in rejoining separated peoples: 'In his [Christ's] flesh he has made both groups [Jew and Gentile] into one and has broken down the dividing wall, that is the hostility between us (Eph. 2.14). The result is a renewed sociality, because Christ has 'created in himself one new humanity [*anthropos*] in place of the two, thus making peace' (Eph. 2.15).

Divine sociality within a dynamic ontology

The sociality of the Divine Being transcends any static ontology, which has no inbuilt capacity for infinite expansive and concentrated presence drawing all things to the Holy God. This suggests that the usual ways in which we have applied the category of 'person' to God is fundamentally too restrictive because the kind of 'person(s)' God is and is becoming transcends anything we might conceive. A dynamic ontology of persons is not necessarily secured by invocation of a raft of associated language of movement and interpenetration such as *perichoresis, relationality and mutuality,* admirable as it is. The danger is that while the language suggests movement and dynamism the framework remains ungrounded and idealistic. It is thus no surprise that it generates an ecclesial form that mirrors these faults.

In the light of the foregoing, the kind of sociality that will generate and expand a true society will have to (a) operate from the ground up rather than top down or more accurately operate with a creative dialectic between top down causality and bottom up emergence and (b) illuminate the dynamic by which Christ and the Spirit belong to the infinite concentration and expansive perfection of the God and Father of our Lord Jesus Christ. What is thus called for, is a dynamic, ground-up ontology of the sociality of God. Such a sociality can provide the appropriate energy and framework for a truly ecclesial sociality. We might say that these two criteria are the minimum requirements for a created and redeemed sociality derived from the Triune God?

The form of the Church: a provisional statement

The Church's double movement

In the light of the above, what might we say concerning the form of the Church? Minimally, we will want to develop an ecclesial sociality that evidences a trace to a dynamic ontology of God as outlined above? The reflections of this chapter suggest an ecclesiology informed by the *logos* of God in creation, incarnate in Christ's life, passion and resurrection and ever active through the energetic ordering of the eternal Spirit. This is a dynamic future-orientated ecclesiology grounded in Christology and pneumatology rather than social Trinitarianism as such. It is a sociality which involves a complex and dynamically ordered relationality. This includes 'being with and for another', but also has the particular qualities of expansive reach, concentrated holiness, and personal relation to the created world of people, things and institutions. We might thus speak of a Triune sociality.

What then are the critical features of a society formed in relation to the sociality of the Triune God as identified above? We recall at this point the earlier depiction of the Holy God as a being of infinitely expansive and concentrated perfection. This double movement is signalled in the concrete acts of Christ and the Spirit in time and space, in creation and redemption. This dynamism of God both *founds* and *fulfils* the form of the Church. What this means is that the Church participates in a double movement of God. So, what we have is the form of a Church that consists of a complex twofold movement of (a) an ever-expanding reach into the world and (b) at the same time an ever-deepening engagement with God and each other through its own inner life. These co-related movements informed by and propelled by the Spirit of the Father's Son provide the basic patterning for the form of a renewed sociality. This can be further explicated in the following terms.

The reach of the Church

In respect to the first movement – that is, outer-directed – the reach of the Church is essentially unbounded and capable of significant expansion under the impress of its life in the eschatological Spirit. The role of the Spirit patterning the life of Jesus offers a theological clue. Luke's Gospel is a good example, for here in the life of Jesus of Nazareth the Spirit overshadows, comes upon, descends, fills, leads, empowers, is released and raises Christ. In the same way, in the Acts of the Apostles the Spirit of the Father's Son is the agent that comes upon, fills, leads, empowers and raises the people of the Messiah. It also means that the Church can be that mode of sociality, which brings into focus the holiness of God in Christ. The form of the Church follows the form of the impress of the Spirit patterning Christ. This means that the Church's life is constantly propelled outwards, crossing boundaries, reconstituting persons, place and society in the process. It means that who is 'of the Church' is an open matter. It can never be a question of 'who is in' or 'who is out', but it always remains an open question; the Church is an unfinished eschatological mystery, which remains in constant movement beyond pre-established boundaries. This is a critical feature of what a renewed sociality looks like and a criterion for discernment of a static or dynamic ecclesiology.

The particularity of the Church

The other dimension of this complex ecclesial movement attends to the Church's internal life. This accords with God's concentrated holy presence. Here is the form of the Church in its intensity mode.[11] This latter move comes to explicit and maximal form in worship of the triune God. On this account liturgy – and in particular the Eucharist – is a concentrated mediation of the world's encounter with Christ and the Spirit (see Oliver

---

11 The distinction between the Church in 'intensity' and 'extensity' mode is developed in Hardy 2001, pp. 109–13.

2008). But precisely because it is a concentration point, it is not the whole but a genuine instance of what society might become as the Church expands though its own inner dynamism in the Spirit. In this double movement, the Church is enabled to display the vitalities and forms of a society renewed and energized by the Triune God.

To the extent that the Church allows itself to be renewed after the pattern of God's life through Christ and the Spirit it is clear that there are no quick and easy routes by which the Church might repair itself, undergo transformation and make an important contribution to the reforming of wider society. The Church is a complex entity and resists attempts to grasp, map and control. This arises because the truth of its life is bound up with the world created and redeemed by God. As a result, any attempt to encase it, silence it, or any action of the Church that signifies a loss of memory of the secret of its own life in God will only undermine the renewal of its life and the world's in which it lives and moves and has its being. To the extent that the sociality of the Church is derived from and related to God's graced sociality the Church will ever remain 'Ecclesia Reformata, semper reformanda', a work in progress.

Questions

1 Why has the doctrine of the Trinity become so important for an understanding of the Church?
2 What are the main problems associated with the social doctrine of the Trinity?
3 What does it mean to speak of the 'reach' of the Church and 'the particularity' of the Church? How is the form of the Church related to an understanding of the doctrine of God?

Further reading

Mark Chapman, 'The Social Doctrine of the Trinity: Some Problems', *Anglican Theological Review* 83:2 (2001), pp. 239–54.

Karen Kilby, 'Perichoresis and Projection: Problems with Social Doctrines of the Trinity', *New Blackfriars* 81:956 (2000), pp. 432–45.

Richard Lennan, 'Communion Ecclesiology: Foundations, Critiques, and Affirmations', *Pacifica* 20 (2007), pp. 24–39.

Jürgen Moltmann, 'The Social Doctrine of the Trinity', in James Byrne (ed.), *The Christian Understanding of God Today*, Dublin: Columba, 1993, pp. 104–11.

6

Measuring the Mystery

Church as mystery

Belief in the one, holy, catholic and apostolic Church is embedded in the ancient Nicene Creed. Importantly, this affirmation of faith is made in the context of statements concerning the Holy Spirit, the third article in the Creed. In the logic of creedal faith, ecclesiology is a subset of pneumatology, which in turn belongs to the creedal statements on the Triune God.

In this chapter, I want to examine the traditional 'marks' of the Church as forms of measurement and assessment. What of course is being measured is nothing less than the Church of the Holy Triune God. In other words, when the subject of our inquiry is the Church, we have to reckon with God, who is the plenitude of being at the heart of all creation. As the Church participates in this fundamental reality, the marks by which we measure the Church's life with God assume a deeper and richer significance in the economy of salvation.

I argue in this chapter, with particular reference to the Epistle to the Ephesians, that *mystery* is a fundamental category for depicting what the Church is. A mystery may be defined theologically as 'something that reveals God to us . . . We can participate in a mystery, but its ultimate depths go far beyond us' (Doyle 2000, p. 58).

The traditional marks of the Church are ways by which the mystery of the Church is measured. I want to examine the ways by which we have attempted to measure the mystery of the Church by reference to the marks of the Church. Two things are involved here. First, treating the *marks as measures* already changes how we might understand and appropriate the marks. Second, as we *measure the marks* to assess their theological weight and purpose we are drawn more deeply into the mystery of the being of the Church. These two aspects – 'marks as measures' and 'measuring the marks' – are related and together illuminate the dynamic way in which the Triune God draws the peoples of the world together for the praise of God (Eph. 1).

I begin with a simple question. In what sense is the Church a mystery? I have suggested above that it is a mystery in the sense that it is *God's* Church. However, for many these days the Church appears as a puzzle and a problem, possibly anachronistic and in some sense shrouded in mystery.[1] But the Church as a fundamental mystery? This doesn't seem to resonate with contemporary sensibilities and experience. This is the case notwithstanding the fact that from earliest times the Church, theologically at least, has been understood in precisely such a way.

When we consider the Church as an historical phenomenon – for example, its visible structures, ministries, and social and political engagements – the language of mystery appears quaint and simply unbelievable. As I noted in Chapter 3, the result of leeching the Church of its mystery is a *de-sacralized ecclesia*. This involves a denial of the theological surplus of meaning pertaining to the Church beyond sociological and phenomenological description.[2]

To speak of the mystery of the Church is an act of faith (Bender 2005, p. 169). This is the case because the Church is 'the unity of a divine action and a human historical existence, and as such it can be perceived in its true nature only by faith'. The mystery of the Church is thus grounded in the work of the Triune God. On this account the

---

1 Such responses may be more than justified considering some of the ways in which the Church has sacrificed its prophetic calling through assimilation to prevailing cultures and values.

2 This has resonances with Jean-Luc Marion's notion of the 'saturated phenomenon' which may be depicted in terms of surprise, superabundance, absoluteness and gift. See, further, Marion 2002. These features of saturated phenomenon, like mystery as used above, radicalize notions of measurement.

Church 'has a two-fold nature that comprises it as a single reality' (p. 169). Thus, Karl Barth could refer 'to the *mystery* of the Church as a divine and human reality in analogy and correspondence to the reality of the incarnation' (p. 174; see Barth 1956, pp. 656–7). This brief discussion develops our reflections from Chapter 1 where the mystery of the Church had to do with its particular relation to God's sacred presence in the world. This, of course, can lead to the *sacred inflation* of the Church (Chapter 3). This cloud hanging over a strong doctrine of the visible Church means that the Church as mystery can easily become the pretext for the exercise of a will to power under the cover of mystery. So from either side of the coin – historical, phenomenological or sacred form of the divine presence – the ascription of mystery to the Church can be problematic.

Church in the mystery of God: the Epistle to the Ephesians

The New Testament Letter to the Ephesians offers some rich resources for reflection on the mystery of the Church (Muddiman 2001, pp. 73f). The writer (in 3.9ff) refers to the 'mystery hidden for ages' being revealed, that is, unveiled, through the Church – *dia tou ecclesia*. And this mystery is gospel – good news. But what is this good news? It is 'the boundless riches of Christ', which corresponds to 'the many varied wisdom of God'. The passage is richly layered interlacing 'hidden mystery', 'riches of Christ' and 'multifaceted wisdom of God'. But, even more remarkably, all this is opened to earth and heaven *through the Church*, not simply that the Church 'is the privileged recipient of the mystery' (p. 74). Furthermore, once the mystery hidden for ages is revealed the mystery does not cease to be mystery. There is absolutely no sense in the New Testament, or for that matter throughout scripture, that the mystery of God's eternal wisdom in Christ ever ceases to be mystery once it is revealed.

In this Ephesians text, the mystery pertaining to God's wisdom cannot be disentangled from the reality of the *ecclesia* of God; the latter mediates the former. There is an appropriate differentiation here between Christ and the Church. However, the organic relation is inescapable for the Church 'is his body [*soma*], the fullness [*pleroma*] of him who fills all in all' (Eph. 1.22). The Church as the fullness of Christ could mean 'completion' or 'complement' (cf. Col. 2.17). Although this is disputed, the text does at least imply that Christ fills the Church that is his *pleroma* (Best 1998, pp. 183–9). From either angle, the text is translucent to the mystery of the reality of the Church. This is the assessment of J.-M. Tillard who, in commenting on the general ecclesiological movement of the letter states that, 'the Church of God appears as the fulfilment of the *mystery*, in other words, the accomplishment in Jesus of the eternal design which forms the course of revelation and whose purpose is to join humanity together again, to unite the universe. The Church belongs . . . to the very reality of the *humanity-according-to-God*' (1992, p. 46).

The above discussion suggests that if indeed the 'multifaceted' wisdom of God is revealed in Christ, it is manifest in the Church, which is Christ's body (Eph. 1.22–3). This represents, according to Rudolf Schnackenburg, a 'decisive theological advance' from the Letter to the Colossians (1991, p. 307). The mystery hidden for ages is manifest through and in the being of the Church. The mystery of Christ constitutes the *ecclesia* as the body of Christ. Accordingly, the mystery of the Church is neither self-enclosed nor self-generated, but arises out of a fundamental relation to God in Christ in the Spirit. The nature of that divine–human relation is the basis for the remarkable statement that those of the body of Christ are 'members one of another' (Eph. 4.25; cf. Rom. 12.5b). This takes a new twist in the marriage bond (two becoming one flesh [*sarx*]) which encodes the mystery of Christ and the Church; the 'great mystery [*mega mysterion*]' (Eph. 5.2). This is followed by the mystery of the gospel itself (Eph. 6.19). Accordingly in Ephesians, the mystery of the gospel includes the Church. The mystery of the gospel and the mystery of the Church are related and interlacing. The 'length and breadth and height and depth' (Eph. 3.18) of the one is woven into the reality of the other. In this way, 'the Church becomes the Mystery of Salvation, and this ecclesiological outlook is what is special and unique in Eph . . .' (p. 141). The Letter to the Ephesians represents a high water mark in the New Testament ecclesiology (p. 293). A letter addressed to a local community points to the universal Church set within a cosmic framework and grounded in the infinite Lordship of Christ.

My concern in this section has been to highlight the significance of the concept of mystery, for understanding the nature of the Church in the ecclesiology of Ephesians (pp. 293–310). The mystery of the *ecclesia* of God belongs to the purposes of God for the cosmos. This purpose concerns the manifesting of divine wisdom in Christ through the Church. While the danger always remains of a too simple identification of Christ with the Church, theologically, the Church is always more than what it appears to be or what is said of it. As a result, there remains a surplus of meaning that arises out of it being 'his body, the fullness of him who fills all in all' (Eph. 1.23). Furthermore, the mystery of the Church cannot be identified solely with a pure heavenly spiritual entity (Eph. 2.6). The reason is that the mystery of the Church is never apart from the earthly visible reality of the Church, even as it is orientated towards the cosmic spiritual realm.[3] A tension remains in Ephesians between a realized and eschatological ecclesiology with the emphasis on the former (Best 1998, pp. 217–23). It seems that the mystery of the Church will have to be displayed in and through the earthly Church or not at all. This is the case notwithstanding the recurring risks this poses for the corruption of the mystery at the heart of the Church.[4]

---

3 The writer isn't working with a Church-militant/Church-triumphant distinction here; the Church on earth *is* the Church seated with Christ in Heaven.

4 Although it is not immediately germane to my discussion, I recognize that the 'high ecclesiology' of Ephesians has been in the course of Church history conscripted into an empire theology, in which the Church has presumed and at times succeeded in assimilating the world into itself for its own aggrandisement on the pretext of its unique place within the cosmic purposes of God. The threat of empire in such a high ecclesiology does not subvert the fundamental theological insight of Ephesians on the nature of the Church. Of course, the ecclesiological reflections in relation to a local and delimited Church in the early years of the Christian movement is a very different context to a fourth-century Constantinian 'Christian' empire seeking ecclesiological justifications for its expansion. For a recent discussion of the dangers of ignoring the ideology of empire embedded within anti-imperial writings of the New Testament, see Fiorenza 2007, Ch. 3.

The appeal to the Church as mystery became increasingly important during the nineteenth and twentieth centuries as a result of significant mission and ecumenical work. These developments generated both new engagements and challenges with the result that the Church had to rediscover the ground of its being in the mystery of God in Christ. Protestantism (in all its varieties) has been generally muted in its deployment of the concept of mystery and tended to find theological solace in notions of 'invisibility', 'spiritual fellowship' and 'communion of persons' though this is changing with greater emphasis on the visible Church, pneumatology and recognition of the concept of mystery (for Barth see Bender 2005, p. 174; Kärkkäinen 2002, pp. 79–94, 126–41; Moltmann 1977; Pannenberg 1998, pp. 38–48; Webster 2005, pp. 96–113). The more catholic wing of Christianity has found language concerning the Church as the mystical body of Christ a helpful corrective to its earlier emphasis on the institution and hierarchy (Dulles 1974, pp. 46ff). This is the context for the 1943 encyclical of Pius XII, in which he defined the Church as the mystical body of Christ and then, somewhat predicably, proceeded to identify this with the Roman Catholic Church. At Vatican II, the Church as mystery was again affirmed though enriched through being conjoined with the concept of the people of God.

Writing in the mid twentieth century, the Anglican theologian E. L. Mascall developed a conception of the Church as 'a reality of the sacramental order, the Mystical Body of Christ, preserved and nourished by the Lord's Body and Blood' (1953). Mascall grounded this conception in the Pauline idea of the body of Christ and understood his own approach as a continuation of a long established Anglican line of theology from Richard Hooker to the late-nineteenth-century Anglican Robert Wilberforce. In more recent international dialogues between Anglicans, Roman Catholics and the Orthodox, the visible Church has been understood 'as a "sacrament" or 'mystery" of Christ's continuous salvific presence on earth' (Locke 2009, p. 165). An interesting example of a more adventurous angle on this ecclesiology is developed in *Radical Orthodoxy*. Here the mystery of the Church is the mystery of the expanding identity of the body of Jesus Christ; a body continually 'transposing and extending its identity'. 'The logic of displacement is now taken up in the limbs and tissue of his body as the Church' (Ward 1999, p. 176).

Perhaps most importantly the Church as mystery has laid the foundations for the emergence of communion ecclesiology. This is probably the most significant ecclesiological and ecumenical development of the twentieth century. It is no coincidence that a scholar of the stature of J.-M. R. Tillard locates the deepest foundations for such a remarkable ecumenical ecclesiology in, among other things, the witness of Scripture to the Church in the letter to the Ephesians wherein is established 'an essential link between *mystery* . . . and the Church of God' (1992, p. 45). An ecclesiology of communion offers both hope and a challenge for the Church in all its diversity to recover the deeper mystery of its life in Christ and the Spirit (Lennan 2007).

Measuring the mystery

Is it possible to measure the mystery of the Church of Jesus Christ? And how might the traditional marks of the Church function as measures? Perhaps it depends on what we mean by measure.

Two kinds of measurement

It is usual to refer to taking a measure as a way of estimating; whether it is quantity, weight, dimensions or movement (Tillard 1992, pp. 45ff). The critical matter is being able to estimate with as high a degree of exactness as necessary. This at least is the familiar sense in which we deploy the notion of measurement and of course it is applicable to an amazing diversity of situations. Moreover, in most disciplines of knowledge and practices of life we are forever taking measures in order to make assessments, understand phenomena better and as a result know better how to live life. The emphasis is on fixed measures for they offer certainty. Thus arises the notion of standard measures, which can be relied upon.

However, the rise of quantum physics at the micro level and the remarkable discoveries in cosmology point to a notion of measurement that cannot trade on fixities any longer. We are led to recognize the complex and ambiguous nature of measurement. Moreover, the world of quantum also highlights the fact that the process of measurement is inherently participative; that we are involved in the very things we measure and that our involvement as participants influences what is measured. The ideal of fixed measure remains attractive, but is of limited usefulness.[5]

The foregoing may seem somewhat tangential to the discussion of the marks of the Church except that it alerts us to a number of things. First, it reminds us that measuring the mystery of the Church will not fit easily with notions of fixity and certainty. Second, because the mystery of the Church concerns its life with *God*, there is a further dimension to the act of measurement. This arises because it is the Lord of the Church who is the primary agent who measures. Our acts of measurement fall under God's measure, for it is God who is the measure of all things and especially the Church, his body.[6] So measuring the mystery of the Church is unwise. Most significantly we come up against our own desire for ownership of all measures and easily overreach ourselves. Humility is the appropriate posture, for who can measure the height, length, depth and breadth of the love of Christ (Eph. 3.18)? Christ can be measured only by himself (Balthasar 1982, p. 468). All our measures will be found wanting and overwhelmed with God's immeasurable grace and freedom for us. The 'power to comprehend' such dimensions of eternal love may be something for which we pray, but, given that the

---

5 I am referring to the conventional aspects of fixed measure – namely that fixed measure is, in fact, a form of arbitrary activity, such as the platinum metre in Paris; the conventions of standard temperature and pressure in physical sciences. Related to such measures is the community for whom these conventions apply, the dynamics of power within those communities, ownership of these measures and who gets to say what counts as a measure?

6 There is an interesting parallel here with 1 Corinthians 2.15 where the *pneumatikos* discerns all things but is discerned by nothing (except other *pneumatikoi*).

kind of knowledge being countenanced 'surpasses knowledge', it is clear that human measures will never be sufficient. Repeatedly, we are reminded in Scripture of the immeasurable nature of God's power, grace and riches, and 'boundless riches' (Eph. 1.19, 2.7, 3.8); of the Spirit given 'without measure' (John 3.34); of the 'eternal weight of glory beyond all measure' (2 Cor. 4.17). The accent is clearly on God's measure of us, and the means by which we are brought to full measure in Christ (Eph. 4.7, 13).[7]

To measure the mystery of the Church has both theological and moral weight for it leads us into a place wherein all our measuring is relativized in the light of God's measurement of us. I have laboured this matter a little, because it is directly relevant to the way that the marks of the Church have functioned in the life of the Church. I want to turn to that matter now.

The marks as measures: a brief history

Jürgen Moltmann notes that the ancient marks are components of the creedal statement of faith and as a result they are not bare marks and nor are they patently obvious (1977, p. 337). Indeed, there are many features of the life of the Church that challenge the reality of the marks of the Church. Thus, from the earliest centuries, when the marks were formalized in AD 380 as creedal statements, they belonged to the 'I believe'. Accordingly, without faith, the marks 'lose their meaning'.

As Hans Küng has shown, from earliest times, the marks were primarily descriptive, indicating the 'properties' (*proprietates*) or characteristic features of the Church (1967, pp. 266f). It was less a question of measurement for apologetic reasons and more a statement of what the one Church was in Christ. However, with the rise of heretical and schismatic movements in the early Church and the need for a robust apologetic the marks of the Church functioned in an apologetic manner. This enabled

---

7 Cf. 1 Corinthians 8 and the contrast between the one who knows and the one who loves and thus is known by God. Cf. also Galatians 4.9.

the Church to be defended against critics from the host culture and offered as measures by which the Church could be distinguished and recognized amidst competing claims for authentic Christianity. This constitutes the first stage in the emergence of the marks as measures in order to clarify identity and sharpen the boundaries of the Church. This was not negative in and of itself, but it did signal a trajectory that gathered momentum over time.

At the time of the sixteenth-century Reformation, the *boundary marking* approach to the marks received renewed emphasis. In a polemical context, the marks became the signs (*signa*) and criteria (*criteria*) to distinguish the true Church from the false. Signs and criteria became, in the course of the sixteenth century, the 'notes' of the Church (*notae ecclesiae*) and the basis for division. The measure of the Church became a highly charged political matter to do with power and control. In this context, fixity of the marks became critical so that clear lines of division could be determined. Yet the attempts to fix the measure of the Church in clear and distinct ways also highlighted the ambiguous nature of the marks as measures of ecclesial identity and fitness. There was little agreement about what constituted the full complement of the marks of the Church. It seemed that in times of crises measures multiplied. The Church of Rome tended to add – was it 6, 7, 8, 15 or 100 *notae ecclesiae* (p. 266)? Luther proposed 'seven chief means of Christian sanctification, or holy possessions' (Hefner 1984, p. 223): the Word, baptism, the Lord's Supper, the keys, the ministry, prayer and suffering.

While the Reformers accepted the four ancient marks of the Creed, they sought a different measure. Their focus was upon the inner ground of creedal marks, that is, preaching of the Word and administration of the sacraments. This is embodied, for example, in Article 19 of *The Articles of Religion* of the Church of England. The twin co-ordinates – Word and Sacraments – functioned as an internal measure of fidelity to the creedal marks of the Church. However, on the basis of these two criteria alone it was inherently difficult to distinguish Protestant, Catholic and enthusiastic sects. Such a measure could not finally determine the matter of ecclesial recognition. What appeared clear and fixed in fact was not. Yet, neither were the four classical marks of the Church convincing measures of catholicity without the dynamism of the gospel and sacraments. In the post-Reformation period, the classical four marks became the standard measure by which churches conducted their apologetic discourse.

Contemporary discussion has attempted to recover the earlier approach to the marks as *theological dimensions* of the Church. This development locates the marks as measures in a more dynamic and less fixed way. This approach admits, in fact requires, creative interpretation and adaptation. The realization of these different dimensions of the Church is, as Küng states, 'an open question' which requires the proof of practice (1967, p. 269). Moltmann, following Küng, orientates the marks of the Church towards performance and as such they become 'the marks by which it [the Church] is known in the world' (1977, p. 361).

It might be said that for much of the history of the Church the marks have operated as fixed measures against which judgements have been often too quickly made regarding other individuals or ecclesial bodies. The marks have been deployed in polemical and apologetic ways that betray an ecclesial immaturity and pride. However, the actual history of the discussion indicates that the tighter the marks operated as fixed and certain measures for apologetic and polemical purposes the more problematic the notion of a fixed measure became. The marks for the most part have been embedded within a notion of measurement that could not do justice to the true mystery of the Church.

The contemporary discussion of the marks appears more attentive to the perils of attempting to deploy the marks as fixed measures of the reality of the Church. What seems to be happening is a search for the deeper basis for the unity, holiness, catholicity and apostolicity of the Church. The main concern seems to be to interpret the marks as dynamic aspects of the life of the Church. In this sense, the marks are measures not of a steady-state Church – in terms of the formal presence or otherwise of certain critical signs of the Church – but of a more open-ended and dynamic ecclesiology.

Increasingly, the focus is on the recovery of practices that display the marks as indicators of action as much as statements of faith and hope. In this sense, the marks become the measure of God's gift to the Church of Christ and the Spirit. In so far as this is God's gift without measure, the marks point the Church towards a yet to be realized fullness of life with God. They are an eschatological sign of the form and shape of the coming kingdom.

Marks as measures of the mystery

Marks as originative gift and future destiny

To treat the marks of the Church as 'measures of the mystery' draws attention to the fact that the marks are neither static qualities nor simply formal criteria, but they already belong to the character of the *ecclesia*. This signals a move from marks as fixed points of measure to marks as dynamic qualities encoded into the very DNA of the *ecclesia* of God. In this dynamic movement, the Lord of the Church is drawing the mystical body deeper into its life in God in the world. In this sense, the marks identify a journey to be travelled rather than a place of rest. From this point of view the marks signal both gifts to the Church and the unfinished business of the Church, work pending, practices to be undertaken. This is a contingent matter and does not describe a smooth progressive unveiling of what has already been predetermined. Rather, the emergent quality of the marks of the Church is a sign of the fundamentally eschatological nature of the Church. The transformation of the Church comes from the future even as it unfolds from within the contingencies of the present.

There are a number of helpful discussions of the marks of the Church. In particular, Hans Küng and Jürgen Moltmann offer creative interpretations of the marks for today's Church. In the post-Vatican II ecumenical climate, Hans Küng attempted to find common ground among the Churches for their mission and future. In characteristic style, he stressed the concrete reality of the Church as the place where the marks had to be reappropriated. Thus we are not surprised when he referred to unity in diversity, catholicity in identity, holiness in sinfulness and apostolicity through witness (1967, pp. 264–359). Division, failure and the paramount importance of joint witness provided the framework for his interpretation of the marks.

From the Reformed wing of the Church, Jürgen Moltmann developed unity in terms of freedom, catholicity as partisanship, holiness in poverty and apostolicity in suffering (1977, pp. 337–61). Moltmann offered a theologically innovative interpretation of the marks against the background of a renewed emphasis upon pneumatology and eschatology encapsulated in the title of his work, *The Church in the Power of the Spirit*.

In these two modern interpreters, the marks become measures by which the whole *ecclesia* is directed towards renewal and engagement in the world. With Küng, the emphasis is on humble recognition of difference, failure, and the common call to recover a whole identity and apostolic witness. The marks are not steady-state guarantees of security but signs of incompleteness and common vocation.

Moltmann's themes of freedom, poverty, partisanship and suffering are the correlates of unity, holiness, catholicity and apostolicity. His approach represents an even more radical reworking of the marks. The accent on engagement and action in the world is unmistakable. To practise the marks of the mystery of the Church is to be in solidarity with a world in pain and searching for hope. Again, we are light years from the polemic and apologetic motives that have been so powerful in the history of the Church. There is no place for complacency; the emphasis is on action and identification with the world under the sign of the cross of Christ. Again, not a steady-state theory of the Church but an ethical imperative to serve a broken world is uppermost.

For both theologians, the marks embody paradoxes of ecclesial faith and practice – such as unity in diversity, holiness in sinfulness, catholicity in partisanship, apostolicity in suffering. For both, the marks point the Church beyond the paradoxes to its deepest mystery. In this sense, the marks belong to a Church lured by the aroma of Christ, who waits in the highways and byways of the world. How the form and content of the marks will unfold cannot be determined with exactness.

To draw attention to the marks as both originative gift and emergent properties of the Church has echoes of a dynamic understanding of the image of God. In Wolfhart Panneberg's insightful exposition of the *imago Dei*, attention is focused on the unfolding and unfinished nature of the *imago Dei* compared to the *imago Dei* as originative gift (1985, Ch. 2). The eschatological focus on our destiny is fundamental. The Church as image-bearer of the divine participates in this same double dynamic of originiative gift and unfolding destiny. What implication does this have for consideration of the marks of the Church? I believe it points to the marks as *emergent properties* rather than fixed and assured measures. The marks are signs of the *destiny* of the Church of Christ as much as they are signs of originative gifts. Thus the marks have dual co-ordinates – originiative and future – and this significantly changes their function and value for the mystery that the Church is. Importantly, it highlights the unfinished and dynamic way in which the ancient creedal statements might contribute to the theory and practice of being the Church in today's world. In in this respect, I have already developed in Chapter 4 an account of the Church as renewed sociality in the world. In the remainder of this chapter, I want to briefly explore how the marks might be understood as measures of such a renewed sociality.

One in expanding connectivity

'There is one body and one Spirit, just as you were called to the one hope of your calling, one Lord, one faith, one baptism, one God and Father of all, who is above all and through all and in all' (Eph. 4.4–6). The accent on unity in this well-known scripture is juxtaposed with one of the more significant attempts in the New Testament to articulate Christ's gift of ministries in the *ecclesia*. Affirmation of the unity of the body of Christ accompanies recognition of an internal diversity, which in turn is integrated into the whole body with Christ as head (cf. 1 Cor. 12: 'many gifts, one spirit; many services, one Lord; many activities, one God activating all in all'). Importantly, when we affirm belief in the one Church we mean more than simply one numerically, that there is only one Church rather than 4, 6, or 460. Rather belief that the Church is one is a statement about the organic wholeness of the Church compared to a mere aggregate of items. Furthermore, it is an organic unity that extends beyond moral and psychological precepts or even attraction between individual members and Christ. Such forms of unity remain within the orbit of human achievement as responses to God's redemptive work in Christ and the Spirit. The one Church is ultimately grounded in what the Anglican theologian E. L. Mascall referred to as the 'supernatural principle' (1953, p. 4). He went on to articulate this with reference to the high priestly prayer of Jesus in John 17 and concluded that the unity of the Church was encoded in 'the self-same act which makes the Holy Trinity a consubstantial unity of love' (John 17.26).[8]

Unity in diversity was the way Hans Küng approached the question of the oneness of the Church in his ecumenical ecclesiology. In the spirit of the Second Vatican Council, Küng rejected notions of enforced uniformity.

The unity of the Church has nothing to do with the mythological magic number one and the intrinsic fascination with oneness. The unity of the Church is not simply a natural entity, is not simply moral unanimity and harmony, is not just sociological conformity and uniformity. To judge it by externals (canon law, ecclesiastical language, Church administration, etc) is to misunderstand it completely. The unity of the Church is a spiritual entity. (1967, p. 273)[9]

---

8 Mascall spoke of the communication of the divine unity by means of 'two arches', that is, first, the arch of the incarnation, the hypostatic union and second, the arch of our adoption into Christ and his human nature (1953, p. 6).

9 Moltmann stresses the move from an 'ecclesiology of tradition, which is orientated to unity' to an 'ecclesiology orientated towards conflict in the world'. This entails a shift from stasis to praxis and engagement beyond ecclesiastical boundaries (1977, p. 342).

Küng, with Ephesians 4.4–6 in mind, stated that '[t]he Church *is* one and therefore *should* be one' (p. 273). However, such a oneness was not set over against diversity – and with Moltmann 'freedom' – but through it. Diversity in worship, theology and Church order coexisted within the parameters of one Lord, faith and baptism (p. 275).

Küng's approach has affinities with Karl Barth who referred to the invisible presence of the One Lord under the form of the concrete historical existence of the Church (see Bender 2005, pp. 162–93). In the latter, the mystery of the Church's unity was hidden and yet to be realized. As a result, there were not two churches – invisible and visible – but one Church constituted by the invisible mystery hidden in the form of the Church.

Both theologians were attempting to make sense of the unity of the Church constituted by the triune God in relation to the evident multiplicity of churches and the forms of historical existence of the Church through time and space. In complementary ways, Küng and Barth represented an ecumenical opportunity for the churches of the world. Moltmann's reflections called the Church to concrete action in the world.

In terms of our reflections on the Church as renewed sociality in Chapter 4, I note the following with respect to the unity of the Church. First, for Barth, Küng and Moltmann, together with most commentators, the focus remains on unity as constituted by redemption as such. However, if the basis of the Church's sociality is to be located first in creation – as argued in Chapter 4 – the question of the Church's unity is first of all a question about createdness *per se*.[10] Christ's gift of unity has its *basis* in creation before it finds its *fulfilment* in redemption. God's gift of unity has to do in the first instance with fundamental connectivity between God, creation and within that human life. When theologians state that the Church is one and therefore should be one, this involves two co-ordinates, creation as well as redemption. The horizon for the mark of unity is wider than we ordinarily assume and

---

10 From this perspective, insistence upon the unity of the Church may be another aspect of its cosmological identity.

stretches from creation through redemption to the consummation when God will be 'all in all' (Eph. 4.6).[11]

Second, and flowing on from the first point, to the extent that unity is both a primal or originative gift of the Spirit and a destiny which is still unfolding we may rightly speak of unity as an emergent property of the Church. It is essentially unfinished; it remains a contested matter and seeks a fuller realization. This is surely the horizon for a great deal of the internal discussions of the churches regarding schemes for greater organic union and all efforts to strengthen cooperation between diverse ecclesial bodies. Of course, this ongoing emergent unity is vital for the integrity and power of the witness of the Church to the gospel (John 17). However, attempts to restrict unity according to predetermined institutional standards presume overly static and fixed measures by which to make judgements concerning the status of ecclesial bodies. This presumes too great a knowledge of the mystery of the Church and insufficient humility about how the Lord may be working his purposes out. This is particularly relevant for our attitude to those ecclesial bodies that are different from the one that any of us may belong to.

Third, because the basis for ecclesial unity is first of all a question of the unity of the created order this suggests rather strongly that the Church is called into a far greater orbit than simply concern for inter Church attempts at greater unity and cooperation. The One who is Lord over the Church is simultaneously Lord over the cosmos. It is the same Lord, and as a result both the world and Church belong within the mystery of this God (Eph. 1.22–3, 3.10). This points us to the horizon of creation itself as a place for the blessing of God's unity. This has practical consequences for how the Churches of the world work together in order to serve the greater connectedness of the whole world and help in the healing of the planet and our relationship with the earth. This gives credence to the idea that the horizon of the Church actually is supposed to coincide with the horizon of creation (see M. Barth 1982).

---

11 The *ta panta en pasin* expression is interesting here, since Paul applies it to the Church in the present (as the sphere of divine activities) and the cosmos in the future (as *basileia tou theou*).

The ecclesial mark of unity is a restless, unfinished and expanding work of the Spirit of Christ. The mystery of the Church's unity unfolds in an emergent, creative and dynamic way at multiple levels: (a) from personal incorporation into the body of Christ; (b) through renewal of the manifold networks of relations that bind the peoples of the Churches together; (c) into ever widening circles of engagement of the *ecclesia* of God with society; and (d) the creation 'which groans with eager longing'. Finding the true measure of the one Church includes and transcends traditional modes of enquiry (such as doctrinal, political, institutional, ethical). To seek an expanded and enriched oneness represents a hazardous journey of faith from the known to the unknown. In this journey, our measure of unity has to be reformed and renewed in accord with the measure of the Triune God.

Holy in transformed community

The Creed refers to 'holy' in two ways: as the 'holy' Church and the 'communion of the saints' or holy ones.[12] Moltmann notes that the former refers to the Church as holy in its 'unity and wholeness', while the latter is in reference to the people of the Church (1977, p. 352). This double reference finds echoes in the New Testament (for example, 1 Cor. 1.30ff, 6.11; 1 Thess. 5.23; 2 Thess. 2.13), where it is abundantly clear that it is God through Christ in the Holy Spirit who is the basis for the holiness of the Church. This means that the Church's holiness is grounded in the holiness of God. Thus Karl Barth argued that the holiness of the visible form of the Church was the result of it being 'co-joined to Christ'. Moltmann refers to the Church being holy, 'because it

---

12 In the Old Testament, *kadad* implies cutting off or separating something for God's service. The New Testament word is *hagios*, which has a similar sense of being set apart for God. *Hagios* becomes *sanctus* in Latin from *sancire* – to limit, enclose, sanctify all of which is opposite of profane – that is what lies outside the holy area, the *fanum*. See Küng 1967, p. 324.

is sanctified through Christ's activity in and on it' (p. 353).[13] In similar manner, Küng can state that 'it is God who sanctifies the Church . . .' (1967, p. 327).

Such affirmations arise out of the fundamental reality of the Church as God's own creation notwithstanding the fact that it is constituted by finite and broken people. As Henri de Lubac once remarked, 'I am told that she [the Church] is holy, yet I see her full of sinners . . . Yes, a paradox is this Church of ours!' (quoted in Doyle 2000, p. 59). In similar vein, Küng could state that 'the Church is a *sinful Church*' and 'the Church which has no sins to confess does not exist' (1967, pp. 320, 322). As a result, '[t]here is only one Church, holy and sinful at the same time, *caste meretrix*'; always holy, always being purified – *sancta simul et semper purificanda*'; always the *communio sanctorum* and always the *communio peccatorum* (pp. 328f.). For Barth, this double reference was a reflection of the Church's humanity and divinity. By analogy with the two natures of Christ, the two dimensions of the one Church could neither be separated nor confused.

There is a particular dynamic at work in the above depiction of the holiness of the Church. For Moltmann, it implies a movement from the Church's past through its confession as the *communio peccatorum* into the future. Its future arises out of its hope and belief in the *communio sanctorum* and the forgiveness of sins. 'In this sense the holy Church is the converting Church of the new beginnings'; a Church, which is *ecclesia reformata et semper reformanda* and is trustworthy as it is *reformatio perennis* (1977, p. 355). Importantly, this is for the sake of witness to the coming *reformatio mundi* and the sanctification of the whole creation.

Belief in the holy Church is an affirmation of both the gift of God and the future into which the Church, as the first fruits of the whole creation, is called. As with the question of the unity of the Church, so with its holiness: we are led to recognize the basic

---

13 The notion of the Church here is identical to that of Israel in Deuteronomy 6 in which Israel as a *yahad* (a oneness) is constituted by her relationship to the *yahad* of God (given in the *shema Yisrael*). This is worked out in terms of holiness: 'you will be Holy as I am Holy'.

structure of the Church's holiness as originative gift stretching back into creation and stretching forward into the fulfilment of all things in Christ. The holy Church represents its destiny as well as its foundation. The eschatological reality is the fulfilment of the originative gift. This dynamic is operating in that well known passage from Ephesians:

> Christ loved the Church and gave himself up for her, in order to make her holy by cleansing her with the washing of water by the word, so as to present the Church to himself in splendour, without a spot or wrinkle or anything of the kind – yes, so that she may be holy and without blemish. (Eph. 5.25b–7)

Here, holiness is an emergent property of the *ecclesia*; at once the gift of God in Christ in time and space and yet a splendour waiting an 'eschatological presentation'.[14] This is a dynamic process through which transformation takes place in people, structure, energy and direction. It is multi-layered, continuous and expansive and, as a result, resists final measure.

What is the nature of this process, and how does it occur? In the first instance and from what has already been said, it is clear that the emergence of God's holiness in life and society is primarily a work of the Spirit of God. As more of creation is drawn towards God through the Spirit, the created order is brought into deeper conformity with the ways of God. The Spirit active in creation, redemption and fulfilment of all things – the One who is 'above all, through all and in all' – is the primary agent in this dynamic process. The form this transformation of created sociality takes is fundamentally Christomorphic; it bears the shape and structure of the crucified Lord of glory. In this sense, the work of the Spirit is to raise all things to the form of Christ.

---

14 Küng quotes Augustine in his *Retractions* thus: 'whenever in my books I have described the Church as being without spot or wrinkle, I have not meant to imply that it was already so, but that it should prepare itself to be so, at the time when it will appear in its glory. In the present time, because of the inexperience and weaknesses of its members it must pray every day anew: Forgive us our trespasses . . .' (1967, p. 327).

From another point of view, the life and work of Christ constitutes the inner form and energy of the Spirit. Holiness occurs as
all things are raised to their fullness of life in God.

Human beings are neither passive observers of God's holy ways
nor the source but they are active (albeit subordinate) agents who
participate in a transformative process. Because the nature of
God's presence and work is so deeply intertwined with creation,
and human participation with God is almost a given of our life
on this planet, though for various reasons – some clear and some
entirely inexplicable – this is resisted as we become turned in on
ourselves. The Church is that body of people who in faith, joy
and love recognize their calling to participate with God in the
movement of holy life in the world. As we shall see in Chapter 8,
this participation operates in various dimensions (such as worship, sacrament, prayer and word, compassionate acts and loving
service in the world of economics, politics, care and compassion,
mission and evangelism, intellectual disciplines). The more deeply
the people of the Church enter into the slipstream of the Spirit's
work the more profound the emergence of holy life becomes. In
fact, it knows no boundaries and recognizes no place as forbid-
den – God will after all be 'all in all'. Yet, as Moltmann reminds
us, 'sanctification does not only come about through active service in the world but is also – and even more – suffered' (1977,
p. 355).

Moltmann's reflections at this point have a certain bite because
the property of holiness draws us deeper into the sufferings of
Christ (Phil. 3.10). If indeed holiness arises out of people attending to those practices which bear witness to the incarnate Lord,
it stands to reason that holiness will be costly for the Church (at
least while the world remains in a state of alienation from God).
The martyrs of the Church bear the sign of God's bruised and broken holy life. And it is not insignificant that in the early Church
martyrdom was valued as a baptism into Christ's death, life and
holiness. Moltmann states:

> The Church is therefore sanctified wherever it participates in
> the lowliness, helplessness, poverty and suffering of Christ. Its

glory is manifest through the sign of poverty. When believers take up their cross, the kingdom of God is manifested to the world. In this sense we can say that the Church is sanctified in this 'perverse world' through the signs of poverty, suffering and oppression. (1967, p. 357)

Moltmann recognized that such poverty could not be restricted to the inner life and attitudes, important as these are. Rather, the Church is called to be the Church *for* and *of* the poor (Gal. 2.10) consecrating everything it has to this service of the kingdom.

Of course, there is much more that could be said on this matter, but the foregoing highlights the way in which the mark of holiness is an emergent property of a community in transformation. But as our reflections on the unity of the Church indicated, this transformation cannot be restricted; it knows no boundaries nor standard measures. God's holy transformative work belongs to earth and heaven. Remarkably, it is the Church, his body that is especially called to display the form and structure of God's holy ways (Eph. 3.10). As the *ecclesia* of God enters into this movement, the Christ-like form of God's life in the world is enhanced and strengthened.

Catholic in embrace

The Greek word *katholikos* means concerning the whole (*kata* – concerning or about; *holos* – the whole, entire, universal). The original sense of the rich experience of the Church in its totality in any particular place echoed the nature of the *ecclesia* of the New Testament. The apostle Paul could write, for example, to local churches at Corinth, Philippi, Galatia and Rome. Such churches constituted the church whole, each *an* entire Church. Though clearly the local church was not *the* entire Church.

However, the original ecclesial sense of catholic as *whole* gave way to a secondary sense of an *orthodox Church* in the polemical contexts of the third and fourth centuries, when schisms raised questions about the whereabouts of the truly whole and authentic Church, that is, catholic.[15] In this context, the idea of catholic in the sense of orthodox teaching of the faith in continuity with the gospel emerged. This later became enshrined in the famous Vincentian Canon much beloved of Anglicans in later times: the catholic faith was that which was 'believed everywhere, always by everyone'. From the Religious Edict of Theodosius in AD 380, Christianity became the only lawful religion and henceforth catholicity received jurisdictional defence. The spread of Christianity across the Roman Empire suggested that *geographical extent* and *numerical size* could become measures of catholicity.

The problem with the above measures of catholicity was that, in the contexts of the great schism between East and West and the later sixteenth-century Protestant Reformation, it became clear that the Church through time and space differed markedly from the early *ecclesia*. This meant among other things that the question of catholicity became embroiled in apologetic and polemical disputes. It became a contested measure of the Church's fidelity to the gospel. Generally speaking, Protestantism retreated into notions of catholicity pertaining to orthodox teaching in continuity with the scriptures and relied on a doctrine of the invisible Church by which to speak of catholicity. Anglicans in time developed what became known as the 'branch theory' to establish its claim to catholicity.[16] Rome, on the other hand, emphasized not only teaching, but space, time and numbers though, as Küng notes, this could also generate difficulties and myriad qualifications (1967, p. 299). Certainly, one outcome of these developments was that the concept of catholicity became unclear and contested, a situation which has remained to this day.

Over time, we can observe a variety of competing measures of catholicity: an original sense of the whole (ecclesiological),

---

15 It is worth noting that unity and catholicity are co-relative concepts. Thus when unity is broken catholicity is immediately under question.

16 According to this theory the Anglican, Roman and eastern Churches 'are authentic "portions" of the catholic Church' (see Avis 1989, p. 179). Avis is discussing the ecclesiology of the nineteenth-century Anglican scholar William Palmer (1803–85).

doctrinal (orthodoxy), special extensity (geographical), numerical size (statistical), cultural variety (sociological), temporal continuity (historical). All of these measures of catholicity may have some value depending on the particular circumstances at any given time. However, none are fool-proof measures, and all betray the fundamental problem associated with the attempt to fix a measure to serve ideological and political interests often under cover of theological claims. The result of centuries of dispute over the mark of catholicity is that the concept is somewhat plastic, essentially contested, often confusing and unresolved.

Küng's own proposal entailed a recovery of catholicity as pertaining to identity. To maintain catholicity means that through time and space the Church in its basic identity in the gospel remains the same. As such, Küng spoke of an 'evangelical catholicity', which transcended short-sighted and exclusive Protestantism and diffuse and confused Roman Catholicism. On this account, true catholicity was a grace given and constantly renewed by the Lord of the Church. This had strong echoes of Barth's view that the ground of the Church's catholicity was derived from the constancy and truth of its Lord. Consequently, the Church's visible form 'reflects and bears witness to its inner catholicity'. On this account, catholic identity is secured christologically.

With Jürgen Moltmann, catholicity or 'inner wholeness' is not a state but an attribute describing a movement following the Lordship of Christ in the world. With Moltmann, catholicity has a more dynamic feel. It points to a universal mission, which expands in ever widening circles. The catholic embrace cannot be fixed and sealed, but is essentially unbounded even as it is inwardly directed by the working of the Spirit. Catholicity is a sign of the ongoing incorporation of the peoples and places of the world under the Lordship of Christ. Yet, Moltmann asks a pertinent question: if we are for the whole, how is this achieved in the present? His answer, like his approach to holiness, is a radical embrace of the oppressed, poor, humble and outcast. The Church finds its catholic identity through partisanship and all that this implies – particularity, limit, boundedness, restriction.

This paradox of catholic embrace retains its universal intent for '[t]he intent is also to save the oppressor'. The analogue is Paul's mission to incorporate the outcast into the kingdom, that is the Gentiles, which he saw as the only hope for Israel (Rom. 11), so that God would truly be 'all in all'. The widest embrace possible through partisanship with the marginalized.

In similar manner to the unity and holiness of the Church, the question of catholicity is first of all a question about God's originative embrace of creation. It is the catholic Spirit which broods and hovers over the abyss in Genesis that brings all things into being through the Word, which creates human society and forms communities of faith and love. This fundamental embrace of God of the whole is indestructible and constant. This comes to concentration in the life of Jesus and the resurrection, wherein the whole creation is reconstituted and orientated towards the consummation of all things. How God brings this rich expanding and transforming embrace about is for the most part beyond human imagining though we have a clue in the *ecclesia* of God. The particular calling and the deepest mystery of the Church is that it belongs to that movement of God to embrace the divided and separated peoples of the world into the one new humanity. In the Orthodox tradition, this catholic impulse constitutes the Church's '*sobornost*' or catholicity (Afonsky 2001, p. 77, quoting George Florovsky).

Excursus: the local and universal Church

Earlier, I referred to the original sense of catholic as concern for the whole. This has two dimensions, the local and the universal. In any one locale, an entire Church is present though this is never the entire Church. The fact of particularity does not diminish the wholeness of the local church. As Küng notes, a church 'does not become uncatholic by being a limited local church, but by being a limited local church which has cut itself off from other churches and hence from the whole, entire Church . . . , [cut] off from the faith and life of the entire Church ("schismatic") or excluded itself from it ("heretical") or even rebelled against it ("apostate")'

(1967, p. 300). The forfeiture of catholicity at the local level occurs through desire (intentional or by consequence) to be self-sufficient, independent and thereby disconnected from the wider *ecclesia*.

The entire Church on earth (that is the total Church visible) is constituted by myriad local Churches. However, this is not by simple addition but 'by being inwardly at one in the same God, Lord and Spirit, through the same Gospel, the same baptism and sacred meal and the same faith'. Accordingly, the total Church is manifest through the local churches, and yet the total Church is more than the sum of the parts and may be rightly referred to as catholic, 'that is the whole, universal, all-embracing Church'. The Lutheran Robert Jensen states it succinctly: 'There are local Churches, each of them the Church, and there is the one Church which each of the local Churches is. The Church is *in et ex ecclesiis* and the Churches are *in et ex ecclesiae*' (1999, p. 234). The ecclesiology of Ephesians offers a rich account of the Church universal, even as the letter is addressed to a local ecclesial community. What emerges is an important dialectic in ecclesiology between the local and the universal, which mirrors to some extent the long-standing discussion in philosophy concerning the one and the many.

A question arises about how these two dimensions of the catholicity of the Church are related. It is easy to ignore the wider social, cultural and political environments in which the churches of the globe exist. For example, in the Western world, there is a strong individualistic and competitive ethos, and this influences the practices of the churches in far more significant ways than we might care to recognize. The fragmentation, isolation and resistance to cooperation among the churches is one sign of a distorted catholicity, which arises in part from the influence of the wider environment and to some extent is bolstered internally by theological justifications for separateness which have longevity on their side but are more brittle in a highly secularised environment, than might be recognized. In this context, it is not uncommon for older disputes about catholicity to reappear (for example, presence or lack of appropriate catholic order and/or adherence or otherwise to catholic teaching).

Underlying such disagreements, we can discern a more pervasive tribalism as institutions and different groups retreat into their
own enclaves in an attempt to shore up identity and respond to
pressure internally and externally. In this context, priority seems
to be given to the local expression of Church. This is not a problem in and of itself for, as noted above, catholicity is not forfeited or disfigured by being limited to the local. However, when
the local functions in an enclosed, self-sufficient and self-assured
manner and fails to acknowledge its wider connectedness, questions about a particular local expression of catholicity ought to
be raised. Of course, when churches of significant numerical and
geographical proportions ignore the plight of the local manifestations of Church and trade on their wider presence and power
and are somewhat dismissive of the local, this too represents a
distorted catholicity.

Full catholicity embraces the dialectic between the local and
wider, more universal, orientation of the Church. Full catholicity
recognizes the mutuality and interdependence that is the mark of
the Church catholic. We are after all 'members one of another'
(Rom. 12.5), and our fundamental connectivity is the basis and
imperative for the truly catholic spirit. Furthermore, a true and
authentic catholicity is an open-ended anticipatory catholicity
actively seeking to follow and embody God's loving reach into
the world. Catholicity is thus an *emergent property* of the *ecclesia*
rather than a secure and fixed entity that churches either have or
do not have. In this way, the mark of catholicity shares with the
marks of unity and holiness an unfinished, restless and future orientated character. Catholicity is both an originative gift of God,
whose love created the world, whose love and embrace of the
whole was decisively manifest in the sending of the Son (John
3.16); whose reconciling love initiated a re-constitution of the
catholic whole in one new humanity (Eph. 2.15–16). This work
of the Trinity continues until the whole creation is brought by
the Spirit of love into the eternal bode of God. A fully catholic
sociality is an eschatological reality that for the moment we only
know 'in part'. These reflections are relevant for my own Anglican Communion. At its best, it aspires to a dynamic catholicity

that involves a creative relationship between a local inculturated Church and the wider Church (cf. IATDC 2007, para. 45).

Apostolic in shared discipleship

Most commentators agree that this mark undergirds the other three ancient marks. The reason is simply that if it were not for the witness of the first apostles of Christ, there would not be on earth one, holy, catholic Church. Of course, that witness is founded upon a prior event well captured in the statement: 'The Church is born in the process that generates our gospel' (Hardy 2010, p. 65). The apostolic witness is a response to this process and in turn is generative of the post-Easter Church. In this sense, apostolicity is foundational for the other marks of the Church.

However, it is also true that in the consummation of all things the mystery of the heavenly Church will be marked by unity, holiness and catholicity. But the apostolic witness will cease as the Church is fulfilled in praise and thanksgiving, or rather the witness born on earth will not be of the same order and purpose as the witness of the heavenly Church.

By what criteria would we measure the apostolic character of the Church? From the Roman Catholic side, Hans Küng finds the category of *witness* central. He notes that the word 'apostolic' does not appear in the Bible and was first used by Ignatius of Antioch and in the martyrdom of Polycarp. The original meaning is 'having a direct link with the apostles of Christ'. If the apostolic nature of the Church is fundamentally to witness to the risen Lord, it is clear that the first apostles provide a prototype of the apostolic calling of the Church. Bearing witness to Christ becomes the apostolic mission of the Church, and while there cannot be any apostles like those who were witnesses to the resurrection, nonetheless a commission and task remains for the Church. Küng thus asks who are the followers of the apostles and concludes that it is the *whole* Church (1967, p. 355). By following the apostles, the Church can learn what real submission and real service mean. Apostolic succession entails a confrontation of the Church with the testimony of the apostles, in a living continuation of the apostolic ministries, with all their various forms of expression' (p. 358).

Küng's exposition of the apostolic nature of the Church might not strike us as particularly radical today. However, half a century ago, even in the liberated air of Vatican II, his approach broke the Catholic mould of apostolic witness being vested in certain hierarchically ordered ministries rather than a responsibility of the whole. The category of witness was a comprehensive, dynamic and freeing one at the time. Theologically it grounded the apostolicity of the Church in the whole people of God. The implications of this for a theology of the laity and the wider *oikumene* were and remain significant.

But what was the *inner form* of the apostolic witness of the Church? Jürgen Moltmann developed the mark of apostolicity in terms of suffering. Moltmann, himself a former prisoner of war and author of books on a theology of hope and the crucified God, now transferred the fruits of his life and thought into a pneumatological ecclesiology which was at once messianic, future orientated, Spirit-led and shaped by the passion of Christ. His approach built upon the foundation of the apostolic mission of the Church so forcefully articulated by Küng. However, such a mission would necessarily encounter resistance from other powers and lead 'inescapably into tribulation, contradiction and suffering' (1977, p. 361). The reason was simple: 'Just as the apostle Paul pointed to his persecutions, tribulations, wounds and scares in order to prove his apostolate (2 Cor. 6 and 7), so persecutions and sufferings will also be the proof of the apostolic Church'. The apostolic character of the Church is thus 'determined' by two realities: (a) eschatologically 'by the Easter appearances of the risen Christ', and (b) 'by the suffering and sacrifice in discipleship of the Christ who was crucified'. Both realities belonged to the whole Christ and hence to the whole apostolate of the Church. The logic of this was that the Church was apostolic when it took up its cross. Moltmann's reflections on the apostolic character of the Church are set within the context of 'a godless and inhuman world', where '"the Church under the cross" shows itself to be the *true* apostolic Church'.

It is clear from Moltmann's approach that the much controverted issue of apostolic succession is located within the wider and richer understanding of 'succession of the passion of Christ'. So much of the history of the debate and controversy about apostolicity as a mark of the Church has been preoccupied with issues of historical lineage from the original apostles somewhat mechanically determined and/or focused on apostolic office within a hierarchically ordered *ecclesia*. Küng broadened the scope of the discussion by applying the category of witness to the whole Church. In this, he was a forerunner of more recent developments that have more firmly embedded apostolicity within the people of God as its fundamental calling and commission (for example, the Anglican report, *Apostolicity and Succession*, 1994). This makes for a more integrated account of the nature of the apostolic office in the Church and recalibrates issues to do with power, authority and responsibility.

Moltmann's reflections offer an even richer account of the *fundamental form* of the apostolic calling of the Church. It is a particular kind of witness so powerfully stated by the apostle Paul: 'I want to know him, the power of his resurrection and the fellowship of his sufferings' (Phil. 3.10). Here is a notion of measurement that goes beyond any fixities and assured guarantees. For example, who can truly and accurately measure the Church's participation in and completion of the sufferings of Christ? Is there a limit? At the extreme end of the scale, it is signalled in martyrdom; not a measure with which the Church is particularly comfortable, but nonetheless it provides the horizon for all consideration of the mark of apostolicity. Apostolic succession in ministry looks very different from this perspective. It is not thereby undermined, but the inner form is allowed to shine more brightly, and the ordered offices of the Church are set against a far more compelling and challenging measure of apostolicity.

The above considerations of the mark of apostolicity highlight not simply the priority of witness and suffering but the fact that this is a shared responsibility of the whole Church. The apostolic calling arises out of incorporation into Christ through baptism in water and the Spirit. This calling is not the preserve of a particular office but fundamentally a commission for the Church. It means that the apostolic mark of the Church is a truly shared mark. As the body is joined and interconnected, so that when one part suffers all parts suffer, so discipleship is not a lonely road but one filled with companions following Christ the great apostle. It is precisely as the road is travelled together in truly shared and collaborative ventures that a new sociality can emerge in the world.

Marks as measures of the mystery

One of the critical challenges for the churches today is to recover the fullness of those practices, which embody the ancient marks of the Church. What is needful in order that the *ecclesia* of God might manifest in its life and witness the unity, holiness and catholicity of its apostolic God? How might these ancient measures of being the Church find fresh forms of embodiment? These are some of the critical issues facing the churches. In this respect, I want to draw this chapter to a close by highlighting one or two areas that may be particularly relevant to the discussion of the marks of the Church.

First, the question of the marks is relevant for many of the new forms of Church which come under the general heading of 'Emerging Church' and 'Fresh Expressions'. In times of challenge and depleted resources, the churches can become embroiled in the minutiae and obsessed with funding, structure and management. These are all signs, among other things of an anxious Church. However, amidst the upheavals both beyond and within the churches, there are exciting new developments; new pathways for the Spirit are being trod and there are myriad new forms through which the mystery of the Church is coming to birth. This is as it should be, but at times it is difficult to discern continuities with the deeper veins of the Christian tradition, and at times such movements become disconnected from the deeper roots of the gospel (Percy 2010, pp. 67–79). For example, in the West, in particular with its deeply competitive and tribal culture – one of the puzzles and contradictions of a global consciousness – the catholicity of new expressions of being the Church can be problematic. Often, fresh expressions and new emerging forms of Church end up with a truncated catholicity, which focuses on the local, but with minimal consciousness of the wider Church. Such churches can easily become uncatholic and self-absorbed and therefore unaccountable. In such environments, unity is an internal quality, but it can sublimate or ignore the yearning for a wider embrace and/or recognition of the whole is forfeited.

Second, what has become known as New Monasticism raises some important and interesting issues in relation to the marks of the Church. How might the marks of a New Monasticism connect with the more dynamic and future-orientated focus for the marks of the Church? The creedal marks provide the basic frame of reference for the life and mission of the Church. Their reinterpretation in each generation occurs at multiple levels from the macro (for example, Küng and Moltmann) to the micro or more intermediate levels found in New Religious Movements such as New Monasticism. Thus, the larger conceptual frames identified by Moltmann – freedom, partisanship, poverty and suffering – receive concrete expression in, for example, the marks of ecclesial life identified by the Rutba House community. Hence, 'catholicity in partisanship' finds concrete expression in 'relocation to abandoned places of empire' and 'holiness in poverty' involves 'sharing economic resources with fellow community members' (Rutba House ed. 2005). Identifying the correlation between developments in wider ecclesiology and its practical expressions at the ground is part of the process by which theology serves the interests of a practical ecclesiology for new apostolic communities.

Third, where the numerically and geographically larger and established churches are engaged in significant internal turmoil and dispute the temptation is again to retreat to a truncated catholicity. An example is the Anglican Communion where, increasingly, final responsibility to determine controverted matters is occurring at the local level, in this case the Province. The proper tension and interdependence between the provinces of the Communion is too quickly forfeited. This impaired catholicity has some of the hallmarks of a schismatic spirit and today in the western churches it is powerfully present, and not simply for the Anglican Communion.

The general condition of the churches of the West as somewhat inward-looking and preoccupied with their internal life means that the marks of unity, holiness and catholicity tend to be unfolded internally as challenges to be addressed at an interecclesial level. While this is important, indeed vital, the marks of the Church are, as Jürgen Moltmann indicated, those measures by which the mystery of the Church will be known in the world. This means that a critical issue for the churches today will be how to ensure that their practices point toward the one, holy, catholic and apostolic Church, which is still unfolding. This, as we have seen above, is a dynamic movement through which the marks move beyond fixed measures of truth and good order and become emergent properties of the renewal of the *ecclesia* of God. This dynamic and emergent quality of the nature of the Church has implications for its structure, the subject of the next chapter.

Questions

1 What are the strengths and weaknesses of such a depiction of the Church as a mystery?
2 The Letter to the Ephesians states that it is 'through the Church that the wisdom of God in its rich variety is made known' (Eph. 3.10)? How can this text assist our understanding of the Church's purpose?
3 How important are the marks of the Church (one, holy, catholic and apostolic) for the doctrine of the Church? In what sense are the marks of the Church God's gift to the Church and in what sense are the marks still developing?
4 How might you apply the discussion of the marks of the Church to your local church? Why do the marks of the Church generate such conflict?
5 How might discussion of the marks of the Church be helpful in the context of Emerging Church, New Monasticism and fresh expressions of Church?

Further reading

Anthony Baker, 'On Making Them All One: Unity, Transcendence and the Anglican Church', *Journal of Anglican Studies* 5:1 (2007), pp. 11–38.

Edith Humphrey, 'One, Holy, Catholic, and Apostolic: Awaiting the Redemption of Our Body', in John G. Stackhouse Jr. (ed.), *Evangelical Ecclesiology: Reality or Illusion*, Grand Rapids, MI: Baker Books, 2003, chap. 5, pp. 135–59.

Henri de Lubac, S. J., 'How is the Church a Mystery', in The *Church: Paradox and Mystery*, 3rd edn, New York: Ecclesia Press, 1969.

Jürgen Moltmann, *The Church in the Power of the Spirit*, London: SCM Press, 1977, Ch. 7.

Wolfhart Pannenberg, 'The Significance of Eschatology for an Understanding of the Apostolicity and Catholicity of the Church', in *The Church*, Philadelphia: Westminster Press, 1983, pp. 44–68.

7

Structured for Freedom

Ordering the mystery

'Measuring the Mystery' (Chapter 6) drew attention to the open and intangible quality of the marks of the Church and also pointed to the dynamic and emergent nature of the unity, holiness, catholicity and apostolicity of the Church. From this perspective, the marks were indicators of a Church on the move rather than stationary.

'Ordering the mystery' draws attention to ecclesial order. This includes matters of polity, governance, accountability and communicative networks and ministries of oversight and care. In this chapter, I consider the purpose of 'ordering the mystery'. Specifically, how might ecclesial polity be structured to optimize the freedom of the baptized to live as the new humanity in Christ (Eph. 2.15)? The question is thus about the possibility of an ecclesial polity of liberty to serve the *missio Dei*. This includes not only a question about the 'what' of polity but the *direction* and *dynamic* of polity. The Church's order and structure is not a steady-state self-enclosed order but ideally operates to encourage faithful following of what God is doing in the world. Accordingly, concern for ordering the mystery reveals itself at a more practical level as a means to enable and hence free the ecclesia to fulfil its calling in the world (Gal. 5.1a). This may seem the very opposite of what many experience as a somewhat wooden and overly constrained and artificial construct that thwarts efforts to live as a Church for the glory of God. The intent of this chapter is to develop a theological account of Church order and structure which shows how it enables the Church to serve the deeper purposes of God in the world.

An ordered structure: polity, faith and ministry

A variety of polities

How might we understand polity, faith and order and how are they related? In introducing the notion of ecclesial order above, I referred to the concept of 'polity'. The concept of polity is an important one in ecclesiology. The English word comes via Latin *polita*, from Greek *politeia*, meaning citizenship or civil administration (*politis* citizen; *polis* city). Polity in a general sense is an umbrella term which concerns the form of government of a nation, state, church, or organization. Ecclesiastical polity is thus the operational and governance structure of a church and includes ministerial forms and authority.

In Christianity, it is usual to refer to three basic types of ecclesial polity: episcopal, presbyterial and congregational. Each of these has a variety of expressions and a diversity of ways in which ministerial authority operates.[1] Episcopally ordered churches characteristically have a threefold ministerial structure (bishops, priests/presbyters, deacons). In a presbyterial structure, there are commonly presbyters (in some cases 'teaching elders' or 'ministers of the word') and lay leaders (ruling elders).[2] Congregational polity focuses on ministerial leadership in relation to the congregation with its council. In all three polities, decision-making takes place at different levels – congregation, synod, province, global – with different weight being attached to decisions at each level. Similarly, at each level there is differing involvement and authority accorded to lay people in deter-

---

1 For example, in episcopally ordered churches there is internal variety: Roman Catholicism views the Church as a single polity headed by the Pope; in Eastern Orthodoxy, the various churches retain formal autonomy, but are held to be unified by shared doctrine and conciliarity (that is, the authority of councils, such as ecumenical councils and Holy Synods); in Anglicanism, the churches are autonomous, though through the connections of the provinces with the See of Canterbury they are united in the Anglican Communion, which has no jurisdictional power.

2 Although the nomenclature varies the common features are no bishops and emphasis on lay elders.

mining church life and decision-making. These differences are not simply congregational versus episcopal but occur within similar polities. For example, in the Roman Catholic Church, lay people play no formal part in synodical government (which is basically bishops in council). By contrast, in the episcopal order of Anglicanism lay people are integral to synodical life. The region of polity is inherently complex both within and between the churches of the one Church of God. In our contemporary context, a critical issue needing to be addressed within any polity is how it provides for structures of accountability throughout the whole ecclesial system especially with respect to lay people (see Lakeland 2004).

Polity and faith

Consideration of polity gives rise to a question: How is *polity* – the particular ordering of the Church – related to *faith*? It is commonplace for churches to differentiate between order and faith. This basic distinction can be observed in the work and literature of the World Council of Churches. Matters of order typically concern how a church is organized and governed; forms of ministry and associated authority it operates under; in short, how it orders its business as the one, holy, catholic and apostolic Church in the world. It may seem that order is of a secondary concern compared to matters of faith. Indeed, this has been an important position in the controversies between and within the churches of the world. Article 20 of the Anglican *Thirty Nine Articles of Religion* states that the Church has power and authority to make judgements and settle disputes in matters of faith and order. Though of course order is a slippery term and it is quite interesting to observe how, in the history of Christianity the boundaries between faith and order have been blurred. Indeed, the relationship between the two is more akin to a weave than we might ordinarily appreciate. Matters of faith find expression through, indeed are manifest in, particular ordering and associated practices. This, of course, makes order a far more contested and conflictual matter than we might care to acknowledge. How a church orders its life is intended to be a way through which the gospel faith might shine.

Order, besides being a highly contingent feature of ecclesial life (it could be otherwise and is affected by circumstances), is an inherently controversial feature of the Church; a fact clearly borne out in the history of Christianity. It puts the lie to any reductionist account of order that might consider it as little more than the peculiar arrangements of a church, which could be easily jettisoned if something better or more useful was found. It was these kinds of considerations that led a former Archbishop of Canterbury, Michael Ramsey, to refer to episcopacy as 'the utterance of the gospel' (Ramsey 1936, pp. 54, 208). Clearly for Ramsey episcopal order was not a 'take it or leave it' option for the Church catholic. In the late sixteenth century in England, the ascendant Puritan sympathizers in the reformation movement took a very different line from Ramsey on the question of episcopacy. However, in doing so they were even more strident in their conviction that the order of the Church of God had to conform to the pattern they considered to have been revealed in Scripture. This, of course, had a decidedly presbyterian appearance.

The various polities of the churches retain great weight for their advocates whether episcopal, presbyterian or congregational. These basic types trace their antecedents to earliest Christianity, and the main lines of each polity can be tracked throughout the Christian tradition. Each of these polities has a number of varieties and each has strengths and weaknesses.

Order may not be coterminous with matters of faith, but neither is it unrelated and simply a secondary accretion. The question of ordering – precisely because it concerns the ordering of the mystery of the Church and the way of salvation – is a matter that remains important, relevant and controversial. And this is only exacerbated in periods of great change and stress for the Church, when adaptation, relevance, identity and mission press in on the Church. Order can be the occasion for significant chaos and new opportunities for freedom for the baptized!

Polity and ministry

Besides the matter of polity and faith, there is also the relationship between *ministry* and *polity*. I have suggested that polity concerns the form of ecclesiastical government. In this sense, ministry or, as it has often been stated, 'an ordered ministry' belongs under the general banner of polity. One might say that ministry is a concrete specification of the form of polity of a particular church. Thus, for example, an episcopal polity will have bishops, priests/ presbyters and deacons ordered in relation to the particular governance of the church. How authority in ministry operates is very much dependent on the particular way in which the polity of a church functions. For example, in an episcopally-ordered church like Anglicanism ministerial authority operates at parish, diocesan, national and provincial levels. Beyond that, there is no existing international canon law or form of government. This reflects what might be termed a provincial ecclesiology appropriate for a fellowship of churches bonded by historical links, common order and fraternal relations. By contrast, jurisdiction in the Roman Communion is centralized with ultimate authority residing in the Pope. While, for everyday matters, ministerial authority operates at the diocesan level with authority focused in the diocesan bishop, nonetheless juridical authority extends wider than this and colours the particular way in which bishops relate to each other and to the Vatican.

It is tempting to locate ordered ministry as a subset of polity, and in some respects this is exactly how it works. However, it is a dynamic and often subtle relation particularly given the fact that from earliest times the accent in the Church was primarily on the ministries as gifts of the Spirit. Polity in important respects represents a more developed, codified and organized form of governance to give focus and strength to the inner life of ordered ministries among the baptized. The reason for raising the question of the relation between polity and ministry is that for too long the two have remained on parallel tracks and the close relation between the two could easily be ignored or considered of little account. All that changes, of course, as soon as the practical life of the churches becomes the main agenda. It is then that polity and ministry within and between churches becomes important.

The dynamic structure of social systems

The concept of structure

Underlying matters of ecclesial polity – governance, ministry, authority, communications – is the question of the dynamics of social structure and its operation in the Church. Ecclesial ordering could benefit from the insights of social theory concerning the constitution and purpose of society.[3] Such an inquiry, though often skirted around in ecclesiology, can illuminate the underlying power that shapes and directs the form and processes of different Church polities. This in turn impacts significantly upon the ecumenical work of the churches as well as their differing modes of engagement with wider society.

A key concept in this regard is 'structure'. Structure essentially means *the way something is put together*. The word is found in late Middle English (1400–1500) for the 'process of building' and is derived from the Latin *structura* (equivalent to *struct*; past participle of *struere* i.e. to put together + *ura* – ure) hence 'the way something is put together' (*Shorter Oxford English Dictionary*). As such, structure

is a fundamental, tangible or intangible notion referring to the recognition, observation, nature, and permanence of patterns and relationships of entities. This notion may itself be an object, such as a built structure, or an attribute, such as the structure of society. From a child's verbal description of a snowflake, to the detailed scientific analysis of the properties of magnetic fields, the concept of structure is now often an essential foundation of

---

3 More usually books on ecclesiology adopt one of two approaches: (a) intentionally distancing themselves from the social sciences in favour of a biblical and/or theological approach; or (b) attempting to incorporate insights from social theorists but in a limited or unintegrated manner.

nearly every mode of inquiry and discovery in science, philosophy, and art. (Pullan 2000, Preface)

The concept of 'form' has in the past played a role comparable to that of structure in contemporary thought. An interesting example in ecclesiology is Gabriel Hebert's *The Form of the Church* (Hebert 1945, p. 9). Concern for structure is concern for how a system is made; what it is made of; and its internal relations. Structures can be hierarchical in form or a network of linkages or cascades with complex or simple connections and components. Not surprisingly the question of structure and its significance in social systems is a matter of controversy among social theorists (see Loyal 2003, Ch. 4).

Structures: containing or enabling

A number of issues arise in relation to the concept of structure (see, for example, Limerick et al. 1998: Chandler 1977 and Chandler and Daems 1980). First, there is a tension between structure as *containment* and as an *enabling* aspect of social systems. Not surprisingly, in contemporary life the containment function of structure is associated with bounded frameworks, restriction of freedom and rather fixed and enforceable rules. This does not necessarily have to be the case, because all social systems require structure, which defines and clarifies limits of diversity and preferred communication flows. However, the containment function of structure does orientate the social system in generally conservative and established directions. When the accent is on structure as enabling, the focus shifts to potentials for new capacity, exploration of meaning and change. The enabling function of structure is associated with more open and dynamic dimensions of structure. In times of institutional stress and challenge, the dialectic between containment and enabling gives way to a one-sided emphasis upon containment. The dynamism of the system structure gives way to steady-state maintenance functions. This usually generates a strong counter-response associated with practices designed to disrupt the stasis of the system and recover capacity for change. These dimensions of structure are evident in the churches today.

Extrinsic or intrinsic structures

Second, structure can be identified in terms of *extrinsic* or *intrinsic*. In the former, structure typically is what is created and imprinted upon an entity; certainly it is not so much given but manufactured. This does not necessarily imply a negative assessment on any structure. While such structuring can provide meaning for a system, nonetheless it does often feed into a view that structure is geared towards status quo operations rather than enabling new possibilities. The extrinsic approach to structure is reflected in analogies of a mechanical kind.

However, structure may not simply be something extrinsic but an emergent property of the system as such. In this scenario, structure is intrinsic to a social system though often inchoate and implicit but gradually emerges. In this case, organic analogies are more familiar. When structure operates in this second manner, the more dynamic aspects of structure come to the fore. An interesting example of the extrinsic/intrinsic approach to structure is reflected in Gabriel Hebert's two senses of *form*: (a) that which was extrinsic to an entity and created to provide sense and meaning; and (b) that form which was intrinsic to the particular entity and in this sense was emergent from within. It raised a question which has proven long running and controversial: to what extent is the complex social structure of the polity of the Church, in all its variety, something imprinted from beyond (for example, by revelation from God); to what extent emergent from within the being of the Church; to what extent is it an entirely contingent matter, an outcome of the historical process as such? The development of episcopacy and episcopal polity is an interesting and controversial example in this regard.

Structure and human agency

Third, and related to the above, is the place of *human agency* in social structuring. Social structures have been conceived as objective features of social organizations and as such 'external to, independent of and determinant upon, [a] freely acting agent' (Loyal 2003, p. 71). This leads to an emphasis on the object over subject, structure over agency and society over individual. Structure became associated with relatively stable or permanent patterns of social relations. In this dualistic account, structure is conceived to operate as a constraint upon human agency (as identified above) and the conditions for transformation become more puzzling. What if human agency played a more constitutive role in the emergence, formation, endurance and transformation of structure?

The sociologist Anthony Giddens developed a theory of 'structuration' to address the way human agents are involved in the 'dynamic process whereby structures come into being and are reproduced recursively through social practices' (Loyal 2003, p. 75).[4] Giddens refers to 'duality of structure' by which he means that 'structure is not external to individuals'; in fact 'as memory traces, and as instantiated in social practices, it [structure] is in a certain sense more "internal" than exterior to their activities' (1984, p. 25). He enlists the analogy of speech and language for social structure. For Giddens, 'speech' (action and interaction) is compared with 'language' (structure) 'the latter being an abstract "property" of a community of speakers' (Giddens 1976, p. 118, quoted in Loyal 2003, p. 72). In the same way that 'language is a structure which forms a condition of possibility for speech (agency), so more generally social structure provides the conditions of possibility for social action' (p. 73). The incorporation

---

4 Giddens identifies (a) 'structure(s)' as 'rules and resources, or sets of transformation relations, organized as properties of social systems', (b) 'systems(s)' as 'reproduced relations between actors or collectivities, organized as regular social practices' and (c) 'structuration' as 'conditions governing the continuity or transmutation of structures, and therefore the reproduction of the social systems' (1984, p. 25).

of human agency into the dynamics of social structuring creates the possibility for structure to *enable* action as well as *constrain*. Structure and agency form two sides of the same coin. In this sense, structure is not simply something *external* and over against human agency; rather the latter is integral (*intrinsic*) to the former and through social acts the whole of structure is instantiated and reproduced. A critical outcome of this rethinking of structure in relation to human agency is to move 'from a fixed and mechanical conception of "structure" to one which emphasizes fluidity and process and dissolves the dichotomy between statics and dynamics' (p. 75).

The work of Giddens and others highlights, among other things, the dynamic nature of social structures and the importance of human agency as an enabling and constitutive feature of social structure. Structure involves people, events and communications. Healthy structures imply the operation of an open, free and competent communicative social order. This involves cultivating hopeful and realistic expectations as an important way by which people inhabiting cultural and religious traditions can participate in change and transformation. It is no longer possible or credible to conceive of social structure as a fixed and external patterning of social relations apart from human agents. To this extent, structures have to be reconceived to recognize that structuring social life includes both permanent patterns of relations and emergent forms of life arising from the very nature of the social structure with social actors. Structure so conceived has the capacity for continual replenishment and transformative power. How might these reflections be relevant for questions concerning the polity and ministry of the Church?

Ecclesial structures, human agency and hierarchy

A transformative ecclesial polity

A number of matters seem pertinent. First, we note that human agency is involved in the constitution of ecclesial polity. This means that polity as a particular form of social structure is not set in concrete, so to speak. Certainly, there are long established patterns of relations and authority that evidence wisdom achieved through well-honed practice. However, because structure is inherently dynamic in its operation and includes human agents 'inside' the structure rather than passive recipients external to it, this means that at any moment new emergent possibilities for social structuring can occur via communicative events between human agents. It means that polity ought to enable transformative action rather than simply lock agents into past patterns of relations. Ecclesial polity operates best when it facilitates enabling action by agents acting with communicative competence.[5] What would the outcome of such action look like? In so far as such action follows the purposes of God, it would generate richer freedom in the Spirit for 'the Lord is the Spirit and where the Spirit is there is freedom' (2 Cor. 3.17). Human agency is not a freewheeling activity but constrained by the Spirit who raises all things to their true order (polity) in God. This does not necessarily mean ancient and well-attested structures ought to be jettisoned but it does mean recovering the enabling function of an inherited polity as a counter to an over-emphasis on containment and stasis.

Hierarchy as ordered structure

Second, the above discussion offers some clues about the much-vexed issue of hierarchy in the Church, especially in relation to ministerial authority. In an important sense, hierarchy concerns system differentiation and is an entirely normal feature of social structure. Indeed, the concept of hierarchy means literally order, that is, the order of things. It is composed of two words, *hieros* (not priestly but *sacred*) and *arche* (not rule but *source* or *principle*), in other words, *sacred source*. In the ancient world, it would have been unimaginable to reject hierarchy as such. The sacred ordering of the world was of divine origin and the basis for its

---

5 I have in mind here the notion of 'communicative competence' developed by the social theorist Jürgen Habermas (1984–87).

intelligibility. As such, hierarchy was not an instrument of power or rule by particular persons such as a priestly elite. Such sacred order was not instituted so that a community could be governed. Rather governance was 'the consequence, not the cause, of order and is defined and given its distinctive form by the pattern of that order' (Horne 2007, p. 20). Accordingly 'Hierarchy is essentially a manifestation of God's providential relationship with the world'; an '"outbreak of God's love" not "a ladder we struggle up by our own efforts' (p. 21). On the other hand, in the modern world, hierarchy has become contaminated by alien notions of 'power over' and often associated with the misuse of power. Under these conditions, hierarchy appears highly problematic and some have wondered whether it ought to be dropped and replaced by the concept of 'ordering' (Greenwood 2009, p. 98).

However, our brief reflections on social structure point to a more dynamic quality for hierarchy in which differentiated order has emergent properties and ever-new possibilities. The patterns of authority within ecclesial polities are not in fact set in place irrevocably (contrary to what many in authority believe), but from within their own life they contain the seeds of new order and differentiated forms. Unfortunately, such possibilities often remain hidden to ecclesial consciousness and to this extent it is difficult for human agents to participate in the renewing work of the Spirit.

Hierarchy as that way of ordering ministry operates with two poles; what is given and established and permanent and also what is emergent, new and transformative. Neither pole exists alone but belongs in tension. What this means in practice is that the ministries of the Churches are interrelated and dynamic. They do not exist outside or above the Church and its polity but are immersed in it. We might want to locate the source of this patterning and differentiation of ministries in a form of sacred order that stretches back to creation as such. This follows the logic of our earlier discussion of sociality in Chapter 4. It is echoed by the Anglican theologian Eric Mascall when he stated 'that the Church has a structure, with a pattern of relations between its members, is only to be expected from its nature as a society of human beings'

(Horne 2007, p. 22, quoting from Mascall 1973, p. 9). For Mascall, such structure and associated hierarchical ordering was an 'inescapable fact of life' and to this extent constituted a 'sacred order' in so far as it 'appears to be a characteristic of the ordering of the world of nature that has its origins in the creative act of God' (p. 22). As Horne notes, this 'inherently hierarchical structure to natural life presents modern men and women with a paradox, one with which they are often extremely uncomfortable. Hierarchy is known as a fact but felt as an embarrassment' (p. 22).

Part of the problem regarding the appeal to notions of hierarchy arises because hierarchy is incorrectly associated with 'power' rather than, as one commentator refers, 'status'.[6] Though in the light of current meanings attached to this word it might be better to speak in terms of 'order' in the sense of how things/people are placed and related within an entity. These two concepts (power and order) may be related, indeed it is unavoidable, but the former flows from the latter and is accountable to it. The latter ecclesial order gives form and shape to the Church's triune identity. This identity is linked to the crucified Lord – embodied in word and sacrament – and hope for the coming kingdom. The ordering is thus Eucharistic and eschatological and those ministries responsible in this order are representative ministries, accountable to the whole people of God.

The above discussion of hierarchy has implications for the nature of ministry. For example, the phrase 'the ministry' has often been invoked to suggest a stream of life and authority distanced from and imprinted upon the *ecclesia*. Such a conception has been powerfully present in the Church and operated in a quasi-mechanical fashion offering certainty and assurance (cf. Pickard 2009). However, in a dynamically structured polity in accordance with the above understanding, the ministries of the Church inhere in each other, emerge out of each other, generate new ecclesial order and enable transformation in social practices. The critical element in this transformative work is the role of human agency seeking to participate in the work of the Spirit.

---

6 The basic distinction is made by Horne, though I have developed it as above.

Brief excursus: Anglican Instruments of Communion

An example of how the above discussion on dynamics of structure impacts on current difficulties in the Church can be observed in the Anglican Communion. In the polity of the churches of the Anglican Communion, there are four 'Instruments of Unity' – the Archbishop of Canterbury, the Lambeth Conference, the Anglican Consultative Council and the Primate's meeting. In contemporary international Anglicanism, there are significant divisions. Furthermore, failures to consult, listen and learn across provinces have rendered the Instruments of Unity, in the view of some, both ineffective and obsolete. In other words, the instruments have lost their *enabling* function. For many, the instruments simply *constrain* and close down rather than free the Church. However, such a view is fundamentally flawed for a number of reasons related to the above discussion. First, the concept of instrument as a part of the social structure (polity) of the Church is suspect to say the least. Instruments of Unity, like distorted views of social structure, are conceived as external to human agents, extrinsic to the processes of ecclesial life, an overlay which, when ineffective, can and ought to be jettisoned. Such an instrumental notion of social structure fails to incorporate the dynamic aspects of human agency. Human beings are not extrinsic to the structure.

Second, the above discussion highlights the fact that structure, like language, awaits repeated instantiation in speech, and it is this which enables a transformed social life. So-called instruments, if that nomenclature is to be retained, have to be incarnated in speech through the actions of human agents. This will be necessarily a slow and difficult process that requires immense patience while new emergent properties of ecclesial life begin to operate. Such an approach is in keeping with wisdom from the social sciences and offers a critical perspective on much current ecclesiological conflict across the churches of the globe. The capacity of the Instruments of Communion to engender new life in the Spirit is related to human agency being patterned after the manner of Christ (Phil. 2.5–11). This draws attention to issues to do with character and the virtues tradition as critical components for the operation of the Instruments of Communion.

Ecclesial structure and the polity of God

God's dynamic ordering

How might the dynamics of ecclesial structuring be understood in relation to the polity of God? This may seem an unusual question though it arises out of the conviction that social ordering including its ecclesial forms is not only a contingent feature of human life but is also related, in ways that are difficult to specify, to God's ways with the world. The polity of God (God's ordered life in relation to the world) can be discerned in creation and traced in the work of God in Christ. This, in fact, has been a critical thread in the argument of this book. The supposition is that a theology of ecclesial polity will be built up through understanding how the dynamics of social structuring are related to and informed by the sociality of God present in creation and redemption. This orientation and patterning informs ecclesial order but it is frequently disfigured and unrecognizable due to human failure. One consequence is that the Church is unable to realize and witness to the secret of its own life, which is nothing less than the beauty of the triune God. However, in truth ecclesial order, because of the complex and remarkable environment of God's love in which it operates, is a dynamically structured ordering of life. This arises in the first place because God 'is a dynamically structured relationality in whom there is an infinite possibility of life' (Hardy 1996, p. 186). The polity of such a being cannot be simply 'read off' from revelation and applied in some kind of blueprint manner. Rather, the way in which God's dynamic ordering, that is, God's polity, is woven into the very fabric of creation is infinitely complex and expansive (see Chapter 5). This means that the discernment of ordering, particularly through the constant fractures and eruptions of chaos and new emergent order, is a highly contingent and complex matter. This invests the world and its social structuring with great significance as the environment in which godly order can be discerned and followed. The polity of God can be discerned in creation and traced in the work of God in Christ. We are not bereft of God's witness in the world; indeed it is richly manifest if we have eyes to see.

In the light of the foregoing, the particular task of the Church is to display in its own order (and hence polity) what is true about the world as beloved of God. This makes knowledge and wisdom discovered from ideal social structuring in society a critical referent in understanding the nature of ecclesial polity, its purpose and orientation. Minimally, it points to a dynamic outward directed polity for the Church as it follows the ways of God in the world. This is invariably a transformative and holy movement of God, and this is the fundamental clue for understanding the purpose of ecclesial polity. How it might strive to achieve this and reform itself according to this purpose is a critical issue for the churches today. It will involve a move from a steady-state to a dynamic outward looking polity. The basis for this movement was discussed more fully in Chapter 4 of this book in terms of a renewed sociality.

Systemic defaults in the social structuring of the ecclesia

The theological ground of ecclesial order – polity and ministry – is to be located in the sociality of God. The dynamic structure and energy of this sociality is instantiated in history in the life of Jesus and the Spirit. Yet, specifying how this sociality unfolds in the ordering of society more generally and in the Church is neither simple nor obvious. Indeed, it is quite complex and resistant to full explanation. Saying this is not a justification for abandoning the task of developing and continuing to develop a structure for the *ecclesia* that seeks to follow God's own dynamic action in the world. It just makes it exceedingly complex and this in turn ought to be the occasion for a greater humility among churches that often behave in a competitive manner as if 'our way is better than your way'. Such attitudes presuppose an ontology of order which is overly static if not moribund and certainly does not measure up to a dynamic social form resonant with the dynamism of the Triune God.

Basic defaults: centralist and fragmented

Often, the reasons for the above attitudes arise from the influence of wider patterns of social structuring that are distorted and truncated. The two basic defaults in this regard are (a) into a formal collective type social structure associated with the primacy of the state and/or Church or (b) fragmentation of social structure such that it devolves to the level of the individual (Hardy 1996, p. 173–87). Both moves represent simplifications that ignore or bracket out the complexity of social structure (p. 184). Furthermore, both exclude the middle area occupied by informal structures that mediate between the fragmented and collective structures. In both these defaults, the human being is related only extrinsically to social structure in (a) a commodity like manner in the service of the collective into which persons are absorbed or (b) as an isolated self in a fragmented social market. In both moves, the resultant social structures become reified and no longer contribute to the unfolding of a true society. The reason for this is that they become their own 'arbiters of social coherence; they are no longer relativized by their obligation to promote an ideal true society which is beyond them' (p. 184). These two kinds of simplifications of society establish social cohesion on their own terms and treat 'complexity, pluralism and changeability of the society' as 'alien aberrations'. In like manner, justice is equated with conformity, 'requiring a return to the norms of society, its identity and its enduring character' (pp. 184ff).

Daniel Hardy sees these developments as signs of the marginalization and transference of God's presence and action into social structuring that no longer refers its own inner reality back to God. Furthermore, this displacement infects the Church. Specifically, God is relativized by being only allowed 'extrinsic and occasional relations with social structures and human beings' (p. 183). In short, the abandonment by society of its own responsibility to 'promote true society, replacing it with its own ideality, reflects the supposition that God *is* disengaged from the world'. A theology of society seems neither relevant nor possible. Ecclesiology as a particular discipline to nurture a theology of society in relation to God suffers as a consequence. This usually is manifest by a retreat into an enclosed ecclesiology of Church and loss of reference to the dynamics of social structuring in the world. To this extent, ecclesiology quickly becomes a self-referencing activity and no longer comprehends the movement of God's life in society and indeed the cosmos (for example, Eph. 3.10).

Primacy of the collective

How do the above developments in society (movement to the primacy of the collective/state and the individual) manifest in the life of the Church? In the former, social structuring gives ultimate weight to the primacy of the whole conceived in a centralist, top down fashion. This can operate at both *macro* and *micro* levels. For example, in the Roman Catholic Church, episcopal polity operates in a strong hierarchical form with ultimate authority located in the Papacy with associated curia. Here is an example of an episcopal polity that accords with a highly structured collective type ecclesiology. The axis of authority and power is centrally mediated top down through the bishops.

The challenge for such a polity is to provide sufficient freedom for an upward movement from the ground to contribute to a true and full sociality. For this reason the concept of the *consensus fidelium* (agreement of the faithful) has been important in Roman Catholicism as a complement to the heavy top down mode of decision making which can easily suppress the voice of the people. This is the reason why, in the mid nineteenth century, John Henry Newman would be moved to write as a Catholic (but not as an Anglican) *On Consulting the Faithful in Matters of Doctrine* (Newman 1992). It is also no coincidence that in more recent times a 'receptive ecumenism project' has been initiated by Catholic scholars seeking greater mutual listening among the churches (Murray 2008). Such things point to the importance for highly centralist ecclesiologies of the issue of 'reception'.[7]

---

7 In an Episcopal polity such as Anglicanism reception remains important but in this case the movement is from local to ever-wider circles of acceptance that is facilitated by complex informal and semi-formal structures at provincial and wider levels.

When ecclesial life gives primacy to the formal collective mode, the dynamic of ecclesial order remains incomplete and distorted. The structuring of ecclesial life is truncated and unable to generate full freedom of the baptized in relation to God. This impacts negatively on the quality of the pilgrimage of the people of God. This top-down collectivist type ecclesial form is mirrored at the micro level where large or for that matter smaller ecclesial units (congregation; independent churches) that eschew episcopal polity nonetheless operate with highly structured top-down hierarchical authority systems that have the same negative impact on the pilgrimage of the people of God.

Primacy of the individual

The other contemporary default into fragmentation with emphasis on the primacy of the individual has numerous ecclesial forms. These are most commonly associated with Protestant and modern Pentecostal varieties. Historically, this default appeared positively as an assertion of the right of *private judgement* in matters of faith and in Pentecostal churches is referred to a theology of the Spirit. This ethos was in accord with an Enlightenment spirit that extolled personal autonomy and freedom from externally imposed authority (Kant 1996). The spirit of the age dovetailed nicely with Protestantism as it developed from the seventeenth century. The plethora of newly emergent denominational churches, while retaining many of the controlling habits of Rome, were always in danger of dissolving and crumbling into smaller and smaller units under the power of the Enlightenment turn to the subject. Polities of a congregational type have on this account struggled to maintain their formal structures. This is evidenced in the repeated divisions and offshoots they have spawned. To the extent that this has been a feature of Protestantism, it bears testimony to the reaction to over formalized institutional ecclesial forms in favour of more fragmented and relatively unstructured ecclesial forms. The challenge has always been and remains for such polities how they can harness the freedoms they espouse in the service of a greater whole. The supposedly freer structured ecclesial forms have not necessarily delivered a Christian pilgrimage marked by true freedom but rather often new kinds of constraints. Freedom from episcopal polity has not ensured freedom for God. The default into more fragmented ecclesial forms, like the particular collectivist type ecclesiology of Rome, fails to generate a rich dynamic ecclesial order.

Informal structures and ecclesial vitality

Interestingly, it is the informal domain of social structuring that appears to be evacuated in the above defaults. However, this intermediate level is a critical component in the healthy functioning of society and especially institutions. The informal is the domain of customs, accepted values, common and/or conventional practices, beliefs, social networks, cultures, and norms (that rest alongside, challenge or reinforce more formal structures), well-formed habits and social relations that are not determined by law and formal rule (cf. Prell et al. 2010). Such informal levels of social structuring generate capacity for social cohesion and provide networks for dealing with conflict and enabling change. Informal social structuring is at least as important as formal structures for the wellbeing of an institution.

In the Church, the domain of the informal is a vital ingredient given the voluntary nature of this society. The informal is the region of shared cultures; of the everyday and 'ordinary' way in which beliefs, values and customs circulate through common practices. It gives rise to notions of ecclesial cultures with their own peculiarities that are full of meaning and emotion and exert considerable influence on individuals and the shape and direction of social action within more formal ecclesial structures of governance.[8] We ignore the importance of the informal at our peril.

In the churches of the Anglican Communion, for example, this informal level has been critical for the wellbeing and mission of the Church. It comes under the rubric of 'bonds of affection'. When

8 For an insightful introduction to the way in which informal Church cultures operate and their significance for the Church and its engagements; see Percy 2005.

these are strained or begin to break down the Church has great difficulty in functioning because it does not have a strong centralized legal structure like Rome (Cameron 2007).[9] Anglicanism typically operates through common practices that resonate across cultures and geographical areas. Moreover it is essentially a 'ground up' ecclesiology most at home in the vernacular rather than through formalized codes of law. This means that it invests heavily in the nurture of an ecclesial intelligence that includes the creation of spaces and places for the free flow of communication, however unwelcome or difficult (Percy 2010, pp. 152–5).

One of the critical challenges for contemporary churches is to develop their particular polities to reflect a multi-layered social structuring that includes the three domains: formal, informal and fragmented. The informal is the domain that connects formal and fragmented; it mediates new possibilities and is focused on high quality face-to-face interactions. It can give substance and integrity to the formal structuring and retrieves fragmented events into the realm of communal action. The domain of the informal operates whether intentionally or not and to this extent is an inescapable feature of social structuring. However, from an ecclesiological point of view the domain of the informal is either accorded programmatic significance in an espoused and operant ecclesiology or it remains muted at best and occurs despite and often in the face of resistance from more formal levels of structure.

How might polity be organized in order to achieve a healthy social structuring for the Church that includes formal, informal and fragmented domains? This remains a task on the agenda of the churches. In our contemporary context – which defaults so easily and 'naturally' into formal and fragmented social forms – it is exceedingly difficult for any particular church to develop its formal governance and ministry in such a way that it facilitates a full and free life for the baptized in their everyday and informal networks

---

9 Interestingly, the 'bonds of affection' seem to belong to the whole of the Communion no matter what particular sectional interest is in mind, whether liberal, conservative or middle of the road. For example, see William 2005.

and interrelations. Yet, this is precisely what ideal polity at the formal levels ought to be geared towards and enable. Specifically, what seems to be required to meet the challenges of an anxious and divided society and Church are polities that intentionally factor into their social structuring significant space for capacity for transformative action and new possibilities to emerge. This accords with an approach to ecclesial polity that is fundamentally emergent and capacity building for the institution and its interaction with the wider environment.

A theology of polity: the ecclesiology of Richard Hooker

Structure and differentiation in the one Church

In the light of the foregoing, I want to briefly consider an example of a threefold form of social structure embedded in the ecclesiology of the late sixteenth century theologian and apologist for Church of England, Richard Hooker (1554–1600). Hooker contributed to an emergent Reformed Catholic ecclesiology at a time of significant upheaval in English Christianity. He attempted to articulate an ecclesiology to make sense of the Church of Tudor and post-Tudor England. From this point of view his ecclesiological interest was in developing a viable theology of polity marked by unity and freedom. Of course, his effort only makes sense within (a) the particular political concerns for the autonomy of a national Church in relation to the excessive claims of jurisdictional authority by Rome, (b) the emergence of tensions within the English reform movement between puritan, traditionalist and moderate positions regarding the polity of the Church and (c) the fact of division between Rome and various Protestant Churches.

Richard Hooker's ecclesiology was carefully articulated in the opening chapters of his Third Book on *The Laws of Ecclesiastical Polity* (1954). The first thing to note is the reference to 'laws of polity'. For Hooker, the concept of 'law' was 'a directive rule unto goodness of operation' (1.8.4). This view was at variance with a notion of law as external authority. Concerning this latter view he had said:

173

They who are accustomed to speak apply the name law unto that only rule of working which superior authority imposeth; whereas we somewhat more enlarging the sense thereof term any kind of rule or canon, whereby actions are framed, a law. (I.III.I)

Accordingly, the laws of polity concerned the inner guidance mechanisms (directive rule) that framed actions that enabled the goodness of an operation – in this case, the good functioning and faithful witness of the visible Church of God. Such law belonged to a rich hierarchy of norms that covered biology, psychology, ethical, social, legal scriptural and angelic law. However, 'Hooker held that all of these norms were creaturely participations in a more fundamental, eternal law based on God's very being' (McGrade 2009, p. 422). Moreover, divine law could not be reduced to a command and obedience type, but also embraced the providential way in which creation was ordered towards its end in God. Already in this, polity and law cannot be restricted to purely formal levels of operation but clearly envisages established custom and ways of relating that bond and orientate the society of the Church.

How did this kind of ecclesial polity unfold regarding the visible structuring of the Church? Hooker made a careful distinction between a 'sound' and a 'corrupted' visible Church:

For lack of diligent observing the difference, first between the Church of God mystical and visible, then between the visible sound and corrupted, sometimes more, sometimes less, the oversights are neither few nor light that have been committed. (III.I.9)

As a result, Hooker considered that heretics, unlike infidels, belonged to the visible Church in its corruption because the former embraced the principles of Christianity though they erred 'by misdirection', and as such remained 'a maimed part, yet a part of the visible Church' (III.2.I). While heresy unrepented of excluded one from the mystical Church, errors and faults, even heretical ones to do with outward profession, only separated one from the visible 'sound' Church. This might not sound that radical to our sensibilities. However, it was controversial in the sixteenth century with regard to the status of Rome. Hooker's argument meant that the Roman Church, though corrupted, nonetheless belonged to the Church visible. Hooker came to this conclusion on the basis that the Roman doctrine of works did not 'directly' overturn the foundation of faith but 'consequently by addition' and thus was lodged in the 'superstructure' at some remove from the foundation of faith which consisted of the 'very few fundamental words' of the Apostolic Creed.[10] An important pastoral implication of this more generous ecclesiology was that 'the fathers of old' could be saved in the Roman Church.

The ecclesiological focus for Hooker was, as identified in Chapter 4, on the unity of the visible Church constituted by one Lord, one faith and one baptism (Eph. 4.4–6). The unity of faith was sufficiently encapsulated in the ancient ecumenical creed and enacted liturgically through baptism. The emphasis was thus upon unity with maximum inclusiveness. This points to a unity grounded in a baptismal ecclesiology that is essentially open and generous.

Polity, scripture and freedom

How was Hooker's ecclesial ideal to be incarnated in a particular polity? The matter came to the fore in Hooker's controversies with 'moderate Puritans' who were part of the Church of England. The issue turned on whether scripture laid down one

---

10 For Hooker's exposition of the doctrine of justification and works and the status of Rome, see his 1585 sermon 'Of Justification, Works, and how the Foundation of Faith is overthrown' in Vol. 1 of the Everyman edition of *Of The Laws of Ecclesiastical Polity*, especially paras. 22–36. This was a more generous view compared to the Anglican divine William Perkins (1558–1602), who wrote in *A Reformed Catholic* (1598) that the errors of Rome had 'razed the foundation' of faith so much so that Rome was no longer a member of the catholic Church. For further see I. Breward, ed., *The Works of William Perkins*, Appleford, Abingdon and Berkshire, England: The Sutton Courtenay Press, 1970, Vol. 3, pp. 263–275, 519–47.

complete form of polity that had to be maintained as necessary to salvation. Hooker's answer was a corollary of his doctrine of the unity of the Church; that is, visible unity was not required in anything more than the outward profession of one Lord, one faith and one baptism. Thus, the Church was free as regards matters of ecclesiastical polity, by which he meant 'a form of ordering the public spiritual affairs of the Church of God' (III.1.14; cf. III.10.20). The necessity of polity in all Churches did not imply 'any one certain form to be necessary in them all' (III.2.1). This approach to polity presupposed a distinction between matters of governance and matters of faith. The former belonged to the 'accessories':

> those things that are accessory hereunto, those things that so belong to the way of salvation, as to alter them is no otherwise than to change that way, than a path is changed by altering the uppermost face thereof; which be it laid with gravel, or set with grass, or paved with stone, remaineth still a path; in such things because discretion may teach the Church what is convenient, we hold not the Church further tied herein unto Scripture, than that against Scripture nothing be admitted in the Church, lest that path which ought always to be kept even do thereby come to be overgrown with brambles and thorns. (III.2.3)

It was a simple enough distinction that continues as a central plank of Anglican ecclesiology and approach to polity. Importantly, for Hooker it was undergirded by a view of the hierarchy of laws of life and being that included both positive commands of scripture and the light of reason. Since neither could be in contradiction to the other because they both derived ultimately from God, the Church could have confidence to make judgements concerning the particulars of polity in the absence of any positive scriptural requirements. The Puritan desire to claim a positive-law-status for what were in fact human laws based on general scriptural rules betrayed a mistrust of the capacity of human reason to participate in things, in Hooker's view, divine (III.7.4).

Of course, in the context of the times, the much vexed question of the legitimacy of episcopal polity represented the sharp point of Puritan criticisms. Hooker offered a rationale for the retention of the ancient order of episcopacy without succumbing to the Puritan argument that such a polity had to be clearly commanded in scripture. For those of Puritan persuasion Presbyterianism was the only legitimate form of polity positively commanded by scripture. While Hooker's own position on episcopacy remains a matter of conjecture, it does seem clear that he viewed episcopal polity as a matter of divine providence and of benefit for the Church over its history and as such to be retained.[11]

Hooker's ecclesiology granted significant freedom to a particular national Church to organize its governance and internal relations. It was an ecclesial vision that presupposed the participation of human agents in the providential ordering of the visible Church of God. This theology of the Church undergirded and nurtured – in principle at least, given the constraints of Tudor England – a relatively free and open ecclesial polity. It invited a fully responsible Church of the baptized and the supposition that the 'full and complete measure of things necessary [for salvation] remained an open matter (1.14.2).[12]

Hooker and contemporary Anglican polity

In the context of a baptismal ecclesiology, with a heavy investment in human participation in the discernment of God's ways

---

11 McGrade states: 'In Book VII, although he claimed divine approval and probable direct divine inspiration for episcopacy, he strikingly did not conclude from this divine right of bishops was immutable. The endurance of episcopal authority has depended essentially on the fact that the Church "hath found it good and requisite to be so governed" (Laws VII.5.8; FLE [Folger Library Edition] 3.168)'. (2009, p. 428). Cf. discussion in Avis 1989, pp. 57–60.

12 Thus the Roman Catholic scholar George Tavard observes that Hooker 'restores to Anglican theology a dimension that has largely been lost: he reopens Anglican thought to a conception of doctrine as a developing awareness of Scripture in the Church's experience' (1963, p. 40).

in the world and an openness to following the truth of God wherever it may be discovered, it was axiomatic that Richard Hooker had sown the seeds for a highly conciliar and public polity intended for the benefit of the whole of society.[13] This, in fact, is precisely what has continued to develop in the history of Anglicanism though never in a smooth and seamless manner. It has meant that present day Anglican polity exhibits a high degree of loose ends, informal networks and heavy reliance on consent, common practices, 'bonds of affection' and 'the practice of the virtues in a political community'. It is thus an example of an ecclesial body that self-consciously includes the three dimensions of social structuring in its life in the world: formal, informal and fragmented.

The development of synodical government at diocesan and provincial levels – including lay and clerical as well as episcopal voices – and a resistance to extra provincial legally binding regulations is entirely in keeping with the ecclesiology of a one and free Church espoused by a theologian of 'classical' Anglicanism. It leads to a polity informed by a 'graced sociality' that is marked by a generous liberty and a commitment to persuasion rather than coercion (Sedgwick 1996, pp. 197, 202). It means that, as Daniel Hardy has stated, 'Anglican ecclesial polity is a sophisticated dynamic of interconnections, one which spells out a theological–ecclesiological contribution to the emergence of civil society. It claims neither completeness nor infallibility, but – in the provenance of God – the capacity to bring free, moral agents together by their common consent in a fashion which mediates the character of God and God's saving grace in human society' (1996a, pp. 338f). Hardy goes on to note that the 'visible means by which it achieves these purposes are not so much theoretical as liturgical and practical–political. These are the ways by which

---

13 Thus Hooker could state in The *Laws of Ecclesiastical Polity*: 'Behold therefore we offer the laws whereby we live unto the general trial and judgement of the whole world' (1.1.3; cf. 1.8.3). In the Preface to *Ecclesiastical Polity*, the issues of publicness and consent are key elements in the establishment of socially binding laws (Preface Ch. 5, paras. 2 and 6).

the purposes of God are enfolded into human community in the created order, and thereby unfolded into human society at large' (p. 339). In short, Anglican polity is orientated to 'affect the whole of life' rather than preoccupation with an enclosed ecclesiastical circle. In this way, the social structuring of its ecclesial life is intended to serve the freedom of society for the purposes of God.

Conclusion: polity within a renewed sociality

This chapter has argued that ecclesial structure – its polity and ministry – is most effective and true to its purpose when it operates as a dynamic and transformative structure at a number of interrelated levels; formal, informal and fragmented. The fact that there are many different kinds of polities among the churches with differing emphases and weighting as regards the above three-fold structuring is to be expected. The social world of the Church generates a variety of institutional arrangements by virtue of differing historical and cultural circumstances. Each particular form of Church governance and associated customs, values and communicative patterns seeks to be faithful to the call of Christian discipleship. This does not mean that all forms of polity are of equal strength. Indeed, the different polities ought to be open to critique and reform particularly as the Church reflects on its encounter with the world. It is also the case that, as I have alluded to in part in this chapter, every form of polity has its particular strengths and weaknesses.

In this chapter, I outlined Richard Hooker's theology of polity as an example of a multileveled structuring of ecclesial life. Other examples might also have been articulated if space had permitted. My purpose in writing about Hooker's vision for the Church was to show how the dynamics of social structuring discussed earlier in the chapter might be understood from an ecclesiological point of view.

However, if there is one aspect of polity that I would want to highlight in these concluding remarks it would be to reiterate the significance of the *dynamic* and *direction* of polity as much as the *what* of polity. I flagged this at the outset. It concerns the orientation of ecclesial polity, that is, the extent to which it gears the Church for an outward and expansive movement following God's purposes in the world. Polity can easily be interpreted as a formal set of rules or legal codes that operate in a highly deterministic fashion. This is similar to the positive command type approach to laws that Richard Hooker expressly rejected in favour of laws that enabled the 'goodness of an operation'. This same kind of dynamic teleological approach to polity emerges in current theorizing about the nature of social structuring. As we have observed earlier in this chapter contemporary social theorists focus on social structure that enables action as well as constrains; that emerges from within the dynamics of societal life as much as is crafted by it; that recognizes the critical contribution of human agency in all social structuring and finally emphasizes communicative competence as a marker of the quality of polity.

It is for the above reasons that the chapter was titled 'Structured for freedom'. The Church of God is not self-sufficient and nor does it exist for itself but as the former Archbishop of Canterbury William Temple once said 'the Church is the only institution that exists for non-members'. This justly famous remark captures the missional mood of our times and challenges ecclesial polity at its core. How might the Church's polity be structured to free the baptized for their calling to discipleship in the world? How might the polity of the Church be structured and operate to enable the Church to display the 'goodness of an operation' in the world for which Christ the Lord died and rose again? In short the Church is called to recover the liberty of the sons and daughters of God. The particular polities it both inhabits and creates ought to serve this end.

The emphasis upon a polity of liberty is a vital component of the kind of renewed sociality discussed in Chapter 4 of this book. Indeed this chapter can be interpreted as a more concrete specification of the form and dynamic appropriate for a renewed ecclesial existence in the world. In terms of Chapter 6 on the marks of the Church, the question of polity has to be assessed in terms of its capacity to exhibit in theory and practice what the one, holy, catholic and apostolic Church might look like. Either from the point of view of a renewed sociality and/or consideration of polity in terms of the marks of the Church, polity is neither an 'add-on' or afterthought. Nor is polity a necessary but not intrinsic dimension to what has become popularly known as 'mission shaped Church'. Rather the form and dynamic of ecclesial polity will be a measure of the capacity and willingness of the Church to be God's agent of freedom for the peoples of the world. However such agency requires considerable energy and discipline and it is to this matter that we now turn our attention.

Questions

1 In what sense must the Church's structure and order be biblical?
2 What is the relationship between the structure of the Church and its mission in the world?
3 'Structure, polity, governance, ministry'; how do these terms relate to each other in the doctrine of the church?
4 What evidence is there in the churches today that structure fulfils an *enabling* compared to a *constraining* function?
5 How important for the purpose of the Church are its 'informal' structures (customs, values, bonds etc)?
6 What are the strengths and weaknesses of Richard Hooker's theology of polity?

Further reading

Leonardo Boff, *Church: Charism and Power*, New York: Cross-road, 1988, Ch. 13 on 'An Alternative Structure: Charism as the Organizing Principle'.
Brad Harper and Paul Louise Metzger, 'The Church as an Ordered Community', in *Exploring Ecclesiology: An Evangelical and Ecumenical Introduction*, Grand Rapids, MI: Brazos Press, 2009, pp. 183–200.
Mary Hines, 'Community for Liberation – Church', in Catherine Mowry LaCugna (ed.), *Freeing Theology: The Essentials of*

Theology in Feminist Perspective, New York: HarperCollins, 1993, pp. 161–81.

Peter Sedgwick, 'On Anglican Polity', in David F. Ford and Dennis Stamps (eds), *Essentials of Christian Community*, Edinburgh: T & T Clark, 1996, pp. 213–25.

Stephen Sykes, 'Episcopé and Power in the Church', in *Unashamed Anglicanism*, London: Darton, Longman and Todd, 1996, pp. 178–98.

Natalie K. Watson, 'Beyond Clericalism: Grappling with the Ordained Ministry', in *Introducing Feminist Ecclesiology*, Cleveland, OH: The Pilgrim Press, 2002, pp. 66–77.

8

Energy for the Journey

The ordered energy of God

An attractive spiritual energy

The late Daniel Hardy stated that:

> there is an ordered energy that is perpetually self-generating
> and fully self-replenishing all the time. We use labels like
> 'ordered energy', or 'word in spirit', 'Trinity', or 'God', but
> these are not just labels for something that is there. They name
> that which of its nature is infinite, endless and expansive, to
> which the only possible response is not to name it but to follow
> it into the depths. You can say of it only that it is what attracts.
> (2010, p. 46)

Hardy's reflection on energy is the point of departure for this
chapter. He wants to speak about the inbuilt created attraction
of all things towards God. Attraction to others 'characterizes the
inherent sociality of all creation' (p. 49). Long before humans
fabricate and construct social processes to generate and shape
relations there is a condition of 'towardness', which is 'even
more basic than creation and redemption', such that one 'cannot expunge towardness from the condition of things' (p. 47).
The reason is that *sociopoiesis* – 'the generation and shaping of
relations' – 'operates in the divine, so that it is a dimension of all
things always' (p. 49). Thus, the movement towards others and
all things towards God is originiative to the divine, and hence,
sociopoiesis 'is always in the divine energy'.

The 'ordered energy' that marks our pilgrimage in the world towards God is a spiritual energy that derives from the energetic being of God (cf. Mills 2011). Precisely because it is from God, it is dynamic and transformative in such a way that creation (including human life) is changed from within. The attractive energy of the Triune God is the original and transformative energy at work in the generating and shaping of a renewed sociality in God (Chapters 4 and 5). *The Church is, on this account, that body of people formed by and drawn towards God through the ordered energetics of God's own life.* The structural forms and polities associated with this ecclesial movement (Chapter 7) cannot be reduced to human constructs designed for pragmatic purposes – they are that but much more. In some sense, structure mediates, embodies and orders divine energy. This means that structure and energy are not antithetical to each other; indeed they are co-related, complementary and mutually involving.

This brief reflection on energy, attraction and ecclesial structure is the backdrop for the concern of this chapter on worship, word, sacraments and witness. I want to develop an understanding of these constituents of ecclesial existence in terms of God's holy energy renewing personal life and society. In this sense, I am concerned to clarify and deepen understanding of those ecclesial means (worship, word, sacrament and witness), through which a renewed sociality is achieved.

Energy as capacity for work

Energy is the capacity to do work.[1] This involves movement and transformation. However, the laws of thermodynamics presume a closed system, which lacks the capacity for self-replenishment and creation of new energy. On the other hand, there are developments in modern science such as the recognition of randomness, chance and chaos that suggest that 'the fundamental state of

---

1 For background to the development of the concept of energy from Aristotle see Smil 2008.

the universe is non-equilibrial' (Hardy and Ford 1984, p. 118). It raises a question: 'What if all the randomness and the constraints point to an inexhaustible capacity for richness, complexity, and order continually transcending itself?' Hardy and Ford conclude that 'it seems more in accord with the overall picture of reality to see the universe as an abundant allowance of space, time and energy through which new abundance can happen'.

The supposition of an energy abundant universe that does not operate in a closed system coheres with a theological vision of a universe, the source of which lies in the indeterminable and infinitely expansive working (energetics) of God (John 5.17). This leads to the possibility of endless capacity for self-replenishment and creation of new sources of energy and consequent capacity to do work and effect change (John 14.12). However, within this wider context for considering energy there is significant scope to draw upon wisdom from the sciences regarding the nature of energy transformation; energy density, conservation and power; the dynamics of energy flows, dispersal and entropy; and potentials for renewable energy. These rich concepts arise from observation and testing of the phenomena of the created order. Yet, this order is itself sustained and replenished by the energetics of God's ways with the world. The conceptual apparatus of energy from the domain of the sciences is similarly available for theological inquiry into the practices of the Church that attend to the crucified Lord of Glory.

Resurrection energy as discontinuity

The Gospel's' climax is the resurrection. In terms of energy, here is a clue to the constitution of the created order; more particu- larly its capacity in God for replenishment and re-creation. This capacity goes beyond the continuities of nature associated with notions of emergence (associated with the First and Second Laws of Physics, which presuppose energy depletion) and suggests the importance of *discontinuity* and *irreducibly new processes* as primary. In this scenario, energy is continually replenished. From this perspective, the resurrection is not an alien intrusion into the laws of science regarding *energeia* but rather a sign of 'a more radical and underlying discontinuity as is denoted by the *transformation* of the universe by a new act of God *ex vetera* (Russell 2002, p. 22). What it leads to, is a conception of the energetics of the paschal mystery of Christ; the source of healing, reconciliation and renewal (see Moule 2010). Characteristically, this involves an energy transfer without diminishment of capacity. In Luke's Gospel power [*dynamis*] flows out from Jesus to repair and transform (Luke 6.19). In this case, the conversion of concentrated energy occurs rapidly which leads to a conception of a 'power flow' (where power is the rate at which energy is converted or work performed).

The capacity for replenishment and expansion of energy characterized the life of the early Church (Acts 1–6). In this case, the expansion of energy from a concentrated source did not lead to less energy available. The good news was transformative and re-creative (without diminishment or lack), and the Apostle Paul was in no doubt that its origin was to be traced to Jesus Christ, '[God's] Son, who was descended from David according to the flesh and was declared to be Son of God with power [*dynamis*] according to the Spirit of holiness by the resurrection from the dead, Jesus Christ our Lord' (Rom. 1.3–4).

In the Christian tradition, energy as the capacity for work undergoes a revolution arising from the energetics of God's holy love in Christ and the Spirit. The Eastern Orthodox appeal to the divine energies might be quite fruitful at this point, for it suggests a 'sort of penumbra of glory, or a field of energy that surrounds the Trinitarian Godhead. In this way, the universe can be considered as lying within God's field of energy or "field of resonance", while at the same time remaining distinct from and contingent upon God's super-essentiality. Within this penumbra or energy-field, there is a resonating and quickening of the natural, material universe, so that the material order is drawn into the experience – however we may understand "experience" – of God' (Reid 1995, p. 133). This perspective on the doctrine of grace presupposes a doxological movement from humans towards God as a complement to a movement of God towards the world in the Trinitarian missions. Both movements are co-present and mutually involving, and both presume a superabundance of God's holy and energetic ordering of all things in heaven and on earth. It is this double energetic movement *from* and *towards* God in the Spirit of Christ, which informs and shapes Christian worship, the media through which this occurs (such as word and sacrament) and witness in the world. In short, the energies of the Triune God are the way, the truth and the life of Christian pilgrimage. The rest of this chapter teases out some of the implications of the foregoing in relation to the basic constituents of Christian pilgrimage beginning with worship.

The energetics of worship

The nature of worship

'Worship is the simplest and most basic constitutive element of religion, and virtually co-extensive with it. In its primary sense, it designates the response evoked by that which is recognized as the source of all order and energy in existence' (Hardy 1996b, p. 896). From an everyday perspective, worship may be described as loving others in the presence of God and loving God in the presence of others. Minimally, this involves an orientation of persons and communities towards the One who calls forth and capacitates such a response. Accordingly, the energetics of worship are mutually involving being at once generated from the divine yet at the same time entailing a human response that emerges from within. Yet, even this response 'is not self-generated but elicited by the quality of what or who is recognized, by a glory whose plenitude elevates the human faculties responding to it'. On this account, worship presupposes divine proximity and grace. This understanding of worship arises from the basic meaning of the word 'worship' from the Old English *weorth-scipe*, 'the condition [in a person] of deserving, or being held in, esteem or repute'. In this approach, the energetics of worship is located in the divine character and leads to a theology of worship grounded in grace.

In another sense, worship is a human activity whereby all life is brought into relation 'to that which has such abundance of being and other perfections as to make it constitutive for life itself'. This leads to a conception of worship as the 'reconstitution of all proximate life' by reference to the divine abundance. This latter understanding of worship is associated with the emergence of the humanistic culture of modern Renaissance Europe. With greater intensity from the twentieth-century worship has been 'assimilated to the human task of constructing a full life'. In this context, worship is the mode that activates, properly establishes and empowers the myriad activities of human life. This includes religious forms such as rituals, symbols, doctrine and moral practices as well as more general features such as reason, understanding and ethical behaviour (p. 897).

The above reflections on worship point to its constitutive role for human pilgrimage towards God. In worship, human beings are maximally opened toward the divine and each other. It is the activity for the recreating and shaping of the manifold relations of life. As such, worship opens the worshippers to the domain of high-density energy. In worship, this is released in an outward directed energy flow. What happens? Essentially, an energy transfer takes place through which life is orientated towards God and reconstituted by God. The change is ongoing and does not dissipate though it resists exact measure and close tracking. Furthermore, in this transfer human beings are raised into the holiness of God's life; akin to the process of sanctification. The Christian pattern of worship follows the resurrection of Christ, where the principal energetic agent is the Spirit of holiness (Rom. 1.3–4). For this reason, in Christian theology, energy is neither content-less nor arbitrary in operation, but turns the body of Christ towards God and the world simultaneously. It does this in a manner, which raises all things to their true being and purpose in God. Worship effects a holy and ordered release of infinite divine energy as worshippers are drawn into the orbit of God's presence through the action of the Spirit. This evokes praise and adoration. Much more needs to be said about this fundamental character of worship as understood in the Christian tradition though space does not permit this.

Worship and the energetics of praise

How then do human beings participate in the activity of worship? Because the source and ground of worship is the infinite beauty, truth and goodness of God the primary mode in which worship occurs is, as stated above, through praise and adoration. Praise of God is fundamental to human existence and is the source of boundless energy. This sense is captured well in Augustine's famous prayer at the beginning of the *Confessions*: 'Great are you, O Lord, and exceedingly worthy of praise; your power is immense, and your wisdom beyond reckoning. And so we humans, who are a due part of your creation, long to praise you – we also carry our mortality about with us, carry the evidence of our sin and with it the proof that you thwart the proud. You arouse us so that praising you may bring us joy, because you have made us and drawn us to yourself, and our heart is unquiet until it rests in you.'

In the twentieth century, Karl Barth stated that the first and 'special ministry' of the community of faith was its 'office to praise God' (1962, p. 865). The orientation of this activity was towards God: 'To praise God, as a function in the ministry of the Christian community, is to affirm, acknowledge, approve, extol and laud both the being of God as the One who in his eternal majesty has become man, and the action in which He has taken man, all men[sic] to Himself in His omnipotent mercy.' Such praise constitutes the purpose and *raison d'être* of the Church, and fills 'a yawning gulf in the life of the world'. The logic of praise – 'praise perfects perfection' – leads to a notion of 'overflow' and 'spiral of praise' and blessing (Hardy and Ford 1984, Ch. 2). However, central in this movement is the origin of praise within the infinite plenitude of the Divine Being. The very act of praise generates awareness of shortcomings and *confession* that opens us to the goodness of God in Christ who forgives and re-energizes us in the Spirit of love. In this process, *thanksgiving* arises as a response to the movement of God towards us; a thanksgiving that issues forth in intercessory prayer and *petition*. This is a way of sharing in the work (*energeia*) of Jesus Christ (Hardy 1996b, pp. 897–8).

The praise of God has a history, and this points to a continuing act of remembering (*anamnesis*) God's ways with the world in Christ and the Spirit. In this re-membering, the richness and vitality of the energies of God the Lord are reappropriated. This reminds us that the energy present in worship comes from an ever-renewable source. This source is nothing less than the holy God and can be tracked in the biblical and liturgical traditions of Israel. This same source is breathed again as blessing upon the world in Jesus Christ and is the ground and possibility of Christian worship.

When worship is manifest in the drama of Christian liturgy, it has the character of 'performance', though this might be more accurately identified as an ongoing rehearsal 'because it [worship] is the place where we rehearse "putting on Christ"' (Ross 2010, p. 195). Rehearsal points to well-honed practice, the formation of habits and orientations and growth in wisdom that has evolved through the joys and sorrows of life in the world. This makes liturgical worship at once 'inescapably *incarnational*' and also orientated to a fuller 'eschatological performance' of the praise of God (p. 196). Worship is the place and the possibility of abundant divine energy.

The media of worship: word and sacrament

The energy for the praise of God is generated by the infinite and all-encompassing plenitude of God. However, this divine energy displays an inner order and structure witnessed to in the Christian tradition. In Irenaean terms, the 'two hands of God' (Word and Spirit) represent the twin co-ordinates for tracking the energetics of divine life in relation to the world. Christian worship is shaped at its core by this double reference to Christ and the Spirit that gives to the body of Christ its charismatic character with its associated sense of 'play' (Suurmond 1994, pp. 189–213). Indeed, it is the deep patterning of divine life manifest in the life death and resurrection of Christ and the ever-replenishing outflow of the Spirit, which have provided a recurring Trinitarian pattern for Christian worship and discipleship. Moreover, this Trinitarian pattern has energized a constant testimony to the ways in which the holy Triune God blesses and transforms the world.

What are the determinate forms through which this pattern is concentrated and hence realized? I state the matter like this because the notion that there is energy floating around in some reified form but essentially unconnected to the material order and the ways in which human beings live is a peculiarly modern and influential notion that lies behind the decline in the significance of worship in the modern period.[2] However, a Trinitarian theology of worship and discipleship informed and shaped by the eternal Spirit of love and the incarnation of the *logos* of God invests the determinate forms of word and sacrament with great significance. Word and sacrament become primary concentrations for the realization of the energy of God. Because this divine energy is ordered in relation to the holy character of Christ, and the power of the Spirit, word and sacrament are properly understood as concentrated forms of divine wisdom to which all things are being drawn and assimilated.

Logos *as energetic wisdom*

Creation is born of the energetic and structured divine word: 'Then God said: "Let there be light"; and there was light' (Gen. 1.3). Chapter 1 of the Book of Genesis reveals a highly differentiated and interrelated cosmos at each stage realizing the character and movement of the originating source. In this way, creation manifests the wisdom of the *logos* of God. Importantly, *logos* and Spirit (*ruach*) are mutually involved in this work of the creator;

---

2 Indeed, a particular challenge in developing a theological understanding of energy (as in the present chapter) is to avoid treating energy as reified or substance-like.

for the word that creates is premised on the Spirit that hovers and moves (Gen. 1.2). Calvin, arguing for the divinity of the Spirit, poetically stated that the Spirit was there at the beginning 'tending that confused mass'.[3] Creation is a form of dissipation into extensity of divine energies; it becomes spread out and available in new forms and places but without diminution of capacity – more like a repetition of plenitude in which it is magnified.

The intrinsic dynamic of this *logos* reality is recapitulated in the prologue to John's Gospel (John 1.1–4). Here, a remarkable energy transfer occurs such that the eternal creative word becomes flesh (John 1.14). The result is a highly concentrated, high-density embodiment of the second person of the Trinity. Unimaginable plenitude in compressed (bodily) form: 'For in him all the fullness [*pleroma*] of God was pleased to dwell' (Col. 1.19) 'in bodily form' (Col. 2.9). What is remarkable is that the plenitude of energy and wisdom that characterizes the work of the *logos* in creation is not dissipated but concentrated in a structured energetic form in the incarnation. God, who is Spirit, is in the second person of the Trinity, embodied in the incarnate *logos*, Jesus Christ. In this movement of God towards creation, the relationship between energy and structure is co-related; the structuring of the energy has a Christ-like form and the energetics of the structure are pneumatological. Word and Spirit cannot be over against one another, nor in parallel but interwoven. Divine energy and structure have a Trinitarian form that is displayed liturgically in the celebration of the sacraments and especially in the Eucharist. But more of this later.

The capacity of the divine word to create *ex nihilo* was the basis for Luther's conception of the Church as a *creatura verbi divini* (creature of the divine word) (Schwöbel 1989, p. 110). This Christological grounding of the Church cannot stand alone without reference to the agency of the Spirit. The reason for this,

---

3 *The Institutes of the Christian Religion in The Library of Christian Classics*, Vol. 20, John T. McNeill (ed.), Ford Lewis Battles translation, Philadelphia: Westminster Press, p.138 (Bk. 1, Ch. 14). Other translations refer to 'cherishing' the creation.

according to Luther, is that the word of God that evokes faith and brings to birth the *ecclesia* 'only happens when the Spirit authenticates the Gospel of Christ as the truth about the relationship of God the creator to his creation'. There is a consistent trace here in the twin co-ordinates for the divine creative energy from creation through incarnation (Luke 1.35) to the Church.

The energy realized through the word of God is multiple rather than singular. It was Karl Barth, in the twentieth century, who referred to the threefold word of God: the eternal word revealed in the incarnate Jesus Christ; the written testimony to the revelation of Christ and the proclaimed Christ (1936, pp. 88–124). This conception of the *viva vox evangelii* – the 'living voice of the gospel' in threefold form – implies a dynamic interplay between the three forms and an associated movement and energy exchange that constantly overflows and expands. In the process, it draws more and more people into the circle of God's trust, freedom and joy (Acts 1–4). These are conditions of high energy density, and remarkable capacity for conversion of potential energy into actual transformation of peoples and places. The result is that the word of God increases (or 'expands' or 'multiplies'; Acts 6.7). Where the dynamic interplay is subverted or blocked – which happens when one form is dislocated or sealed from the other forms of the word – the first thing that occurs is dissipation of energy. The natural replenishment of energy is blocked, because the focus shifts from the source in the plenitude of God's being to the forms though which this plenitude is realized. This can be observed, for example, in certain forms of scripturalism wherein the richness of scripture is reformatted into standard doctrinal themes that leech out the vitality and energy of the written word.

Holy Scripture

The foregoing dynamic of the *logos* suggests that the Holy Scriptures represent a rich and powerful source of energy and wisdom. It is for this reason that Scripture is so vital for the Church's worship, discipleship, evangelism and mission. Much of course has been written concerning the Scriptures, and space is limited here.

I want to consider briefly how we might understand the way in which Scripture represents a form of energy for life. To this end I am struck by the words of the Anglican Collect traditionally used on the Second Sunday in Advent and now on the Last Sunday after Trinity (*Common Worship: Daily Prayer* 2005, p. 442). It is a prayer that reveals the mode in which energy transfer takes place in relation to Scripture and hearer:

Blessed Lord,
Who caused all holy Scriptures to be written for our learning:
Help us so to hear them,
  To read, mark, learn and inwardly digest them
that, through patience, and the comfort of your holy word,
we may embrace and forever hold fast
  the hope of everlasting life,
which you have given us in our Saviour Jesus Christ.

This rich theology of scripture takes us beyond statements of what we believe *about* the Bible. Perhaps more importantly the prayer invokes the analogy of Scripture as food for the journey of faith. Through hearing, reading, noting and learning the prayer invites us to 'inwardly digest' the holy word. It is, if you like, the Eucharist of the word; a feasting and ingesting. When Scripture is likened to food, we are in the region of energy and the conditions under which it is released.

The Anglican poet and priest George Herbert likewise finds the food analogy with Scripture illuminating and powerful:

Oh Book! infinite sweetnesse! let my heart
  Suck ev'ry letter, and a hony gain,
  Precious for any grief in any part;
To cleare the breast, to mollifie all pain.
Thou art all health, health thriving till it make
  A full eternitie: thou art a masse
  Of strange delights, where we may wish & take.
Ladies, Look here; this is the thankful glasse,
That mends the lookers eyes: this is the well

That washes what it shows. Who can indeare
Thy praise too much? Thou art heav'ns Lidger here,
Working against the states of death and hell.
Thou are joyes handsell: heav'n lies flat in thee,
Subject to ev'ry mounters bended knee. (Herbert 1941, p. 58)

Herbert enjoins the human heart to 'suck every letter' of Scripture in order to 'hony gain'. To ingest the word is to enter into wisdom though it is clear that this process goes beyond mere cognition. Moreover, the focus is on the effect of Scripture on the believer. It points to a transfer of concentrated energy that is released for the reordering of life towards God. Herbert obviously believed that the richness of God is encountered through and in the medium of Holy Scripture. Furthermore, the metaphor of eating taps into an ancient biblical tradition of eating the scroll, which could be sweet (Jer. 15.16 and Ezek. 3.3) or both bitter and sweet (Rev. 10.8–11). Interestingly, in these contexts the ingestion of the word releases a prophetic word; again energy transfer and expansion without diminution but with radical effects for society.

It is easy to forget that throughout history it is through the liturgical rhythms of the Church that the energetic wisdom of the word tradition is rooted and effects change. Over millennia, this has meant that the people of God are primarily hearers of the word before they are readers, interpreters, students and scholars. Accordingly, '[t]he first and foremost doctrine *de scriptura* is therefore not a proposition *about* Scripture at all. It is rather the liturgical and devotional instruction: Let the Scripture be read, at every opportunity and with care for its actual address to hearers, even if these are only the reader' (Jensen 1999, p. 273). It also means that word and prayer are deeply intertwined, with the result that Scripture traverses the range of ways in which human beings in their personal and corporate worship and discipleship are drawn imaginatively into the movement of God's Spirit. This raises an interesting question about whether Scripture is a sacrament. Barth himself considered that the history of Jesus Christ – 'of His resurrection, of the outpouring of the Holy

Spirit' – was the only sacrament Protestantism had left.[4] The Lutheran Robert Jensen offers a nuanced approach noting that the 'liturgical or devotional reading of Scripture is not "sacrament," by any usual enumeration . . .' (1999, p. 260). However, Jensen recognizes that 'the coincidence of heaven and earth, future and past, sign and *res* is the truth of Scripture's role and power' and concludes that Scripture is one of the 'mysteries of communion'. Yet, it is never a static mystery but a highly concentrated and dynamic form of divine energy. As such Holy Scripture has more of the character of the travelling cloud of Exodus, and the luminous but mysterious cloud of the Transfiguration that protects, surrounds, leads, accompanies, bears witness while remaining luminous, inspires awe, assures yet convicts, and humbles even as it remains unable to be fully comprehend (Thomson 1996, pp. 199–203).

The word tradition in Christianity has many interlinked and multi-layered forms. Besides the obvious liturgical expression there are numerous others such as creeds, confessions, prayer, teaching, doctrines and the work of theology. These all participate in the energetic wisdom of the *logos* of God embodying testimony to the *viva vox Christi*. Some of these forms of the word tradition are compressed into short forms, such as statements of belief, songs and hymns, preaching. Some forms have more of the character of extended theological inquiries leading to particular teachings and/or doctrines. All belong within the symbolic region of the *ecclesia*, and all forms of the word tradition concern communication and energy. Indeed, 'in the most fundamental sense, communication consists in the transmission of energy in a form' (Hardy and Ford 1984, p. 157). This means that the word tradition in Christianity is a tradition of movement, change and transformation. When it becomes locked in a steady-state repetitive communication system, energy transfer

---

4 See Barth 1981, p. 102f; cf. 1956, p. 296, where Barth refers to the humanity of Jesus Christ as 'the one mysterium, the one sacrament, and the one existential fact before and beside and after which there is no room for any other of the same rank'.

ceases, there is no longer replenishment and entropy occurs. This occurs when the determinate media (Scripture, creed, doctrine, prayer, liturgical form, hymn) become the focal awareness of the body of Christ or individuals. In other words, the focal awareness shifts from God – who is the fullness and goodness of the source of wisdom and energy – to the determinate media. Under these conditions, the divine is effectively relegated to subsidiary awareness. The dynamic interplay between divine grace and human participation becomes skewed towards human preoccupation with their own engagements rather than upon the One, who energizes and bestows wisdom. This is not just an issue for the word tradition in Christianity but also operates in the sacramental tradition.

Sacraments and celebration: transformative energy flows

The subject of sacramental theology is complex and immense, and my purpose in the brief comments, which follow, is to identify some of the ways in which sacraments might be understood as transformative energy flows. Such a conception may not immediately resonate with usual discussions of sacraments. However, I hope to show that far from being a tangential concern the purpose and intent of the celebration of the sacraments is to effect transformation through release and dispersal of energy. Such an understanding is not entirely novel. For example, some theologians have asked in relation to the Eucharist: 'Is it to be seen mainly as an historical memorial, or in sacrificial terms, or as a sacrament of human fellowship, or as communion with the crucified and resurrected Lord, or as a source of spiritual energy?' (Hardy and Ford 1984, p. 18). But how are sacraments a source of spiritual energy and effective in a transformative way? The matter needs teasing out and prompts an associated question: how might the theme of energy be relevant to a theology of the sacraments?

In this respect, the Eucharist is instructive. Although *time* (past, present and future and the concept of *anamnesis*) and *spatial* categories (debates about real presence, location of the risen body of Christ) have been critical in the conflicts of the sixteenth-century

Reformation, perhaps the most significant, though most easily missed, issue in eucharistic theology concerns the nature and manner of energy transfer and its effects. For example, the Reformation controversies about the presence and sacrifice of Christ in the Eucharist – such as Catholic 'transubstantiation'; Lutheran 'consubstantiation' or 'sacramental union'; Zwinglian 'receptionism' – can be understood as disputes about how divine energy was transferred, what transformations occurred and their effects for participants. For the most part, discussion about the Eucharist in Western theology has presupposed Aristotelian understandings of substance and accidents. This meant that the focus was inevitably on the eucharistic elements of bread and wine and their status as signs representing the *res* signified. This focus entailed a certain confinement of the dynamics of spiritual energy, a problem observed in the preoccupation with the conditions necessary for sacramental efficacy. The relationship 'between efficaciousness and effectiveness of the sacramental celebration of the Church' was marginalized (Prétot 2008, p. 27). One consequence of this was that the sacramental celebration itself, the field of energy in which this occurred and the divine energetics of the transformative presence of the risen Christ were obscured and/or unattended to. The restricted role for the Spirit in this eucharistic theology[5] was very different from the focus in Eastern Orthodoxy on the *epiclesis* of the Spirit in relation to the ecclesial body. My point is a simple one at this stage, namely, that attention to energy and its transformations offers a way to examine the nature of sacraments. And there is evidence for this in contemporary ecumenical discussions.[6] My thesis in what follows is that the concept of energy can provide fresh insight into the nature of the Church's

---

5 Calvin's theology of the Spirit in relation to the Eucharist is somewhat of an exception here and deserves more attention.

6 This underlies the ARCIC 1 *Agreed Statement on Eucharistic Doctrine 1971*, where one purpose of the Eucharist is 'to transmit the life of the crucified and risen Christ to his body, the Church, so that its members may be more fully united with Christ and with one another' (para. 6).

sacramental celebration and deliver it from preoccupation with elements as such.[7]

Sacraments in intensity mode

There are two basic domains within which sacraments operate in the life of the Church, *intensity* and *extensity*. The former (*intensity*) identifies the *concentration* and *density* of God's life in relation to the world and human affairs. Prayer and the spiritual life, worship, sacramental celebration, Scripture attentiveness, and an 'earnest desire, that is rational, passionate intensity of heart, soul, mind and strength' all offer 'intimations of the deeper treasures of the wisdom of God' (Hardy and Ford 1984, p. 111). A fully human relational life with God and others in the world involves living 'in the intensity of God's gift of truth and holiness, in the inner dynamic of the wisdom of God'. Without this engagement with intensity, 'we will have neither the possibility of understanding and interpreting the Scriptures and tradition nor the means to relate deeply to one another'; in short we can become distracted by the 'extensity of life' (p. 112). Intensity identifies the quality of divine richness and is pursued within worship 'where the interwoven involvements of God, community, world and self are most fully expressed, where the "spread-out-ness" of life in *situ* is returned in thanks and the compassionate gift of truth and holiness is most fully realized'.

In terms of intensity, sacraments are richly concentrated forms of God's loving purposes in Christ. Baptism as incorporation into the body of Christ and Eucharist as the embodiment of God's gracious self-giving through the death and resurrection of Christ constitute sacramental celebrations through and in which the reality of God in Christ is encountered. The high-density energy

---

7 There has been a shift in Roman Catholic sacramental theology from sacraments as 'ecclesial operations' centred on Christ and those who act in his place to sacraments operating in a richer Trinitarian network in which they are celebrations of the paschal mystery with radical consequences. For further discussion, see Prétot 2008, pp. 25–32.

embodied sacramentally (in the celebration as such in all the details including but not restricted to the elements of bread and wine and water) mirrors the potentialities of the Genesis account of creation when light is spoken forth. In the Eucharist, the great acts of God in creation, in the story of Israel, in Christ and the Church and the world are re-narrated. In this 'eschatological performance', the past is reconstituted in the present as an anticipation of the coming Kingdom of the reign of God to which all creation is being drawn. In terms of the present discussion, the sacraments are sources and embodiments of spiritual energy. However, the dynamic nature of this sacramental reality can easily default into preoccupation with the sacramental moment as such (such as the conjunction of matter, form and minister in consecration) with consequent inattention to the temporal unfolding and emergent quality of the sacramental celebration. Rather the *celebration* of the sacraments is the occasion for a remarkable release – explosion-like – of concentrated divine energy. This has a transformative effect on the worshippers who become participants in an energy transfer witnessed to in the flow of the Spirit evident in the new possibilities for faith and service.

Sacraments in extensity mode

Clearly, the dimension of intensity is only half the story here. The other domain relevant to sacraments is extensity, that is, the spread-out-ness of life. The energy flow of the Spirit of Christ released in word and sacrament has a particular pattern, form and dynamic which is deeply Trinitarian. Divine energy is never potential energy but always actual and necessarily expansive. The risen Christ in the power of the Spirit is the mode in which divine energy draws all things on earth and in heaven towards their consummation in the perfection of God the Lord. This is a fully energetic movement and highlights the second dimension relevant to a theology of sacraments, that is, the mode of extensity. Extensity is necessary to the human condition for it is the way in which we 'carry out God's command to "go forth" and to engage all his creatures' (Hardy 2010, p. 69). As such, extensity refers to the 'spread-out-ness' of things. Creation represents the dispersal, flux and change of all things. The fact is 'that human beings live in extended time, and so learn of the movements of God's truth and holiness to them in the course of time' (Hardy 2001, p. 109). Following Christ necessarily means living in *situ* in the complexities and puzzles of life in the world. Extensity refers to the 'sheer polyformality of things', which is fascinating, engaging, alluring and, because of the associated chaos and unavoidable distractions, also 'our malaise and tragedy' to the extent that it makes it difficult for us to maintain 'our unity with God' and our sense of God's presence (Hardy 2010, pp. 23, 69).

The dimension of extensity is the region in which Baptism and Eucharist are constantly repeated in the ebb and flow of discipleship in the world. For example, the energy flow released in the eucharistic celebration embodies liturgically the continuous and emergent nature of divine energy that sustains creation and human movement towards God. The correlate of the intensity of worship through word and sacraments is discipleship of the body of Christ in extensity. The effectiveness of the sacraments is discerned in extensity and the ongoing transformations of societal life, in which the body of Christ lives and moves and has its being.

If celebration of the sacraments is a celebration of transformative flows of divine energy, which generate new life, the celebration is incomplete and unformed, until it finds form in the transformation of the world after the sacramental pattern embodied in Baptism and Eucharist. By its very character, this embodiment remains incomplete and purposive; always orientated towards a yet-to-be realized future, when Christ will one day be 'all in all'. This is more than simply a formal process. The energy of God in sacramental mode is characterized by abundance, generosity and unconditional blessing. This means that the sacraments are signs and symbols of a distributive justice that is always seeking fuller and richer blessing in the world. The energies of God celebrated in word and sacrament seek transposition into political, economic, legal, communicative, symbolic and interpersonal dimensions of life in extensity. If sacraments in the narrow sense identify the holy energy of God in rich intensity, this same energy for life and holiness is manifest in its reach through extensity. In both modes, the future fullness of holiness and truth of God is anticipated and longed for.

Sacraments of renewable energy

A number of implications flow from this brief reflection on sacraments and energy. First, clearly, there is need for a delicate balance between intensity and extensity in human life and therefore in Christian pilgrimage in the world. The need for balance operates in every area, and hence it is not surprising that the sacramental life of the Church ought to find embodiment and release in both concentrated forms – that is, sacramental celebrations – and in dispersal in the world in extensity. In our current situation in the West, this balance is sorely needed. We are acutely aware that our lives are continuously dispersed and distracted in a market-driven competitive environment, in which the lure of the next interesting and fascinating thing grasps our attention and distracts us into innumerable unfulfilling activities and ventures. This can cause a basic fracture in our relationship with God, others and ourself. The fragmented self played out in extensity has no capacity to recover inner centredness or constancy of self. Under these conditions, energy dissipates, entropy sets in and anxiety increases. As a consequence people search ever more furtively for ways to sustain, renew and replenish lost capacity for engagement. One response to this situation is observed in the flight into interiority, which is a particular kind of intensity. However, this can become excessively turned in on the self in a twisted manner that is equally unsatisfying and certainly disconnected from rich relations with others, the world and God. Worship can easily be colonised by this narcissistic self. So, there is no guaranteed blueprint for finding the appropriate balance and poise between intensity and extensity.

How might our reflections on the sacraments and the Eucharist in particular be relevant to the above matter? If, as proposed above, the Eucharist is a transformative energy flow derived from nothing less than the heart of God such a flow does not cease at the end of the celebration but in fact gathers momentum signalled in the words at the end of the celebration 'Go in peace to love and serve the Lord'. What is released through eucharistic celebration and praise is a form of divine energy, which is infinitely replenishing for human life in the world. The Eucharist has a double coordinate of intensity and extensity. Moreover, it joins the two and directs both modes towards the other. This is the way the sacrament becomes a source of constant renewable energy for people in society. On this account, the eucharistic celebration is an instance of God's holy intensity and properly directed extensity.

Second, the foregoing gives a particular significance and urgency to the immersion of the Church in the world in all its dimensions. The new sociality embodied in the eucharistic form of the Church is an essentially unfinished and expansive dynamic arising from the basic movement of divine energy. The communal practices of the Church, in particular those central sacramental practices that encode the wisdom and energy of the Triune God, offer a radical alternative as 'signs and instruments of the formation of a new social reality' (Izuzquiza 2009, p. 201). The transformative energy flow of sacramental celebration spreads out and into social, cultural, economic and political domains. In this dynamic, the risen Christ is 're-membered'; an *anamnesis*, which, for example, in the context of the trials and tribulations of oppressed people, provides the energy and endurance for 'a counter-discipline to state terror' (Cavanaugh 1998, pp. 229f). This requires the eucharistic body of Christ to become visible in the world, 'not secreted away in the souls of believers or relegated to the distant historical past or future' but in the present time where bodies are constantly disappearing due to violence and terror (p. 234). For William Cavanaugh, this constitutes the eucharistic discipline and discernment of the body. It means that the Church 'does not simply perform the Eucharist; the Eucharist performs the Church' (p. 235). The energetics of eucharistic discipline constantly direct the Church into extensity, where Christ's broken body is also to be discerned.

Third, though related to the above point is the theme of energy and food, already identified in the discussion on Scripture. This is focused in the concept of 'manna from heaven' prefigured in the

Exodus story and the Johannine feeding story (John 6.1–15), and concentrated in the Eucharist as heavenly manna. In all cases, we have to do with multiplication and the superabundance of God, and always with plenty left over (Mendez Montoya 2009, pp. 113–56). Divine replenishment of human capacity is neither bounded nor complete but overflowing and infinite. Manna symbolizes 'the always more than enough to share'. The Eucharist is thus a sacramental sign of the plenitude of God's provision and the source of renewable energy for the world.

Fourth, the foregoing presupposes a particular Trinitarian dynamic, which drives and informs the flow of energy through successive concentrations in Word and Sacrament and ever-expansive movement outwards into creation. It is an energy flow which arises from the particular presence and action of Christ and the Spirit. However, the 'and' is precisely the issue. The reason is that the relationship and dynamic is much richer than any joining word can identify let alone track. We might say that Christ incarnate and risen is the structured form of the Spirit, while the Spirit of Christ is the energetic ordering of creation and thus of the Church of God. The *perichoresis* of the Trinity is an open and world involving movement and never a self-enclosed performance (Chapter 5). Word and sacrament represent and embody this complex and dynamic energetic ordering of God in a highly concentrated form. In this way, Word and Sacrament constitute a genuine sign, symbol and foretaste of God's ever replenishing presence and action in society and creation. A renewed sociality is at once both baptismal and eucharistic in form and substance; emblematic of the divine pattern in creation and redemption.

Energy in overflow: sacrament of towel and witness

The foregoing reflection on the energetics of Christian pilgrimage have focused on those activities and modes through which the energy of the Holy God is released and does its work, that is worship, word, sacrament. The energy associated with these three fundamental practices and modes of encounter with one another and God provides the energy for the journey of faith in the world.

The way that the energetics of word, sacrament and worship actually works is indeed complex and never simply in one direction only; as if energy flows down from God and through such media without a corresponding energetic movement back towards God. When people are drawn into the energetic life of God and as a result are empowered for discipleship in the world, something quite remarkable occurs. There is an overflow of energy that is constantly replenishing and indeed expanding. The law of entropy or dissipation of energy no longer operates at least as long as the movement from God to humans and from humans towards God continues. It is a double movement but always buoyed along by the presence and working of the Spirit of love. The release of divine energy is concentrated in worship, Word and Sacrament and is enmeshed in the interactions of human beings with one another and the world created and loved by God. The manner in which the energy of God's life is continually doubled and continually overflows is a matter of awe, wonder and joy.

Those who worship the living God, hear the living voice of God through word and are nourished through the Word made visible in sacrament are continually directed beyond themselves and into the world to serve as faithful disciples. The energy released through worship, praise, word and sacrament overflows into the life of discipleship. The pattern of God's love towards the world – a life of outpouring, self-emptying; a life of abundant holiness – that is concentrated in worship, is repeated in an extended manner in the world. As I mentioned above, this does not cause a dissipation of energy but in fact becomes the mode in which the release of divine energy is extended, indeed doubled. A life of service and care, friendship and practising justice, and bearing witness in word and deed to the hope of Christ; these are the constituents of Christian discipleship. And as disciples of Christ live out the pattern of Christ's life in the world they discover, often much to their utter surprise, that the energy available for life, love and care increases and is replenished by entering into the pattern of Christ's life. This is the remarkable ecology of holy energy that overflows and carries people and all things with it.

The logic of this pattern of discipleship is encoded into the gospels. It is sharply and poignantly present in the Johannine Last Supper when Jesus 'got up from the table, took off his outer robe, and tied a towel around himself. Then he poured water into a basin and began to wash the disciples' feet and to wipe them with the towel that was tied to him' (John 13.4–5). Here the Lord and teacher performs the most menial and lowly of customs of the day and thereby points his followers in the same direction: 'you also ought to wash one another's feet' (John 13.14b). This 'sacrament of the towel' is the key to blessing (John 13.16). In terms of our discussion on energy, we might say that this humble service of the towel is the means by which the holy energy of the Lord overflows for blessing for recipients and givers. To be blessed implies 'an abundance of joy, a beatitude, a participation in the joy of God' and it leads to an overflow of love. Assuming the lowest place following the pattern of Christ has a transformative effect and ongoing blessing.

The founder of L'Arche, Jean Vanier, comments that '[t]he history of humanity has changed since God has knelt humbly at our feet, begging our love. We can accept or refuse. Jesus is chained to our freedom' (2004, p. 226). This divine move to the lowest place, to those at the bottom of the societal pyramid is a move that transforms human society from a pyramid to a body in which 'There is no "last place"' (p. 227). John's Gospel encodes foot washing as a counterpart to the breaking of bread. They are, in fact, mirror images and companion symbols for both involve the giving of Jesus' body for others: 'communion at the table of the Lord cannot be separated from communion lived in washing each other's feet. . . To wash a person's feet is a gesture that creates and expresses a communion of hearts' (p. 231).

The foot washing of John 13 is a concentrated symbol of the life of service, care and friendship in the world. It is the way of communion with the lost, broken, fearful, anxious, victims, oppressors and violent, downtrodden and forgotten. In more recent decades, it is the earth itself that has increasingly become the subject of the tender care symbolized in the foot washing. In this way, the gospel of God is announced in deeds of love. It is the natural complement to a life of witness through words of love and truth. Here too is an overflow of joy in God that generates joyful energy as the message is received and embodied in lives of thankfulness and praise.

As disciples of Christ bear witness to the hope God gives, they participate in the slip-stream of God's renewing energy which bubbles up and out and over. The energetics of communication cannot be reduced to practical methods of telling the gospel though it includes this. Telling the story, rehearsing it multiple times in myriad ways and contexts is a lifelong vocation soaked in the prayer of the whole Church. It takes us into the heart of the mystery of the gospel (Eph. 6.19). This too releases new energy and the logic of overflow means that energy is not dissipated even through difficult circumstances, suffering and evil (see Pickard 1999, pp. 91-7).

Conclusion

This chapter has offered an approach to those ecclesial practices that have been central to Christian pilgrimage throughout history. Worship, word, sacrament, service and witness have been developed in terms of the energy empowering life on the 'Way' (Acts 9.2). The energetics associated with these activities coheres and generates a continuous source of replenishing and sustaining capacity to live as disciples *en route*. Divine energy in its concentrated and dispersed forms (intensity and extensity) is transformative at all levels of life. When entropy and diminution of energy occurs pilgrimage suffers; it stagnates, ossifies and implodes. In short, the *ecclesia* moves into a steady-state mode of operation. The anxieties that arise as a result generate hyperactivity. This masks real energy depletion in the Church that impacts upon its leadership, the functioning of ecclesial communities and the capacity for discipleship in the world (Chapter 3).

The Emmaus Road story of Luke 24 suggests to me a paradigmatic story of divine energy and the dynamic, in which human beings participate in the energetics of God's presence and action in the world (Pickard 2011, pp. 251-62). Here is a story of the unfolding word of truth on the journey towards Emmaus generating fire in the heart; of table fellowship in which the guest becomes host and faith is born; of renewed energy for a return to Jerusalem to share the news; of overflowing joy in the presence of the risen Jesus; of blessing and orientation towards the world. The Emmaus Road journey of discipleship is a journey by way of worship, word, sacrament, care and witness. In these specific and particular forms, the energetics of God's love is the reason for an ongoing and constant energy flow embodied in the discipleship of the coming Church. It is to this Church that I now turn to conclude.

Questions

1 What is the relationship between energy and structure in understanding the nature of the Church?
2 'Worship is the place and the possibility of abundant divine energy'. Why is this the case? How is this energy of God present and mediated in Christian worship?
3 In what way is Scripture food for the journey?
4 What are the strengths and weaknesses of the metaphor of scripture 'as a cloud'?
5 The Eucharist 'is the pure primal event by which righteousness was constituted in Jesus' time, and it is fully recalled each time it is re-enacted' (Hardy 2010, p. 65). How do you understand this statement?
6 What is the theological significance of Jesus' washing the disciples' feet in John's Gospel? How is it relevant for evangelism and seeking justice in the world?

Further reading

Ellen T. Charry, 'Sacramental Ecclesiology', in Mark Husbands and Daniel J. Treier (eds), *The Community of the Word: Toward an Evangelical Ecclesiology*, Downers Grove, IL: Inter Varsity Press, 2005, pp. 201–16.

Rebecca S. Chopp, 'The Power of Freedom: Proclamation and Scripture', in *The Power to Speak: Feminism, Language, God*, New York: Crossroad, 1991, pp. 40–70.

Marva J. Dawn, 'God as the Centre of Worship: Who is Worship For?', in *Reaching Out without Dumbing Down: A Theology of Worship for This Urgent Time*, Grand Rapids, MI: Eerdmans, 1995, pp. 75–104.

Robert Jensen, 'The Church and the Sacraments', in Colin Gunton (ed.), *The Cambridge Companion to Christian Doctrine*, Cambridge: Cambridge University Press, 1997, pp. 207–25.

Fergus J. King, 'Mission-Shaped or Paul-Shaped? Apostolic Challenges to the Mission-Shaped Church', *Journal of Anglican Studies*. 9:2 (2011), pp. 223–46.

Jean-Jaques Suurmond, 'The Church as the Body of Christ', in *Word and Spirit at Play: Towards a Charismatic Theology*, London: SCM, 1994, Ch. 3, pp. 189–213.

Stephen Sykes, 'An Anglican Theology of Evangelism', in *Unashamed Anglicanism*, London: Darton, Longman and Todd, 1996, pp. 201–10.

Susan J. White, 'What is Liturgical Spirituality?', in *The Spirit of Worship: The Liturgical Tradition*, London: Darton, Longman and Todd, 1999, pp. 13–33.

9

Slow Church Coming

Postscript for a travelling ecclesiology

Brief overview

In the preceding chapters, I have offered a theological account of the character and dynamics of the Church of God. The themes in this systematic ecclesiology have been varied and interlacing: sociality and communion, emergence and growth, sociality and trinity, structure and freedom, energy and mystery. These themes have provided the interpretative mechanisms for more traditional ways of speaking about the Church, such as its unity, holiness, catholicity, apostolicity; its polity and ministry; its worship, scripture, and sacramental traditions and its commitment to care and witness. I have tried to recast these familiar elements on a broader conceptual canvas in order to create a more open space for dialogue, both within the Churches and between the one Church of Jesus Christ and the manifold wisdom to be found in society, other religions, academy and personal life. In a sense, this book is preparatory to such dialogues; an attempt if you like to get the ecclesiological house in order.[1] Above all else, I hoped by this method to draw attention to the unfinished, future-orientated, joyful freedom into which the Church is called as it follows the ways of God in the world.

Much of what I have written in this book has focused on the 'not yet Church'; the Church that is still unfolding. This is the

---

1 For example, it could be an interesting and important project to explore the inter-religious value of the themes of energy and structure in relation to the divine life and human society.

reason for the emphasis upon the dynamics of a renewed sociality; on the emergent unfinished character of the marks of the Church; of ecclesial structures serving the freedom of the baptized; on renewable energy as the underlying reality of worship, word, sacrament, care and witness. In this way, I have offered an ecclesial heuristic, that is, some clues about how we might seek and find the Church afresh as we are attracted to God.

But what portrait or depiction of the Church might make sense of the approach of this book? I would hope that what I have developed in the preceding chapters could generate a multiplicity of imaginative constructs concerning the nature of the Church. In this final chapter, I want to offer one such portrait/depiction of the character of the coming Church; a portrait that I trust is faithful to the theological trajectory of this book. Central to my portrait is the idea of 'slow Church'. I distinguish such a Church from, on the one hand, the frenetic over-functioning Church and, on the other hand, the fast-asleep Church whose pace and pulse are difficult to detect.

The coming Church

The 'coming Church' is not the Church which is, though there are anticipations in the present. The 'coming Church' is not to be identified with the kingdom, though again there are intimations and clues in the unfolding form and movement of the Church, which point to the kingdom of God. Yet, the 'coming Church' does signal a movement from God to the world – a sign that the people of the world are not bereft of God's love, and that there remains an ever-present surplus of goodness, truth and beauty to enrich our lives. However, the 'coming Church' is meant to indicate that the movement is not simply from God to the world but also from the future towards the present.[2] This belongs to a dynamic call and response in which those called by God move towards God

---

2 For an important discussion of the concept of God's re-creation from the future as it is developed in the theology of Wolfhart Pannenberg, see Mostert 2002, pp. 161–75.

and into the future at the same time. While the kingdom is an eschatological reality partially realized in any present, the coming Church is the reality of the new thing God is doing from the future and coming to birth in the unfolding present. The coming Church comes from beyond even as it emerges from within and transcends what already is. In this sense, we might speak of an ongoing ecclesial granulation; a process that occurs from within and generative of renewal which can only be recognized as the gift of the transcendent Spirit of holiness.[3]

The 'coming Church' is the Church, which yearns and longs for new life in the midst of the old. I have in mind the transformation referred to in Revelation 21.5: 'Behold, I am making everything new'. The sense here is something new *from* something old rather than something new, entirely distinct from what is already present. So, rather than making 'a new thing' it is, as the text indicates, 'every-thing new'. Where the creative activity of God is transforming existing structures, the process will take some time and require great patience and courage. There is no room for the idealist's flights of fancy. We are in a state of radical transition, during which we wait with eager longing, fully awake to the present realities and hopeful that the coming Church will prove to be a sign and embodiment of the character of the kingdom of God. But all of this takes time for good things take time.

Seeking the Church requires a Church that can be found; one that moves at a pace that is not easily missed in the busyness of life. Other attractive substitutes for true community with God lure many a passer-by. To be a seeker of the Church and the mystery it lives by is a lifelong journey. To be a pilgrim of the coming Church requires patience, for good things take time.

---

3 Daniel Hardy refers to the medical process of granulation, which occurs below the wounded area of the body and by which inner healing takes place. There is something about the character and quality of the human body that effects healing from within (2010, p. 64, cf. pp. 81, 118–19).

Travel slowly for good things take time

Some years ago, when I was involved in organizing a day retreat for some theological students, I said: 'It is not a quiet day, it's a slow day'. It rang a bell for many, certainly for me. A major task for a travelling Church is to find the optimal pace for the journey. Any long-distance runner knows how critical it is to pace themselves in order that they will have sufficient energy and stamina to finish and can respond to unforeseen contingencies on the way. By 'slow Church coming', I wish to flag the importance for the Church of recovering a pace and rhythm for people on the Way. When the Church moves out of the fast lane, leaves the motorways for the B roads, looks beyond the quick-fix consumer and entertainment models for religion, and begins to follow in the footsteps of Christ, it really has to be one step at a time.

It is a truism that 'nothing can be loved at speed'.[4] A colleague once said to me: 'the older I get the more I have realized that good things take time'. Were these the words of someone who had lost energy? I doubt it, for I too have discovered that the things that are really worthwhile are things that require commitment, energy, resilience and time. Nurturing good-quality friendships, suffering with another in trouble or pain, working patiently to see a dream or vision for a community realized, taking time to celebrate and laugh, attending to the welcomes and farewells of life, planting and watering seeds of new ideas, living with conflict while trying to harness it for good, working with others to effect change in Church, society, politics all requires perseverance, energy, and time.

Good things require a 'longish moment'; long enough for individuals and communities to listen to their souls, to feel the deeper impulses and questions; long enough 'for some of our demons to walk away' (Williams 2002, p. 81). For example, within the

---

4 The Australian writer Michael Leunig writes in his poem 'Another Way of Being': 'Nothing can be loved at speed. God lead us to the slow path; to the joyous insights of the pilgrim; another way of knowing: another way of being. Amen' (1991).

tradition of biblical lament, the primal cry 'How long, O Lord?' presupposes a lengthy period of faith and then disillusionment. In similar vein, Thomas Merton once said that for every step of faith there is a corresponding step of doubt. Hence, only as we journey in faith can we gain the confidence to ask of God the really tough questions, those found in lament. This makes sense of Jesus' cry of dereliction, 'My God, my God, why . . .?' This then is the sign of the deepest faith ever lived, because it is so secure, so deep, so grounded, that it could ask, with sincerity, at the moment of crisis the hardest question of all – have I been abandoned? But this involves discovering and nurturing a cultivated pace and rhythm in order to inculcate freshness, replenishment of energy, vitality of spirit and love of one another; all such things fall to my mind under the heading of 'slow Church coming'.

When I attended the UK Greenbelt Festival in 2011, Rob Bell, an American author, spoke about his life as a Christian and at the end read from Psalm 119: 'Your word is a lamp unto my feet.' His exegesis was simple and yet profound. Basically, you can't see far with a lamp; it's not a torch nor is it a searchlight; it's just a lamp. Following the light of God sheds light for the way but it is a light sufficient for the next step. This again struck a chord with me as someone who has been a disciple since the cradle. We pray 'give us this day our daily bread' though we might just as easily pray 'give us this day sufficient light for the path we are to tread'.

The above anecdotal comments provide a springboard for the kind of ecclesial portrait I want to sketch in this final chapter. Good things do take time, and however urgent we may feel the demands of our time, nonetheless 'hasten slowly', represents a greater wisdom than anxiety-driven Church pragmatics. To my mind, 'slow Church coming' captures well the kind of travelling ecclesiology, which underlies this book. I have suggested that the coming Church will be a Church that emerges slowly. This entails a major task to think through. The remainder of this chapter is a brief sketch of what slow Church coming is about and as a consequence points to work on the theological agenda for the coming Church.

In praise of slowness

In Praise of Slowness by Carl Honoré (2005) had the subtitle, *Challenging the Cult of Speed*. Against a culture of 'everything faster', Honoré proposed 'slow is beautiful', the 'importance of being at rest', 'raising an unhurried child', 'the benefits of working less hard', 'doctors and patience', etc. The inside cover offered an apposite word from Gandhi, 'There is more to life than increasing its speed.' Not surprisingly the book is full of anecdotes about the consequences of living life at speed without developing the capacity to slow down. Honoré quotes from the 1996 novel *Slowness* by Milan Kundera, 'When things happen too fast, nobody can be certain about anything, about anything at all, not even about himself' (p. 9).

For Honoré, fast and slow 'are shorthand for ways of being or philosophies of life. Fast is busy, controlling, aggressive, hurried, analytical, stressed, superficial, impatient, active, quantity-over-quality. Slow is the opposite: calm, careful, receptive, still, intuitive, unhurried, patient, reflective, quality-over-quantity' (p. 14). Slow was about connections real and meaningful with everyone and everything. The author noted the paradox that 'Slow does not always mean slow'. For example, doing a task in a slow manner can often yield faster results; a 'slow frame of mind' may be perfectly congruent with doing things quickly or dealing with significant stress. In short, the 'slow movement' is not a recipe for living at a snail's pace nor an attempt to turn the clock back with respect to technology to some imagined utopian past. For Honoré, the key word is *balance*. This includes learning to live at a speed appropriate for the occasion, and this in turn required a 'slow frame of mind'. Honoré's proposals point to the importance of developing a certain habit and character that gives strength and resilience; those necessary virtues that breed freedom to find an appropriate pace and presence in the world. His book sparked a whole literature, and his ideas resonate with many today. It may even be good news for the Church!

When I suggested to someone that I wanted to finish my book with an ode to slowness, they looked worried, assuming that in my latter years I had lost the passion and drive and was simply reacting to the hectic pace of life. Nothing could have been further from the truth. I responded, 'slow Church, like the slow food movement; local, fresh and organic'. What would it look like for the Christian Church to recover a discipleship that was truly local, fresh and organic? Again this takes patience and requires generous helpings of time and commitment.

Fast-asleep Church

The Church in the West appears at times to be in a deep sleep; a Rip-van-Winkle Church. Such a Church is no longer reading the signs of the times and remains locked in a steady-state condition. This occurs when the Church recycles the habits and ways of the past without attention to the changing contexts. Such a Church is dying or in a comatose state. It lacks resilience, determination and joy. For the most part, we inhabit a Church culture, which appears at times wilfully blind to the precariousness of its situation and apparently content to remain on the well-worn paths of yesterday. Permanence, fixity and constancy are prized above all else.[5]

Frenetic Church

One response to this not-untypical situation is to react in the opposite direction. In this scenario, the Church and especially its leaders furtively begin the search for the program or action plan that

---

5 At one level, it is entirely understandable that people try to preserve the good things of the past by creating structures of permanence – doctrinally, legally, in terms of property, liturgically. In fact, such a move is quite necessary for institutional wellbeing and strong networks of relationships. The danger arises when this move over-reaches itself. It fails to take account of the immersion of the idea of the Church in history, cultures and society. Or rather, immersion is identified with the implanting of a fixed and unchangeable code of doctrines, rules and practices. But when this occurs, the dynamic of the Church is short-circuited; no account can be given of how God might be unfolding something new.

will arrest decline, turn the ship around, and rebuild the Church. They slip into over-functioning and become exhausted or exhaust others. The diagnosis of the presenting ills of the Church may be quite accurate. The problem arises in the recommended course of treatment. Unfortunately, the response to a dying Church is anxiety and an overreaction that easily succumbs to the values of the host culture. The consumer, fast lane management approach, results and outcomes driven strategic plans operating within a competitive market driven culture is the environment in which we live and move and have our being (see Cowdell 2008, Ch. 1). It infiltrates the Church's often admirable attempts to recover the energy and vitality of the gospel, engage people and be involved in mission for the sake of the kingdom.

I heard recently about a church leader (Anglican) extolling the virtues of such a pragmatic approach to evangelism. In response to a question about the gospel requirement for faithfulness in such a situation, the leader replied with words to the effect 'faithfulness is a mask for failure'. He may have been half right with respect to some people but it is hard to reconcile his response with the message of the Scriptures, and there is wisdom in the poster that said, 'Failure is maintaining enthusiasm from one failure to the next'. Much has been written about the above issues, and my point in raising them here is to say that such a response to a moribund and flagging Church will only hasten the death of the Church. For leaders the critical issue is how energy is deployed, what forces skew the direction and form it assumes, and how such activity is aligned with the pattern of Jesus' life.

Recovering an ecclesial pace

Is there a third way beyond the moribund and/or the over-functioning Church? The purpose of this chapter is to explore an alternative pace, rhythm and presence for the Church. This third way is the 'slow Church coming', and it has echoes from an earlier period in the Christian tradition.

Monastic slow

In his classic work *Transforming Mission*, David Bosch discusses the 'extraordinary resilience and recuperative power' of Christian monasticism (1991, pp. 230–6). Bosch quotes from an earlier writer, Christopher Dawson, who stated that even if 99 out of 100 monasteries were burnt down and the monks killed or driven out, nonetheless,

> [t]he whole tradition could be reconstituted from the one survivor, and the desolate sites could be repeopled by fresh supplies of monks who would take up again the broken tradition, following the same rule, singing the same liturgy, reading the same books and thinking the same thoughts as their predecessors. (Dawson 1950, p. 72, quoted in Bosch 1991, p. 232)

Bosch's comments are apposite.

> The monks knew that things took time, that instant gratification and a quick-fix mentality were an illusion, and that an effort begun in one generation had to be carried on by generations yet to come, for theirs was a 'spirituality of the long haul' and not of instant success. Coupled with this was their refusal to write off the world as a lost cause or to propose neat, no-loose-ends answers to the problems of life, but rather to rebuild promptly, patiently, and cheerfully, 'as if it were by some law of nature that the restoration came'. (p. 232)

Holy Saturday slow

If slow Church was the order of the day in an earlier monastic era, is it relevant any longer? George Steiner, in his remarkable *tour de force* of western culture in the twentieth century, gives the theme of slowness a much broader canvass (1989). In a celebrated final few paragraphs, Steiner speaks about the 'transitional circumstances' of our times. He proposes that we are a culture and a people who are in-between the old and the new, we are waiting in between. It is a place that is full of pain and the occasional glimmer of hope. Such a context requires, above all, patience and perseverance and a reticence for quick-fix solutions. At the end of his work, Steiner searches for a symbol to situate our times and the form of life it requires. He finishes his book thus:

There is one particular day in Western history about which neither historical record nor myth nor Scripture make report. It is a Saturday. And it has become the longest of days. We know of that Good Friday which Christianity holds to have been that of the Cross. But the non-Christian, the atheist, knows of it as well. This is to say that he knows of the injustice, of the interminable suffering, of the waste, of the brute enigma of ending, which so largely make up not only the historical dimension of the human condition, but the everyday fabric of our personal lives. We know, ineluctably, of the pain, of the failure of love, of the solitude which are our history and private fate. We know also about Sunday. To the Christian that day signifies an intimation, both assured and precarious, both evident and beyond comprehension, of resurrection, of justice and a love that has conquered death. If we are non-Christians or non-believers, we know of Sunday in precisely analogous terms. We conceive of it as the day of liberation from inhumanity and servitude. We look to resolutions, be they therapeutic or political, be they social or messianic. The lineaments of that Sunday carry the name of hope (there is no word less de-constructible).

But ours is the long day's journey of the Saturday. Between suffering and aloneness, unutterable waste on the one hand and the dream of liberation, of rebirth on the other. In the face of the torture of a child, of the death of love which is Friday, even the greatest art and poetry are almost helpless. In the Utopia of the Sunday, the aesthetic will, presumably, no longer have logic or necessity. The apprehensions and figurations in the play of metaphysical imagining, in the poem and the music, which tell of pain and of hope, of the flesh which is said to taste of ash and of the spirit which is said to have the savour of fire, are always Sabbatarian. They have risen out of an immensity of waiting which is that of man [sic]. Without them, how could we be patient? (pp. 231–2)

The waiting that Steiner speaks of is not passive. It is a cultivated waiting that brims full of vigour, life and resilience. It is waiting that does not glory in triumphalist claims. Nor is this waiting one of infinite emptiness and uselessness. He recommends a hopeful waiting that breeds holy patience as the new life emerges from the old. But it is not an easy, comfortable waiting, how can it be amidst the endless round of pain and violence in this world? Thus he concludes: 'But ours is the long day's journey of the Saturday'. The slow of Holy Saturday becomes a paradigm for a culture in need of recovering its own humanity in the midst of our inhumanity to one another and the earth.

Jesus slow: walking and healing

How might the Church recover the secret of its own humanity bound as it is to the glorified humanity of Jesus Christ? The humanity of God entailed a journey of the Son of God 'into the far country',[6] for 'though he was in the form of God, he did not think equality with God a thing to be grasped, but emptied himself taking the form of a servant and being found in human form he humbled himself and became obedient to the point of death – even death on a cross' (Phil. 2.6–8).[7] This constituted a journey into finitude, lack and limitation, yearning and suffering. God in

---

6 This was Karl Barth's well-known depiction of the incarnation as the journey of the second person of the Trinity into the world with allusion to Luke 15. Barth speaks of 'the character of the divine condescension, that takes place as God goes into the far country' (1956, p. 168).

7 Precisely because he was in the form of God, he chose the path of humility. In other words, Christ was true to form in this *kenosis*.

Christ embraced the slow lane, which went by way of Holy Saturday but is rooted in incarnation. In Christ, God pitched a tent among the peoples of the world (John 1.14). In the Christian tradition, the 'long day's journey of the Saturday' of which Steiner speaks is a journey that is first of all a divine pilgrimage. This is a pilgrimage with others that embraces but is never enclosed by Holy Saturday. Holy Saturday slow opens up into a consideration of the slow God.

A slow God may appear at first sight a challenge. Indeed, a reading of the Gospels suggests a Jesus always on the move from one village to the next; up to Jerusalem, down by the Sea of Galilee; on the borderlands between Judea and Samaria; at table, at parties, constant engagements, disputes, controversies, teaching, healing. Mark's Gospel is instructive in this respect, for here there is a note of urgency and movement in Jesus' ministry. It could be compressed into a few months. In this Gospel, Jesus is a man on a mission, and slow is not a word one would readily associate with his ministry, at least according to Mark.

Yet the Gospels as a whole, including Mark's Gospel, also record a Jesus who sought solitude, knew how to relax and refused to rush but appeared purposeful even as he moved about. We might say he inhabited the 'slow frame of mind', even in his active ministry. More particularly Jesus walked. His was a peripatetic ministry – quite normal for the time and hardly worth commenting on, except for the fact that this mode of travel all over the land provided the space and rhythm for his ministry of saving presence. The significance of Jesus walking is beautifully captured in the Emmaus road story of Luke's Gospel. The scene of companions on the road in conversation; gathering at the table, touched so deeply by Christ's presence that the only response they can imagine is to set off again on a return journey to Jerusalem to share the story. From the seedbed of such journeys with companions, Christian pilgrimage has gone to the ends of the earth.

The deeper significance of Jesus walking impressed itself upon the theologian Daniel Hardy:

I woke one night with a strong sense of the power of Jesus walking. It wasn't theory; it wasn't theology or doctrine. He was walking, step by step through the land, and after every set of steps he met someone, stood by someone, one to one, and in some way touched and healed each one . . . God's presence is outworking among us in a low-key way [a code for slowness?], and we may not have been looking for so modest a way; as simple as the quality of Jesus' walking, the way people respond to him, the way he is present to them and the way they are deeply healed. (Hardy 2010, p. 80)

Moreover, the healing that emerged in this pattern and pace of ministry constituted 'a powerful presence, which goes down to the depths, *surfaces slowly* and attracts a kind of healing' (p. 81, my italics).

'Jesus slow' indicates a particular kind of pace and presence that enables healing and transformation. It is embedded in his walking on the land in the company of others. In like manner, the 'pilgrim who finds him or herself walking–healing is not alone but travels with the Church' (p. 85). It gives rise to the idea of a 'moving ecclesiology'; '*the wandering* ecclesia: *measured by Jesus' steps*'.

Eucharistic slow

The slow of Jesus is remembered and celebrated in the Eucharist. Here is displayed and enacted through word and sacrament, the way of Jesus slow. Eucharist 'names the element of Church practice that most clearly typifies the whole: the name *per se* of God's redemptive presence in the life of the Church . . . [the Lord's Supper] . . . is the pure primal event by which righteousness was constituted in Jesus' time, and it is fully recalled each time it is re-enacted' (p. 65). Participating in the risen life of the walking and healing Jesus generates thanksgiving on the part of the pilgrim. In terms of our reflections on slowness, the Eucharist may be understood as slow release energy giving rise to gratitude and praise. This is sufficient to carry the pilgrim through 'the long day's journey of the Saturday' in faith and hope and love.

Recovering ecclesial presence

The difficulty with 'community'

I have suggested that 'slow Church' is in fact a code for the recovery of an appropriate pace and rhythm. I have differenti-ated slow Church from (a) the fast-asleep Church that remains locked in idealizations of permanence and (b) the anxiety driven frenetic Church associated with a competitive, constantly innovat-ing, success-orientated consumer society. If the former appears as 'dead man walking' functioning zombie like, the latter is often dif-ficult to differentiate from a surrounding host culture of fast food, entertainment and high-octane charismatic leaders. The pace of the former is barely recognizable, while the pace of the latter is almost guaranteed to exhaust energy. Both paces are life threatening!

However, 'slow Church' not only attends to the issue of ecclesial *pace*, it also is a code for the way in which ecclesial *presence* might be reconceived. Pace and presence are co-related. The Church has to travel at a pace that makes for the optimal instantiation of ecclesial presence. It takes time and a cultivated rhythm in order to achieve a rich ecclesial presence for the sake of the gospel; to secure a grip and strength for the journey. A kind of ecclesial torque is required! When Christianity operates in the fast lane as per the second scenario identified above, there is little prospect of the Church taking root and developing a genuine inculturated presence. On the other hand, the Church that is trapped within its own walls, sealed from the contemporary host culture and to this extent disengaged, embodies an ecclesial presence, which is essen-tially irrelevant to its host culture. In this latter case, the Church is out of step with the times, most probably dead slow and certainly unable to mediate a genuine ecclesial presence.

At one level, the subject of ecclesial presence does not seem to be a problem. The Church in its diversity has a strong and unmistakable institutional appearance and manifests the behav-iours of such an entity. It is not difficult to identify structures of permanence in, for example, polities for governance, ministries, sacraments, mission programs, doctrine and moral standards. The question of ecclesial presence considered from an institutional and empirical point of view seems assured. The Church is evidently still in existence and in the West asset rich.

However, when presence is restricted to an institutional matter it hides the significant disintegration of the Church in the West over recent centuries. Church contraction, decline and loss of vitality are common observations. Responses to this have been noted above (that is, Church fast asleep or Church in frenetic mode). These and related issues about the Church's role and place in society have been the subject of important theological and socio-logical scrutiny. One consequence is that the question of ecclesial presence is now a contested matter. What does it now mean to speak about the presence of the Church?

The anxiety that attends the question of ecclesial presence inter-estingly presents itself through the rise of the quest for community. The language of community has become the default for those of the Church who are desirous of recovering an ecclesial presence, which is authentic and faithful to the gospel of Jesus. Ecclesial presence has become a question of authentic Christian commu-nity (see Kirkpatrick 1986). It might even be possible to speak of an obsession with community or at least an obsessive fixation on creating community, often with little understanding of how this occurs and endures. In this respect, Martin Buber's comments in the early twentieth century are apposite:

> The true community does not arise through peoples having feelings for one another (though indeed not without it), but through, first, their taking a stand in living mutual relation with a living Centre, and, second, their being in living mutual rela-tion with one another. The second has its source in the first, but it is not given when the first alone is given . . . The community is built up out of living mutual relation, but the builder is the living effective Centre. (Buber 1937, p. 45)

The communitarian approach to ecclesial presence has been recently critiqued by the American theologian Peter Dula (2011). Dula examined the idea of ecclesial community in a number of contemporary theologians from different ecclesial traditions, including Stanley Hauerwas, Alasdair MacIntyre, John Yoder, John Milbank and William Cavanaugh. Dula notes their critiques of Church and society and observes that each in their own way identify periods where ecclesial presence accorded most nearly to their understanding of what it means to be an ideal community of the gospel. For example, Yoder identifies the optimal period of Christian community with the sixteenth-century Anabaptists, Milbank the eleventh century and Cavanaugh in Chile under the Pinochet regime. Dula recognizes that these theologians represent a more general desire to 'find the pristine, the pure, the traditional' (p. 97). Implicit in this is a view of the Church in its pure form, which is essentially a passing phenomenon, momentary and episodic. Thus Milbank states, 'We are forced to admit that it [the Church as he understands it] can only have been present intermittently during the Christian centuries' (quoted on p. 98). For someone like Milbank in the Anglo-catholic tradition, this is a serious conclusion though from the perspective of Yoder or Barth such a conclusion might be expected (p. 110).[8] Problems with the search for a pure period of the Church lead Dula to critique the idealist communitarian ecclesiologies implicit in the above approaches to the Church. Instead he proposes the notion of the 'fugitive ecclesia'.

Fugitive *ecclesia*: elusive pace and presence

The episodic Church

Dula argues that the communitarian approach exemplified in the positions of the above theologians trades on notions of purity. They make the mistake of identifying particular periods in history that embody the marks of the pure Church. In terms of our

---

8 For Barth, the Church is witness to rather than the embodiment of the marks of the Church. From this point of view, there can be no particular time or place, which is particularly privileged for the Church, contra Milbank. Barth's Christological ecclesiology almost requires a notion of fugitivity.

foregoing discussion, it is a matter of specifying when and where the *pace* and *presence* of the slow Church is optimized. Dula is critical of all such attempts to specify pure community. Indeed, from his perspective 'community' is itself fleeting and unsatisfactory, and this is not compensated for nor overcome by strong assertions to the contrary. Such protestations, however nuanced and sophisticated, simply confirm the deep unrealized longing for the elusive experience of true community. Dula develops the notion of the episodic or fugitive Church, which is always disappearing, on the run, fugitive.

In developing this position, Dula draws upon the writings of the American philosopher, Sheldon Wolin, and in particular his 1996 essay 'Fugitive Democracy'. Dula notes the 'mood of disappointment' and 'despair about the possibility of democracy' in Wolin's essay and he echoes Wolin's sense that democracy 'can only be momentary, occasional, sporadic, and evanescent' (p. 96). Wolin distinguishes between the *political* ('the idea that a free society composed of diversities can nonetheless enjoy moments of commonality when . . . collective power is used to promote or protect the wellbeing of the collective') and *politics* ('legitimized public contestation'). Wolin states that '[p]olitics is continuous, ceaseless, and endless. In contrast, the political is episodic, rare'. Dula notes that in Wolin's assessment the significant moments of the genuinely political (such as Poland's Solidarity Movement) have been 'fleeting, fugitive' and often 'degenerated into something authoritarian and reactionary'.

The burden of Dula's argument is that the fugitivity associated with Wolin's notion of political is in fact the trajectory of the arguments of Milbank, Hauerwas, Cavanaugh and others. The fact that they seem reluctant to say so explicitly leads Dula to state: 'They seem caught between the inescapability of the fugitive and the promise to Peter . . . theology is faced with the unbearable suggestion that modernity/late capitalism/postmodernity/the secular/neo-neo-neo-Constantinianism, pick your epithet, is tantamount to the gates of hell' (p. 97). Dula is mindful of Milbank's comment that 'Either the Church enacts the vision of paradisal community . . . or else it promotes a hellish society beyond any terrors known to antiquity'.

The problem with the fugitive *ecclesia* is that it does not seem capable of bearing the weight that is placed upon the Church's witness. This is especially the case for people like Milbank, Hauer-was, and many others, it needs to be said, for whom 'everything hangs on Church being what they say it is'; that the meanings of the word God 'are to be discovered by watching what this com-munity does' and that 'the Church is the organized form of the Jesus' story'. What credence can be placed upon such claims, if the community, which instantiates such things, is 'episodic, eva-nescent, fugitive'? Hence the reticence to state the full implication of their critique of Church and society. Dula notes that a 'bleak account of modernity is essential to their ecclesiology' (p. 98). But they end up with a significant difficulty: 'things have to be bad enough to justify the rigid Church–world dualism but not so bad as to make Church impossible'. There seems no way out of a choice, 'either Church is possible and therefore things are not so bad, or things are every bit as ugly as they often seem and therefore we should give up hope for anything other than fugitive *ecclesia*'.

No *unambiguous ecclesial presence*

There are a variety of possible options in relation to the fugitive *ecclesia* ranging from abandonment of the Church to full accep-tance of its fugitive status (with accompanying attitudes of resig-nation and/or joy). However, as I mentioned above, the idea of the fugitive Church trades on notions of purity and primitiveness. This may give a rather skewed picture of the reality of the Church that, even in its imagined pure manifestations, inevitably has had elements of violence that have been too easily overlooked. The notion of ecclesial presence would have to be modified to take account of the fact that there is probably not one particular time or place that represents the pure spring of the Church. *On this basis, there is no unambiguous ecclesial presence.* The Church may well have an episodic character woven into and through some constant practices and forms of life. This gives rise to the notion of levels of intensity of being the Church in any time and place. This ought to generate a degree of humility that even if everything is not in a state of flux nonetheless we cannot rest assured that at any one moment the Church can settle back and rest on its achievements.

Fugitive ecclesia: a cautionary note

Dula's critique of communitarian ecclesiology is helpful in so far as it highlights the dangers of an over-idealized view of the *ecclesia* which can mask such things as structural violence, discrimination and loss of energy. From Dula's point of view, it seems that the concept of 'community' is made to bear too great a load and disappointment is almost hard-wired into the Church. But is 'fugitive *ecclesia*' an adequate response? Dula's position may be another version, albeit quite sophisticated, of the Protestant suspicion of the visible Church.

The theology of sociality developed in this book ought to make us wary of discounting the work of God in creation constantly drawing all things back to the Lord. The orientation towards community is encoded into createdness as such and this means we ought to expect intimations of ecclesial presence everywhere that people are being raised to fullness of life together. The Church is that company alive to this work of God in the world and who intentionally attend to this work through worship and discipleship. How does it do this? I have suggested in this chapter that it is a matter of slow Church coming. The Church attends to its incarnate and living Lord at a pace that enables genuine recognition and discipleship to occur. This takes time and attention and hence it is a slow unfolding work (Mark 4.26–9).

I have also suggested that the Church is always coming; that it remains incomplete and contingent. There can be no pure embodiment of the ecclesial community past or present, precisely because it remains a work in progress. That is why the Eucharist is so critical for the ongoing life of the Church. In this primal practice of the Church, the community of faith is able to acknowledge its incompleteness, fracture and hope for a new time. It can do this precisely because the Eucharist bears witness to and embodies the true and abiding life of the *ecclesia*, which is Christ the Lord in the midst. If the Church is fugitive *in some sense*, it is so not because it is always disappearing but because it seeks to embody in its life the slow Church coming. The fullness of its true life lies ahead or in what is coming from the future.

In this chapter, I have also argued that slow Church is a matter of presence as well as pace. I drew attention to the fact that the plight of the Church in our present western context has meant that the question of ecclesial presence has increasingly become bolted onto the concept of community and the ways through which community is spread – for example, by social agency. The search for the Church has become a search for authentic community. This has set many theologians – not to mention vast numbers of the people of God – on a trajectory towards what Dula calls 'fugitive Church'. The supposition is that ecclesial presence has to be understood in an episodic, momentary manner. The danger is that this presumes either (a) the identification of certain times and places as evidence of the pure (as with Milbank, Cavanaugh, Yoder) or (b) leaves the matter entirely without concrete form and location (such as Barth) (Dula 2011, p. 110). Neither approach does justice to the character of created and redeemed sociality developed in the earlier chapters of this book. The possibility for new community as a work of the Holy Spirit cannot be restricted to the enclosures of the visible institutional Church, nor to some supposed episodic outbreak of new ecclesial life. Such views trade on a false dichotomy between creation and redemption. This is not to say that the Church lacks visibility; nor that history gives evidence of repeated renewal of the *ecclesia*. However, the boundaries of being the Church are necessarily more porous, elusive and open than we might have believed. This is good news for all!

Does this render the notion of fugitive *ecclesia* valueless? Given the parlous state of so much of the western Church such a conclusion is hard to justify. But the fact that the fugitive Church has such traction in ecclesiology and more general ecclesial sensibilities is indicative of a deep dis-ease with much that goes under the banner of the institutional Church. The fugitive Church represents a search for a truer, more authentic and genuine sociality that operates under the skin of and even in spite of the constraints of the institutional Church. The episodic character of this renewed sociality may operate in tension with the institution and beyond its scaffolding, but this is not necessarily evidence of a *parallel ecclesia*.

Fugitive *ecclesia* may perhaps function as the renewing dimension within the Church as it is. It is precisely at this point that the default to community is important for this is the clue to what is being sought in the so-called fugitive *ecclesia*; not a parallel Church but a search for community with God and others. This belongs to the deeper mystery that the Church is. Fugitive *ecclesia* is an expression of the deep human desire for true community. However, what if the hoped for community that undergirds much of contemporary ecclesiology is largely rhetorical masking deep uncertainties about what is really possible?

My concern with the emphasis upon community as the mode through which we now make judgements regarding ecclesial presence, is that community itself is easily colonized by host cultures and can quickly become the habitations of the 'like-minded' or as Peter Berger once called it, 'lifestyle enclaves' (Bellah et al. 1985, pp. 71–5). This has echoes of Derrida's reflections on the '*paralysis* of community' arising from the fact that a community 'must limit itself, [to] remain a community while remaining "open," forbidding itself the luxury of collecting itself into a unity' (Caputo 1994, Ch. 4, p. 113).[9] In this vein, Derrida refers to 'an *open* quasi-community' that is always 'a community to come', 'another community' with 'loose ends', a 'com-*manus*, with munificence and extravagance' (p. 124). This paradoxically is 'weak community' that requires considerable strength and resilience. The danger Derrida,

---

9 For Derrida, it is about a community opening itself to difference and hospitality even as it lives out a 'common identity'. The sign of the responsible community is that such a community lives with the tension between open hospitality and holding a common identity without predetermining in advance how that tension must be settled (p. 121).

Bellah and others allude to is that the language of community can function as rhetorical language that unintentionally masks a hermetically sealed, non-porous sociality that trades on dualisms between the Church and the world, an 'us-and-them' notion, which has little if anything to do with the good news of the hospitality of the kingdom of God. Maybe things are worse than we have thought and even the ideal of community is vacuous. The slow Church coming will have to reckon with the critique of community and find a form that finds a pace and presence that is hospitable.

The idea of community as it is currently deployed may be made to bear too much weight for the being of the Church. Another way to regard the matter is that there may be more originative modes of life, which provide the seedbed for the slow Church coming. Prior to communitarian emphases, underlying notions of fugitive Church and most certainly providing seedlings for a renewed sociality, there is companionship as the form through which ecclesial presence is ignited and expands into full-orbed ecclesial practices. If you like, companionship is a bedrock condition without which the Church cannot be the Church.

Companionship: on slowing the rush to community

At this point in his discussion of fugitive *ecclesia*, Dula turns his attention from *community* to *companionship*. In doing so, he invokes Aristotle's appeal to 'friendship' as the means by which people are helped to attain virtue. Dula notes that, for Aristotle, if the state fails to achieve true polity – good ordering for the welfare and maturation of its citizens – this task can at least be achieved through friendship. 'His [Aristotle's] turn to friendship, however, is not an abandonment of the polis in favor of friendship because it carries with it the hope that friendship is the seed of the polis' (2011, p. 113). Dula is in company with theologians like Hauerwas, who argue that with the failure of the modern state, the only political alternative we have is friendship. However, he parts company with them, when they weld friendship to Church.

proper acknowledgement of fugitivity suggests that friendship is an alternative not just to the collapse of the polis, or to the war machine of the modern state, but also to the Church when it has become fugitive, or when theologians realize that it has always been fugitive.

This does not represent an abandonment of the Church—or the *polis*, or even the state – but it does imply beginning 'at a narrower, reduced level'. Dula is wary of a too smooth and unproblematic transition from companionship to community. In the case of Hauerwas, according to Dula, Church is assumed to 'make friend-ship possible, instead of the other way around' (p. 202).[10] The danger is that companionship might become entangled within dis-torted forms of community that aspire to conformity and suppress the affirmation of otherness. Such things, Dula argues, are too high a price for community. Companionship lives by and grows through the affirmation of otherness while community can too easily function as a rhetoric for new forms of control and suppres-sion of difference. Dula desires to give an account of companion-ship 'to slow us down on our rush to community' (p. 117).

This slowing down 'on our rush to community' strikes a chord with me at many levels not least in a chapter on slow Church com-ing. It is the key features of companionship – acknowledgement of otherness; capacity for self-reliance as a counter to conformity; appreciation of other selves and our humanness; recognizing and welcoming difference; the joy of the bonds of affection – that are only what they are as time goes by, as we learn patience as per-sons, as we bump up against the imponderables, disappointments and failed expectations in relation to self and other selves. Com-panionship crafted in such circumstances of life in the world can't be rushed; rather it has an emergent gift-like character that con-tinually surprises and lures us towards each other and God. Per-haps the slow Church coming will be the kind of Church which is

---

10 More accurately we might want to speak of a dialectical process whereby companionship both generates and is in turn nurtured through the Church.

formed and nurtured through intricate and complex webs of companionship. It will be a Church which lives with a certain restraint regarding its own claims and efforts at self-promotion.

It may be that friendship/companionship is the inner power of ecclesial granulation; working below the surface of the wound, healing society from within. Perhaps it is more accurate to speak not of a fugitive Church but a travelling Church, not an episodic explosion of new life but more a travelling caravansary nurturing companionship, collecting pilgrims on the journey, sharing food, attentive to God and others, discovering the secrets of a life of praise.

Such a portrait of the Church resonates with the general trajectory of this book with its emphasis on the unfinished nature of the Church, the essential dynamic of its structures and energy sources and the ways in which the sociality of the Church is renewed through being with God in the world. Such a portrait moves beyond a steady state Church to a dynamic ecclesial ontology. The principal features of this are movement, renewable energy, and elastic structures that seek to embody the height, depth, length and breadth of the mystery of the life of the Church.

Travelling companions

Searching for the sacred

A travelling ecclesiology will have time to gather the seekers of God. In the slow Church coming, such people are not so easily missed, and in a slow Church, there is time for friendships to grow, and justice and peace can find a place in the ecology of discipleship. The slow Church coming will be a Church which is always discovering a pace that enables the presence of God and life with others to be optimized. The seekers of God are more often those seeking a genuine life together, where people are honoured within the ecology of praise to God. The pace and presence of the coming Church has to be such a community, where such an honouring and praise is possible and can expand.

That there are many seekers of God in our contemporary world is patently obvious. The fact that many do not normally come by way of the Church as we know it ought not fool us into thinking they do not exist. Indeed, the Australian writer David Tracey refers to the search for 'primal spirituality', and he notes that the 'return of the religious' continues unabated (2003). It is the reason why, notes American theologian, Harvey Cox, Pentecostalism has exercised such a potent force throughout the world, and, in its more domesticated forms, why the charismatic movement and its offshoots provided such an important impetus for renewal in the late twentieth century (1996).

How well the mainline churches of the world will be able to connect people with the deep realities of human need expressed through such a 'primal spirituality' is an important issue. It is a problem, for increasingly the traditional institutional embodiments for such religious instincts are being jettisoned by the younger generations. Furthermore, as Philip Jenkins has convincingly argued, the Christianity of the twenty-first century will be significantly influenced by the religious and spiritual impulses from the southern globe (2002).

Richard Roberts contends that for the secular west the sacred has not been lost or abandoned so much as migrated (2001, pp. 178f). In this context, the Church has to rediscover its significant resources to make it possible for the people of the world to encounter a radical otherness beyond the 'sacralization of the self' and 'self-religion'. This will require a significant reorientation, and as I have suggested above it requires a different pace, rhythm and presence, which I associate with slow Church. Indeed, slow Church may turn out to be a prophetic response to an anxious quick-fix, solution-driven culture, where people become quickly worn out and fall by the wayside as unproductive units.

Pilgrims and nomads

Who are the travellers on the slow route to God? The philosopher Zygmunt Bauman identifies four types of travellers:

pilgrims, nomads, vagrants and tourists (1993, Ch. 8). Pilgrims are those who have clear intent and a final destination. They are on a journey to somewhere quite specific for a specific purpose. Their way appears stable and rich in meaning. They follow an order of things along pre-established tracks. They are travellers along well-worn tracks and obediential following is their defining mark. So goes the post-modernist take on the pilgrim. It resonates, but it also jars. The pilgrims' acts are innovative, but their path is chosen for them; pilgrims gain deep satisfaction and consolation from knowing that others have passed before and will travel again. Pilgrims are fundamentally guests, and the path the host. I remember reading Bunyan's *Pilgrim's Progress* as a young man. I was totally captivated by the rich imagery and symbolism. However, pilgrimage more often appeared fraught and dangerous. Bunyan's pilgrim lived by grace and at any moment the ground could open up and consume the hapless pilgrim. Bauman's depiction appears idealized and self-assured compared to Bunyan's.

In the post-modern environment, Bauman wondered whether pilgrims had been eclipsed by nomads. Such persons are always on the move but they circle around well-structured territory. This territory has stable meanings in each fragment. There is no final destination for nomads but rather a constant covering of the same tracks within a bounded area. No place is privileged. The nomad moves in a regular succession following the order of things. Nomads usually have an itinerary and the appearance of aimlessness can be deceiving.

Vagabonds and tourists

However, in Bauman's analysis, the nomad failed the post-modern test or rather was eclipsed by another type closer to the post-modern archetypal traveller. The vagrant or vagabond appears. The vagrant or vagabond is also on the move; all three types share that in common. We have to do here with a fundamentally seeker-spirituality rather than a dweller-spirituality (Wuthnow, 1998, Ch. 1). It is a religious sensibility, which is restless and on the move. But the vagabond does not know how long he or she will be staying in a place. Moreover, it is rarely up to the vagrant to decide how long. Others will make that choice. Vagabonds have no itinerary. They set their destination as they travel by reading the signs. Essentially, the vagrant is uncertain where, how long, and with whom the roving goes. Vagabonds move on because they are dissatisfied with the last place at which they stopped. Their frustration pushes them on. They hope that the next place might be free of the faults of the previous one. They are driven by untested hope. They journey through unstructured space, quite different to the nomad. The vagrant is a pilgrim without destination and a nomad without itinerary. Vagrants wander through life and the only tracks they have are their own, which are always vanishing behind them and do not in the nature of the case reach before them. They inhabit each space in an episodic fashion. They structure the site in which they happen to stay in for a time, and then they dismantle it and leave. The vagrant or vagabond resembles an aimless wanderer. Maybe such a traveller is one in whom the hope of promise of something better has not been totally obliterated. Hope is the prime mover, disillusionment the constant companion. We are close to our contemporary person who may indeed pass by the Church looking for something.

There is one final metaphor that fits post-modern life, the tourist. The tourist, like the vagabond, will not stay long in any place. But the only time constraint is his or her biographical time. The tourist invests all places with maximum pliability. Places are like soft putty in the hand. It is at the tourist's discretion which spaces come into the tourist's world. So, the tourist can disregard natural locations, the uniqueness of a place and its intrinsic meanings. None of this necessarily counts for the tourist. The tourist is driven by the aesthetic, the quest for pleasurable and novel experiences, as he or she moves through alien spaces. There is curiosity, the need for amusement and almost total freedom of space in the tourist's world. This is where tourist and vagabond part company, for the latter only dream of such freedom. The tourist on the other hand pays for it! The tourist pays for the freedom to disregard native concerns, natural locations with meaning and claims of a moral kind. The tourist has freedom from all this via contractual agreements. Tourists are essentially extra-territorial with a privilege and right to restructure the world in which they live and move and have their being. The world is the tourist's oyster full of exotic thrills.

Both tourist and vagabond move through the spaces occupied by others. Both have mis-meetings with the other or perfunctory encounters of a highly episodic kind. The tourist can be physically close and spiritually remote. The seductive charm of the tourist is that physical proximity does not allow or require moral proximity. Freedom from moral duty has already been paid for. The charm of tourism is total negation of moral responsibility. As Bauman states, 'the tourist is bad news for morality. The moral conscience has been given a good dose of sleeping pills. The tourist is in but not of the world' (1993, p. 242). Freedom to be seems to be the key. The really worrying thing about the tourist as type is that it infects the western world, and it is not simply for holiday time but has become the normal life. For the tourist, the social space is grazing ground; the aesthetic space is the playground. In all spaces, the mode of engagement is unadulterated voyeurism. For the tourist, churches may be grazing-grounds or playgrounds.

Bauman suggests that the tourist and vagabond are here to stay. 'The vagabond and tourist are no more marginal people or marginal conditions. They turn into moulds destined to engross and shape the totality of life . . . They set the standard of happiness and successful life in general'.

An ecclesiology for pilgrims

Bauman's four types identify well the travellers that are the concern of the slow Church coming. The pilgrim is a far more complex figure than Bauman's portrait and is always in danger of morphing into one of the other three types. It may be more accurate to see the pilgrim as an interesting and complex blend of all four types. How can it be otherwise within the context of the late or post-modern west? It is no exaggeration to say that churches are inhabited by many tourists or ecclesial voyeurs who have all the characteristics of people window-shopping. What will draw them beyond their self-enclosed worlds into relation with others and God? How might the tourist become a true pilgrim? The vagabond and nomad types can also appear along the road. Indeed, the aimlessness that afflicts the vagabond is deeply ingrained in the western psyche, and many a pilgrim is at heart an aimless wanderer seeking a more hopeful outcome. This condition often expresses itself in its opposite in forms of religious fundamentalism. Here, the lure of certainty appears as an attractive antidote to an aimless life without hope.

What kind of Church, if any, will such people seek? This book is written in the conviction that the *ecclesia* of God is a natural companion for our post-modern types because it too is a travelling people. Moreover, the secret of its own life, its deepest mystery is neither owned nor can be claimed by anyone. Rather, the secret of its life is the attractive love of God; a divine lure, which draws people to each other and at the same time to the God in whose image we have been made. Furthermore, this Church moves at a pace that gives time for wisdom to be found, take root and expand among people. It is the pace and presence of the slow Church coming that carries in its corporate memory the faithful of the past. The Church at any time is always travelling with the saints and sages of past time and space.[11] In such an ecclesial environment, organizational structures and ministrations of ancient lineage can take on a new significance as enablers for deeper freedom and peace. The remarkable thing about such an *ecclesia* is the presence of a surplus of renewable energy, which is continually released through attentive listening to God and one another; to re-membering and celebrating and to care, service and joyful telling of the story of Jesus. This is the unfinished Church of Emmaus Road companions; the slow Church coming on a journey with the peoples of the world.

---

11 In this sense, the episodic church is a theological impossibility.

Questions

1 How might 'slow Church' be a counter-cultural prophetic Church?
2 What are the implications of 'slow church' for the Church's engagement with society and the environment?
3 What are the strengths and weaknesses of the appeal to the Church as a community?
4 How important is the concept of companionship for a travelling ecclesiology?
5 What are the implications for the life and mission of the Church of Bauman's four travellers in the post-modern (pilgrim, nomad, vagrant and tourist)?

Further reading

Scott Cowdell, 'The Emerging Church', in *God's Next Big Thing: Discovering the Future Church*, Mulgrave, Victoria: John Garrett Publishing, 2004, pp. 74–111.

Veli-Matti Kärkkäinen, 'A Post-Christian Church as "Another City"' and 'Lesslie Newbigin, Missionary Ecclesiology', in *An Introduction to Ecclesiology: Ecumenical, Historical and Global Perspectives*, Downers Grove, IL: Inter Varsity Press, 2002, pp. 221–30, 151–9.

Stephen Pickard, 'Unfinished Emmaus Journey: Discipleship for Pilgrims', in *In-Between God: Theology, Community and Discipleship*, Adelaide: ATF, 2011, pp. 251–62.

Bibliography

Gregory Afonsky, *Christ and the Church: In Orthodox Teaching and Tradition*, New York, Crestwood: St Vladimir's Seminary Press, 2001.

Apostolicity and Succession, House of Bishops Occasional Paper, London: Church House Publishing, 1994.

Paul Avis, *Anglicanism and the Christian Church*, Edinburgh: T & T Clark, 1989.

Paul Avis, 'Ecclesiology', in A. McGrath (ed.), *The Blackwell Encyclopedia of Modern Christian Thought*, Oxford, Blackwell, 1993.

Hans Urs von Balthasar, *The Glory of the Lord: A Theological Aesthetics Vol. 1, Seeing the Form* (1961), Edinburgh: T & T Clark, 1982.

Karl Barth, *Church Dogmatics* I.1, Edinburgh: T&T Clark, 1936.

Karl Barth, *Church Dogmatics* IV.1, trans. G. Bromiley and T. F. Torrance, Edinburgh: T & T Clark, 1956.

Karl Barth, *Church Dogmatics* II.2, Edinburgh: T & T Clark, 1957.

Karl Barth, *Church Dogmatics*, IV.3, trans. G. Bromiley, Edinburgh: T & T Clark, 1962.

Karl Barth, *Church Dogmatics* IV.4, trans. G. Bromiley, Edinburgh: T&T Clark, 1981.

Karl Barth, *Dogmatics in Outline*, trans. G. T. Thomson, London: SCM Press, 1966.

Markus Barth, 'Christ and All Things', in Morna Hooker and Stephen G. Wilson (eds), *Paul and Paulinism: Essays in Honour of C. K. Barrett*, London: SPCK, 1982, pp. 160–72.

Zygmunt Bauman, *Postmodern Ethics*, Oxford: Blackwell, 1993.

Robert Bellah et al., *Habits of the Heart: Individualism and Commitment in American Life*, New York: Harper & Row, 1985.

Kimlyn J. Bender, *Karl Barth's Christological Ecclesiology*, Aldershot: Ashgate, 2005.

Ernst Best, *Ephesians*, ICC series, Edinburgh: T & T Clark, 1998.

M. Bockmuehl and M. Thomson (eds), *A Vision for the Church: Studies in Early Christian Ecclesiology*, Edinburgh: T & T Clark, 1997.

Leonardo Boff, *Trinity and Society*, Maryknoll NY: Orbis, 1988.

BIBLIOGRAPHY

Roberta Bondi, *To Pray and to Love: Conversations on Prayer with the Early Church*, Minneapolis: Fortress Press, 1991.

Dietrich Bonhoeffer, *The Communion of Saints: A Theological Study of the Sociology of the Church*, trans. Reinhard Krauss and Nancy Lukens, Minneapolis: Fortress Press, 1963.

David Bosch, *Transforming Mission: Paradigm Shifts in Theology of Mission*, Maryknoll, NY: Orbis, 1991.

Martin Buber, *I and Thou*, Edinburgh: T & T Clark, 1937.

Rudolf Bultmann, *Theology of the New Testament*, trans. Kendrick Grobel, 2nd edn, Vol. 1, London: SCM Press, 1965.

Gregory K. Cameron, 'Ardour and Order: Can the Bonds of Affection Survive in the Anglican Communion?', *Ecclesiastical Law Journal* 9 (2007), pp. 288–93.

Helen Cameron et al, *Talking About God in Practice: Theological Action Research and Practical Theology*, London: SCM, 2010.

John Caputo (ed.), *Deconstruction in a Nutshell: A Conversation with Jacques Derrida*, New York: Fordham University Press, 1994.

William Cavanaugh, *Torture and the Eucharist: Theology, Politics and the Body of Christ*, Oxford: Blackwell, 1998.

Alfred D. Chandler, *The Visible Hand: The Managerial Revolution in American Business*, Cambridge, MA: Belknap Press, 1977.

Alfred D. Chandler and Herman Daems, *Managerial Hierarchies: Comparative Perspectives on the Rise of the Modern Industrial Enterprise*, Cambridge, MA: Harvard University Press, 1980.

Mark Chapman, 'The Social Doctrine of the Trinity: Some Problems', *Anglican Theological Review*, 83:2 (2001), pp. 239–54.

Sarah Coakley, *Powers and Submissions: Spirituality, Philosophy and Gender*, Oxford: Blackwell, 2002.

L. Coenen, 'Church, Synagogue', in Colin Brown (ed.), *The New Dictionary of New Testament Theology*, 4 vols, Grand Rapids, MI: Zondervan Publishing, 1975, Vol. 1, pp. 291–307.

Adela Yarbro Collins, *Mark: A Commentary*, Minneapolis: Fortress Press, 2007.

Raymond Collins, *The Many Faces of the Church: A Study in New Testament Ecclesiology*, New York: Crossroad, 2003.

Scott Cowdell, *Abiding Faith: Christianity Beyond Certainty, Anxiety and Violence*, Eugene, OR: Cascade Books, 2008.

Harvey Cox, *Fire From Heaven: The Rise of Pentecostal Spirituality and the Reshaping of Religion in the 21st Century*, London: Cassell, 1996.

Christopher Dawson, *Religion and the Rise of Western Culture*, London: Sheed & Ward, 1950.

Dennis Doyle, *Communion Ecclesiology: Vision and Versions*, Maryknoll, NY: Orbis Books, 2000.

Peter Dula, *Cavell, Companionship, and Christian Theology*, Oxford: Oxford University Press, 2011.

Avery Dulles, *Models of the Church*, New York: Gill and Macmillan, 1974.

Edward Farley, *Ecclesial Man: A Social Phenomenology of Faith and Reality*, Philadelphia: Fortress Press, 1975.

E. Feil, *The Theology of Dietrich Bonhoeffer*, Philadelphia: Fortress Press, 1985.

Anthony Giddens, *New Rules of Sociological Method*, London: HarperCollins, 1976.

Anthony Giddens, *The Constitution of Society: Outline of the Theory of Structuration*, Cambridge: Polity Press, 1984.

Paula Gooder, 'In Search of the Early "Church": The New Testament and Development of Christian Communities', in Gerard Mannion and Lewis S. Mudge (eds), *The Routledge Companion to the Christian Church*, New York and London: Routledge, 2012, pp. 9–27.

Norman K. Gottwald, *The Tribes of Yahweh: A Sociology of the Religion of Liberated Israel, 1250–1050 BCE*, Maryknoll, NY: Orbis Books, 1979.

Robin Greenwood, *Parish Priests: For the Sake of the Kingdom*, London: SPCK, 2009.

Stanley J. Grenz, *Theology for the Community of God*, Grand Rapids, MI: Eerdmans, 1994.

Colin Gunton, 'The Church on Earth: The Roots of Community', in Colin Gunton and Daniel Hardy (eds), *On Being the Church: Essays on the Christian Community*, Edinburgh: T & T Clark, 1989, pp. 48–80.

Colin Gunton, *The One the Three and the Many: God, Creation and the Culture of Modernity*, The 1992 Bampton Lectures, Cambridge: Cambridge University Press, 1992.

Colin Gunton, *The Promise of Trinitarian Theology*, Edinburgh: T & T Clark, 1993.

Jürgen Habermas, *The Theory of Communicative Action*, trans. Thomas McCarthy, 2 vols., Cambridge: Polity Press, 1984–7.

Daniel Hardy and David Ford, *Jubilate: Theology in Praise*, London: Darton, Longman and Todd, 1984.

Daniel Hardy, 'Created and Redeemed Sociality', in Colin Gunton and Daniel Hardy (eds), *On Being the Church: Essays on the Christian Community*, Edinburgh: T & T Clark, 1989, pp. 21–47.

Daniel Hardy, *God's Ways with the World: Thinking and Practising Christian Faith*, Edinburgh: T & T Clark, 1996.

Daniel Hardy, 'A Magnificent Complexity: Letting God be God in Church, Society and Creation', in David F. Ford and Dennis L. Stamps (eds), *Essentials of Christian Community*, Edinburgh: T & T Clark, 1996a, pp. 307–56.

Daniel Hardy, 'Worship', in P. B. Clarke and A. Linzey (eds), *Dictionary of Ethics, Theology and Society*, New York and London: Routledge, 1996b, pp. 896–900.

Daniel Hardy, *Finding the Church: The Dynamic Truth of Anglicanism*, London: SCM Press, 2001.

Daniel Hardy, 'Anglicanism in the Twenty-First Century: Scriptural, Local, Global', unpublished paper delivered at the Anglican Group, American Academy of Religion, Atlanta, 2004.

Daniel Hardy, 'John Macquarrie's Ecclesiology', in Robert Morgan (ed.), *In Search of Humanity and Deity: A Celebration of John Macquarrie's Theology*, London: SCM Press, 2006, pp. 267–76.

Daniel W. Hardy with Deborah Hardy Ford, Peter Ochs and David F. Ford, *Wording a Radiance: Parting Conversations on God and the Church*, London: SCM, 2010.

Nicholas Healy, *Church, World and Christian Life: Practical–Prophetic Ecclesiology*, Cambridge: Cambridge University Press, 2000.

Nicholas Healy, 'Practices and the New Ecclesiology: Misplaced Concreteness?', *International Journal of Systematic Theology* 5:3 (2003), pp. 287–308.

Gabriel Hebert, *The Form of the Church*, London: Faber and Faber, 1945.

Philip J. Hefner, 'The Church', in Carl Braaten and Robert Jensen (eds), *Christian Dogmatics* Vol. 2, Philadelphia: Fortress Press, 1984.

George Herbert, *The Works of George Herbert*, ed. by F. E. Hutchinson, Oxford: Clarendon Press, 1941.

Peter C. Hodgson and Robert C. Williams, 'The Church', in Peter Hodgson and Robert King (eds), *Christian Theology: An Introduction to its Traditions and Tasks*, London: SPCK, 1996.

Carl Honoré, *In Praise of Slowness: Challenging the Cult of Speed*, New York: HarperCollins, 2005.

Richard Hooker, *Of the Laws of Ecclesiastical Polity*, 2 vols., London: J. M. Dent & Sons, 1954.

Brian Horne, '*Homo Hierarchicus* and Ecclesial Order', *International Journal for the Study of the Christian Church* 7:1 (2007), pp. 16–28.

IATDC, '*Communion, Conflict and Hope*, The Kuala Lumpur Report of the Inter-Anglican Theological and Doctrinal Commission (IATDC), London: Anglican Communion Office, 2008.

Daniel Izuzquiza, *Rooted in Jesus Christ: Toward a Radical Ecclesiology*, Grand Rapids, MI: Eerdmans, 2009.

Philip Jenkins, *The Next Christendom: The Coming of Global Christianity*, Oxford: Oxford University Press, 2002.

Matt Jensen and David Wilhite, *The Church: A Guide for the Perplexed*, London: T & T Clark, 2010.

Robert Jensen, *Systematic Theology* Vol. 2, 'The Works of God', New York and Oxford: Oxford University Press, 1999.

Joachim Jeremias, *New Testament Theology*, London: SCM Press, 1971.

Elizabeth Johnston, *She Who is: The Mystery of God in Feminist Theological Discourse*, New York: Crossroad, 1993.

Immanuel Kant, *An Answer to the Question: What is Enlightenment?* 1784 (pub. 1798) in 'Immanuel Kant' trans. and ed. M. J. Gregor, *Practical Philosophy*, Cambridge: Cambridge University Press, 1996.

Veli-Matti Kärkkäinen, *An Introduction to Ecclesiology: Ecumenical, Historical and Global Perspectives*, Downers Grove, IL: InterVarsity Press, 2002.

Ernst Käsemann, *New Testament Questions of Today*, London: SCM Press, 1969.

Karen Kilby, 'Perichoresis and Projection: Problems with Social Doctrines of the Trinity', *New Blackfriars*, 81:956 (2000), pp. 432–45.

Frank Kirkpatrick, *Community: A Trinity of Models*, Washington DC: Georgetown University Press, 1986.

Hans Küng, *The Church*, trans. R. Ockenden, London: Burns & Oates, 1967.

Catherine LaCugna, *God For Us, The Trinity and Christian Life*, San Francisco: Harper, 1991.

Paul Lakeland, *The Liberation of the Laity: In Search of an Accountable Church*, New York and London: Continuum, 2004.

Richard Lennan, 'Communion Ecclesiology: Foundations, Critiques, and Affirmations', *Pacifica* 20 (2007), pp. 24–39.

Michael Leunig, 'Another Way of Being', in *The Prayer Tree*, North Blackburn, Victoria: Collins Dove, 1991.

D. Limerick, B. Cunnington and F. Crowther, *Managing the New Organisation: Collaboration and Sustainability in the Postcorporate World*, Sydney: Business and Professional Publishing, 1998.

Kenneth A. Locke, *The Church in Anglican Theology*, Farnham: Ashgate, 2009.

Alfred Loisy, *The Gospel and the Church*, Philadelphia: Fortress Press, 1976.

Steven Loyal, *The Sociology of Anthony Giddens*, London and Stirling, VA: Pluto Press, 2003.

A. S. McGrade, 'Richard Hooker on Anglican Integrity', *Anglican Theological Review* 91:3 (2009), pp. 417–32.

Alister McGrath, *Christian Theology: An Introduction*, 4th edn, Oxford: Blackwell Publishing, 2007.

Alister McGrath, *Heresy: A History of Defending the Truth*, London: SPCK, 2009.

John McIntyre, *The Shape of Pneumatology*, Edinburgh: T & T Clark, 1997.

Gerard Mannion and Lewis S. Mudge, 'Ecclesiology – the nature, story and study of the Church', in Gerard Mannion and Lewis S. Mudge (eds), *The*

Routledge Companion to the Christian Church, New York and London: Routledge, 2008.

Jean-Luc Marion, *God Without Being*, trans. Thomas Carlson, Chicago and London: University of Chicago Press, 1991.

Jean-Luc Marion, *In Excess: Studies of Saturated Phenomenon*, trans. Robyn Horner and Vincent Berraud, New York: Fordham University Press, 2002.

E. L. Mascall, *Corpus Christi: Essays on The Church and the Eucharist*, London and New York: Longmans, Green and Co, 1953.

Eric Mascall, 'Ministry and Priesthood', unpublished paper, 1973.

Angel F. Mendez Montoya, *The Theology of Food: Eating and the Eucharist*, Chichester: Wiley-Blackwell, 2009.

Daniel L. Migliore, *Faith Seeking Understanding: An Introduction to Christian Theology*, 2nd edn, Grand Rapids, MI: Eerdmans Publishing, 2004.

Peter Mills, 'The Metaphysics of Energy', *Modern Believing* 52:4 (2011), pp. 32–9.

Paul Minear, *Images of the Church in the New Testament*, London: Lutterworth Press, 1961.

Jürgen Moltmann, *The Church in the Power of the Spirit*, London: SCM Press, 1977.

Jürgen Moltmann, 'The Social Doctrine of the Trinity', in James Byrne (ed.), *The Christian Understanding of God Today*, Dublin: Columba, 1993, pp. 104–11.

Christiaan Mostert, *God and the Future: Wolfhart Pannenberg's Eschatological Doctrine of God*, London: T & T Clark, 2002.

Christiaan Mostert, 'The Kingdom Anticipated: The Church and Eschatology', *International Journal of Systematic Theology* 13:1 (2011), pp. 25–37.

Common Worship: Daily Prayer, London: Church House Publishing, 2005.

John Muddiman, *The Epistle to the Ephesians*, London and New York: Continuum, 2001.

Lewis S. Mudge, *Rethinking the Beloved Community: Ecclesiology, Hermeneutics and Social Theory*, Lanham MD: University Press of America, 2001.

Paul Murray (ed.), *Receptive Ecumenism and the Call to Catholic Learning: Exploring a Way for Contemporary Ecumenism*, Oxford: Oxford University Press, 2008.

John Henry Newman, 'On Consulting the Faithful in Matters of Doctrine', *The Rambler*, July 1859, reprt. in James Gaffney, (ed.), *John Henry Newman, Conscience, Consensus and the Development of Doctrine: Revolutionary Texts by John Henry Cardinal Newman*, New York: Image/Doubleday, 1992.

David Nicholls, *Deity and Domination: Images of God and the State in the Nineteenth and Twentieth Centuries*, London and New York: Routledge, 1989.

Colm O'Grady, *The Church in Catholic Theology: Dialogue with Karl Barth*, Vol. 2, London: Geoffrey Chapman, 1969.

Simon Oliver, 'The Holy Trinity and the Liturgical Subject', in James Leachman (ed.), *The Liturgical Subject: Subject, Subjectivity, and the Human Person in Contemporary Liturgical Discussion and Critique*, London: SCM, 2008, pp. 226–241.

Neil Ormerod, 'Ecclesiology and the Social Sciences', in Gerard Mannion and Lewis S. Mudge (eds), *The Routledge Companion to the Christian Church*, New York and London: Routledge, 2008, pp. 639–54.

Wolfhart Pannenberg, *Anthropology in Theological Perspective*, Edinburgh: T & T Clark, 1985.

Wolfhart Pannenberg, *Systematic Theology*, Vol. 3, trans. Geoffrey Bromiley, Grand Rapids, MI and Edinburgh: Eerdmans Publishing, 1998.

George Pattison, *The Being of God*, Oxford: Oxford University Press, 2010.

Jaroslav Pelikan, *The Christian Tradition, A History of the Development of Doctrine*, Vol. 5, *Christian Doctrine and Modern Culture (since 1700)*, Chicago: University of Chicago Press, 1989.

Martyn Percy, *Engaging with Contemporary Culture: Christianity, Theology and the Concrete Church*, Aldershot: Ashgate, 2005.

Martyn Percy, *Shaping the Church*, Farnham: Ashgate, 2010.

Stephen Pickard, *Theological Foundations for Collaborative Ministry*, Farnham: Ashgate, 2009.

Stephen Pickard, *In-Between God: Theology, Discipleship and Community*, Adelaide: ATF Publishers, 2011.

Michael Polanyi, *Personal Knowledge: Towards a Post Critical Philosophy*, London: Routledge and Kegan Paul, 1958.

C. Prell, M. Reed, L. Racin and K. Hubacek, 'Competing structure, competing views: the role of formal and informal social structures in shaping stakeholder perceptions', *Ecology and Society* 15(4): 34 (2010). Online: www.ecologyandsociety.org.vol 15/iss4/art34/.

Geoffrey Preston, *Faces of the Church*, Aidan Nichols (ed.), Grand Rapids, MI: Eerdmans, 1997.

Ronald Preston, 'A Theological Response to Sociology', in Leslie J. Francis (ed.), *Sociology, Theology and the Curriculum*, London and New York: Cassell, 1999, pp. 50–61.

Patrick Prétot, 'The Sacraments as "Celebrations of the Church": Liturgy's Impact on Sacramental Theology', in P. Bordeyne and B. T. Morrill (eds), *Sacraments: Revelation of the Humanity of God*, Collegeville, MN: Liturgical Press, 2008, pp. 25–41.

Wendy Pullan (ed.), *Structure*, Cambridge: Cambridge University Press, 2000.

Karl Rahner, *Foundations of Christian Faith: An Introduction to the Idea of Christianity*, trans. William V. Dych, London: Darton, Longman and Todd, 1997.

Michael Ramsey, *The Gospel and the Catholic Church*, London: SPCK, 1936.

John Reader, *Constructing Practical Theology: The Impact of Globalization*, Aldershot: Ashgate, 2008.

Duncan Reid, *Energies of the Spirit: Trinitarian Models in Eastern Orthodox and Western Theology*, Atlanta, GA: Scholars Press, 1995.

Alan Richardson, *An Introduction to the Theology of the New Testament*, London: SCM Press, 1958.

Richard Roberts, *Religion, Theology and the Human Sciences*, Cambridge: Cambridge University Press, 2001.

Melanie C. Ross, 'The Serious Drama of Worship', in Melanie C. Ross and Simon Jones (eds), *The Serious Business of Worship: Essays in Honour of Bryan D. Spinks*, London: T & T Clark, 2010, pp. 185–98.

Robert Russell, 'Bodily Resurrection, Eschatology, and Scientific Cosmology', in Ted Peters, Robert Russell, Michael Welker (eds), *Resurrection: Theological and Scientific Assessments*, Grand Rapids, MI: Eerdmans Publishing, 2002, pp. 3–30.

Rutba House (ed.), *School(s) for Conversion: 12 Marks of a New Monasticism*, Eugene, OR: Cascade Books, 2005.

Edward Schillebeeckx, *Church: The Human Story of God*, London: SCM Press, 1990.

Friedrich Schleiermacher, *The Christian Faith*, English translation of the second German edn 1830, by H. R. Mackintosh and J. S. Stewart, Edinburgh: T & T Clark, 1928.

Rudolf Schnackenburg, *Ephesians: A Commentary*, trans. H. Heron, Edinburgh: T & T Clark, 1991.

Elisabeth Schüssler Fiorenza, *The Power of the Word: Scripture and the Rhetoric of Empire*, Minneapolis: Fortress, 2007.

Christoph Schwöbel, 'The Creature of the Word: Recovering the Ecclesiology of the Reformers', in Colin Gunton and Daniel Hardy (eds), *On Being the Church: Essays on the Christian Community*, Edinburgh: T & T Clark, 1989, pp. 110–55.

Peter Sedgwick, 'On Anglican Polity', in David F. Ford and Dennis L. Stamps (eds), *Essentials of Christian Community*, Edinburgh: T & T Clark, 1996, pp. 196–212.

Vaclav Smil, *Energy in Nature and Society: General Energetics of Complex Systems*, London and Massachusetts: MIT Press, 2008.

George Steiner, *Real Presences*, Chicago: Chicago University Press, 1989.

Georg Strecker, *Theology of the New Testament*, trans. M. Eugene Boring, Louisville: Westminster John Knox Press, 2000.

Jean-Jacques Suurmond, *Word and Spirit at Play: Towards a Charismatic Theology*, London: SCM Press, 1994.

Kathryn Tanner, *God and Creation in Christian Theology: Tyranny or Empowerment?*, Oxford: Basil Blackwell, 1988.

George Tavard, *The Quest for Catholicity: A Study in Anglicanism*, London: Burns & Oates, 1963.

William Thomson, *The Struggle for Theology's Soul: Contesting Scripture in Christology*, New York: Crossroad, 1996.

J.-M.-R. Tillard, *Church of the Churches: The Ecclesiology of Communion*, Collegeville, MN: Liturgical Press, 1992.

J.-M.-R. Tillard, *Flesh of the Church, Flesh of Christ: At the Source of the Ecclesiology of Communion*, Collegeville, MN: Liturgical Press, 2001.

David Tracey, *The Spirituality Revolution: The Emergence of Contemporary Spirituality*, Sydney: HarperCollins, 2003.

Jean Vanier, *Drawn into the Mystery of Jesus through the Gospel of John*, Ottawa: Novalis, Saint Paul University, 2004.

Miroslav Volf, *After Our Likeness: The Church as the Image of the Trinity*, Grand Rapids, MI: Eerdmans, 1998.

Howard Wallace, 'Adam', in D. N. Freedman et al. (eds), *The Anchor Bible Dictionary* , Vol. 1, New York: Doubleday, 1992, pp. 62–4.

Graham Ward, 'Bodies', in John Milbank, Catherine Pickstock and Graham Ward (eds), *Radical Orthodoxy: A New Theology*, London and New York: Routledge, 1999, pp. 163–78.

Natalie K. Watson, 'Reconsidering Ecclesiology: Feminist Perspectives', *Sexuality and Theology* 14 (2001), pp. 59–77.

Natalie K. Watson, *Introducing Feminist Ecclesiology*, Cleveland, OH: The Pilgrim Press, 2002.

John Webster, 'The Visible Attests the Invisible', in Mark Husbands and Daniel J. Treier (eds), *The Community of the Word: Toward an Evangelical Ecclesiology*, Downers Grove, IL: InterVarsity Press, 2005.

Claude Welch, *The Reality of the Church* (New York: Scribners, 1958), reprt. Eugene OR: Wipf & Stock, 2004.

Carroll R. William, 'Restoring the Bonds of Affection', *Anglican Theological Review* 87:4 (2005), pp. 619–28.

Rowan Williams, *Writing in the Dust: Reflections on 11 September and its Aftermath*, London: Hodder & Stoughton, 2002.

Marvin R. Wilson, *Our Father Abraham: Jewish Roots of the Christian Faith*, Grand Rapids, MI: Eerdmans, 1989.

Sheldon Wolin, 'Fugitive Democracy', in Seyla Benhabib, ed., *Democracy and Difference: Contesting the Boundaries of the Political*, Princeton, NJ: Princeton University Press, 1996, pp. 31–44.

Robert Wuthnow, *After Heaven: Spirituality in America after the 1950s*, Berkeley and Los Angeles: University of California Press, 1998.

John Zizioulas, *Being as Communion, Studies in Personhood and the Church*, Crestwood, NY: St Vladimir's Press, 1985.

Index

Church
belief in 23–4
as body of Christ 34–6, 40,
43–4, 92, 121–4, 131
called 5–7, 37
catholicity 16, 139–45
coming 211–12
as communion 102
as community of sinners 136
double movement of 114–16
emergence of 8–14
as eschatological community
37
as extension of the incarnation 87
founded by Jesus 14–19
founded also by the Spirit
18–19
fugitive 225–33
as herald 41
holiness of 135–9
humanity of 64
images of 33–9
marks of the 118–50, 225
as mediation of divine
presence 62
as mystery 118–24
as mystical communion 42
order and structure 152–81
as people of God 39, 40, 44
as pilgrim community 7, 36
as pioneer people 39
as proclaimer 14
purpose 7
as sacrament 41, 42
as servant 43, 44

as sign of the kingdom 20–2
slow 210–38
as social form of Christianity
85–99
sociology of 67–8
unity of 10, 70, 93–9, 131–5,
175
see also ecumenical
movement
and world 65–6, 73–6
Clarke, Sathianathan 3–4
clergy, separated from laity 65
Coakley, Sarah 105–6
Coenen, L. 6
Collins, Adela Yarbro 12
communion see koinonia
communion ecclesiology 36
community 224, 228–32
companionship 1–2, 231–5
consensus fidelium 169
consumerism 217
Counter-Reformation 43
Cox, Harvey 234
creation 88–9, 142
logos in 90, 91, 191–2
creeds 23, 118, 127

Daly, Mary 106
Dawson, Christopher 218
Derrida, Jacques 230–1
Docetism 59–60, 61, 63–6, 70,
74
and institutional control 76
Donatist heresy 57
Dorotheos of Gaza 1–2, 87
Dula, Peter 224–33

Dulles, Avery 33, 39–42
dynamic imagery 6–7, 21,
    110–11
  and social structures 157–8,
    169

Ebionite heresy 60, 71–2, 75
ecclesia, etymology 5–6
ecclesial bond *see* Church,
    unity of
ecclesiology
  and society 84–5
  task of 29–30
ecumenical movement 27, 36
election
  of the Church 11
  of Israel 10
Emerging Church 148–9
Emmaus Road story 37, 207–8
energy 183–208
eschatology 19–22, 37
  realized 64, 122
Eucharist 197–9, 200, 202–3,
    222, 229

failure 217
faith and order 154–5
Farley, Edward 75–6, 86
Farrer, Austin 110
feminist theology 43, 46, 51–3
Florovksy, George 142
foot washing 206–7
frameworks 45
Fresh Expressions 148–9
friendship 231
fugitive *ecclesia* 225–33

Giddens, Anthony 160–1
Gottwald, Norman K. 9
grace 92
Gregory of Nyssa 106
Gunton, Colin 19
  Christology 63
  on sociality 94–5
  on Trinity 62, 103–4

Hardy, Daniel
  on the Anglican Church 112,
    178–9
  on Bonhoeffer's ecclesiology
    86, 89
  on ecclesiology 26–7, 30, 88
  on God and social structures
    168
  on healing 212
  on Jesus walking 222
  on mystery of God 110
  on ordered energy 183
  on seeking God 3
  on sociality 94, 96
  on society 90–1
Hauerwas, Stanley 48, 50, 231
healing 212, 220–2
Healy, Nicholas 46–51
  on blueprint ecclesiologies 63,
    70
  on Church's faithfulness 65
  on models of Church 46–8
  on prophetic ecclesiology 29
  on sociology of the Church
    68
  on turn to practices 48–51
Hebert, Gabriel 158, 159

Printed in August 2022
by Rotomail Italia S.p.A., Vignate (MI) - Italy